Review Copy –

Ralph Adams Brown, Sp. (I)'c

A. Ä.: Prep – Inst.
USCG – Groton, Conn.
4 January. 1945

GREAT SOLDIERS
OF WORLD WAR II

GREAT SOLDIERS OF WORLD WAR II

By Major H. A. DEWEERD

Associate Editor, Infantry Journal

W · W · NORTON & COMPANY · INC · *New York*

A WARTIME BOOK

PRINTED IN THE UNITED STATES OF AMERICA
FOR THE PUBLISHERS BY THE VAIL-BALLOU PRESS

TO

N. K. D. W.

FOREWORD

☆

DESPITE the inevitable imperfections of such an account, there is something to be said for attempting to evaluate the military leadership of the war while it is still going on. It will be many years before a final estimate can be made of the leaders treated in this book. The war has already undergone marked changes in character and will probably continue to do so in the future. So much has happened since 1939 that it will come as a shock to some to recall that in those days General Gamelin was widely regarded as the "finest professional soldier in the world." Without some kind of background to help him the best-intentioned civilian reader can find little meaning in the day-to-day summaries of the war. Therefore an attempt to get away from the spot-news mentality and place some of the leaders of World War II in a broader perspective against the changing background of military events may be helpful. It may contribute to a better understanding of the present and future stages of the war.

While the tentative nature of these portraits is acknowledged, it would be unrealistic, I think, to assume that the ultimate verdict of history will present striking deviations from the general conclusions one is able to draw now. Some of the soundest observations about the nature of the last great war were drawn up while the guns were still hot. Professor Robert M. Johnston's *First Reflections on the Campaign of 1918,* published before his untimely death in 1920, is as penetrating an account of the last phase of the war as can be found anywhere. Events themselves are often more eloquent and dependable than documents. This is particularly the case in military history, a fact that has led to the old saying: "Truths can be seen wandering about the battlefield naked on the night after an encounter but by the next morning they are all in uniform!"

The professional historian who thinks of examining *all* the relevant documents before writing military history or weighing a leader, simply has no conception of what modern military records are like. He can have only the faintest idea of their staggering bulk and why they are necessarily fragmentary in nature. There is rather general agreement among those who work with these records that even after they are available, the whole and true story of what took place cannot be built up from them alone. Anyone who has worked in the War or Navy departments during the present war knows that there is a vast "literature" of unwritten material relating to the war and its leaders that will never become a part of the "record."

One additional reason for writing now is that war has never been waged with more elaborate journalistic, pictorial, or radio coverage.

While the author has had access to a great deal of classified material as a necessary part of his work on the staff of a military periodical, every attempt has been made to base these sketches on material already published. It is, of course, impossible to forget what one has read, but if the result of this reading appears at all in these pages, it is in the negative sense of correcting or omitting what one might otherwise write. I wish to stress the fact that the opinions expressed and the conclusions drawn are those of the writer alone and do not represent War Department views or those of the service at large.

If the inclusion of portraits of Hitler, Churchill, and Chiang in a book entitled *Great Soldiers* seems a bit unusual, it is because we have not accustomed ourselves to the functions of the statesman-soldier in modern war. When war became total, it was inevitable that the heads of states, who alone can marshal and direct the whole mobilized political, economic, and military power of their countries, should become in reality commanders in chief. Upon their decisions, more often than upon the actions of their professional military chiefs and advisers, rests the issue of national survival or downfall.

The reader or reviewer may ask, "Why a portrait of Church-

ill, Hitler, and Chiang, but none of Marshal Stalin or Tito?"
Or one may wonder why a sketch of General Eisenhower is
included and one of General Marshall omitted. What about
General Arnold and Air Marshals Harris and Tedder? The
answer must be that the major work of these men is still incomplete. It is possible to say *now* that Churchill has led Britain
from a condition of real but unacknowledged defeat to one
where victory is inevitable. Eisenhower has not completed his
work in Europe, but he has already conquered French North
Africa, Sicily, and has conducted the operations that knocked
Italy out of the war. The great work of General Marshall will
not become fully apparent until the whole pattern of the American war effort is clear. The same observation holds for Marshal
Stalin, Tito, General Arnold, Air Marshal Harris, General Alexander, and others. It has not been possible to write about the
younger Russian leaders because there is no material on
them at present. The writer hopes to expand and revise
these interim sketches when fuller information is available. At
that time it may be possible to complete the gallery by adding
new portraits.

Four chapters of the present work appeared in the author's
Great Soldiers of the Two World Wars (1941), but that book
is now out of print and these chapters have been substantially
revised or rewritten. Acknowledgment is made to the editors of
the *Yale Review* and the *Infantry Journal* for permission to re-
print material that first appeared in their journals.

MAJOR H. A. DeWEERD

Washington, D. C.

CONTENTS

☆

Foreword   7

GAMELIN   15

DE GAULLE   39

WAVELL   56

ROMMEL   81

MONTGOMERY   102

HITLER   126

CHURCHILL   166

TIMOSHENKO   190

MacARTHUR   213

CHIANG KAI-SHEK   241

EISENHOWER   264

Bibliography   299

Index   309

ILLUSTRATIONS

☆

	FACING PAGE
GAMELIN	16
DE GAULLE	41
WAVELL AND AUCHINLECK	56
ROMMEL	96
MONTGOMERY AND ALEXANDER	104
MONTGOMERY	121
JODL, HITLER, AND BRAUCHITSCH	128
HITLER, THE FELDHERR	128
CHURCHILL	168
STALIN, ROOSEVELT, AND CHURCHILL	185
TIMOSHENKO	192
MACARTHUR	224
MACARTHUR WATCHING THE LANDING OF ALLIED PARA- TROOPS NEAR LAE	238
CHIANG KAI-SHEK	241
EISENHOWER	264
EISENHOWER AND MARSHALL	281

MAPS and CHART

	PAGE
THE WESTERN FRONT	29
THE BATTLE OF FLANDERS AND THE BATTLE OF FRANCE	33
THE LIBYAN CAMPAIGN	66
THE ETHIOPIAN CAMPAIGN	72

	PAGE
SIDI REZEGH—TOBRUK	90
KNIGHTSBRIDGE—TOBRUK	93
THE BATTLE OF EL ALAMEIN	112–113
MARETH AND WADI AKARIT	122
ORGANIZATION CHART OF THE GERMAN HIGH COMMAND 1944	163
THE BATTLE FOR MOSCOW	204
SOUTHWEST PACIFIC AREA	235
THE CHINA WAR ZONE	262
THE NORTH AFRICAN THEATER	274
THE END IN NORTH AFRICA	287

GAMELIN

☆

"He was a cold light, an abstraction."

FATE played one of its tragic, inscrutable tricks on France in 1935 when, into the office of the vice-president of the Supreme War Council at No. 4 Boulevard des Invalides, just vacated by General Maxime Weygand, walked a short, grayish officer: Maurice Gustave Gamelin. General Weygand's retirement from the control of the French army at the age of 68 was a military event of more than average importance. Famed, perhaps unjustly, as the military brains and alter ego of Marshal Foch (who left the advice: "Call Weygand if trouble comes"), Weygand was long regarded as the symbol of France's military supremacy on the Continent. It was known that the retiring commander in chief was not enthusiastic about his successor and would have preferred General Alphonse Georges, but that was frequently true of commanding officers and their successors. Time had not yet healed the wounds of the bitter wartime quarrels between French generals. Weygand was a Foch man, Gamelin a Joffre man. Joffre's treatment of Foch just before his own retirement in 1916 (Foch was placed on the inactive list on the grounds of ill health) had never been forgiven. Even after both marshals were dead their widows passed each other on the street without speaking. Weygand may have preferred Georges (who had worked with both Pétain and Foch) not because he loved Pétain more, but Joffre less.

On his record Gamelin seemed to possess all the formal qualifications for his important office. From a strictly professional standpoint he appeared to be the most accomplished officer in France—or in Europe for that matter. Had he assumed command of the French military establishment at a less critical time, he doubtless would have carried his brightly burnished professional reputation with him to the security of the grave. Instead, it was his tragic destiny to face one of the few great revolutionary changes in military methods and concepts with the weapons and concepts of an earlier and happier day. As a result, the story of his leadership in 1939–40 is one of measureless disaster for the country he loved.

Gamelin came from a military family. His father, Zephirin Auguste Gamelin, served in the wars of the Second Empire, was wounded at Solferino, and ultimately rose to the rank of comptroller general of the French army. Maurice was born within the shadow of the War Ministry at No. 262 Boulevard St. Germain in Paris in 1872. His education was given a strong Catholic bent in Collège Stanislas, where he fell under the influence of Henri Cardinal Baudillart. He demonstrated a taste for philosophy and a talent for memory work which enabled him to graduate from St. Cyr in 1893 first in a class of 449. For three years he served in the 3rd regiment of the *Trailleurs Algériens* and put in an additional three years in the cartographic section of the army geographic service. Here he developed a fondness for painting and an interest in the topographic features of the French frontiers. As captain of a company of *chasseur à pied* he was detailed to the École de Guerre, where Foch was making a name for himself as the foremost lecturer on military problems in France. Gamelin's record at St. Cyr and his promising showing at the École de Guerre brought him to the attention of General Joffre, whose star was rising in the military firmament of France. In 1906 Joffre, commanding the 6th Division in Paris, made Gamelin his aide. He stayed with Joffre when the latter rose to the vice-presidency of the Supreme War Council in 1911. He was thus prepared to play a conspicuous role in the events of 1914.

Employing the tenacious memory he had developed at Collège Stanislas by memorizing 10 lines of prose each night before retiring, Gamelin made himself master of the military literature on Napoleon. It was widely believed that he could repeat verbatim every order the emperor ever issued. Such erudition was uncommon, even in an army that made a fetish of the study of

GAMELIN

Napoleon. Two years' service with the line from 1912 to 1914 made him available for staff duty when the crisis came in 1914. Gamelin was a trim, sleek, taciturn, quick-witted major of 42 who had given considerable study to the problem of countering a German attack from the direction of Belgium. Joffre loved to have sharp-witted young men around him, possibly as a foil for his own ponderous mental processes. He brought Gamelin ("one of my red corpuscles") back to his staff in August, 1914.

The events of August and early September, 1914, gave Gamelin a chance to utilize his early study on a German attack from the direction of Belgium. Plan XVII, the French program that called for a concentric advance by the First and Fifth French armies in a brutal and relentless manner (*l'offensive brutale et à outrance*), broke down with heavy losses in the face of German machine guns and artillery. With the apparently irresistible force of an avalanche, the gigantic German armies of Kluck and Bülow rolled through Belgium into northern France. Berthelot was Joffre's chief of staff, but it was Gamelin who on August 25 wrote the famous "Instruction No. 2" which admitted that the French plan of offensive war had failed and which announced the general plan of building up a sufficient force on the French left wing to menace the German right when the time arrived for the counterattack. For more than a week the victorious German armies rolled on, driving before them what appeared to be "the beaten French armies." By September 4 it was apparent not only to Gallieni, military governor of Paris, but also to Gamelin, that Kluck's force would not envelop Paris, and that the time had come to throw Manoury's Sixth French Army, which was concentrating at Meaux, against the flank of Kluck. Though historians have found it difficult to determine just who was responsible for the famous Marne maneuver, Joffre's *Memoirs* make it clear that Gamelin understood the situation fully and explained it to a group of officers in his presence at the operations room of the general headquarters on September 4. He urged that the counterattack be delivered the next day. Illustrating his points on a huge operations map Gamelin raised his voice (a thing uncommon with him) and firmly declared: "Now is the time to bottle them up!" Joffre pleaded for greater delay so that the Germans might be more definitely drawn into the trap. But when reports from French army commanders and the British Expeditionary Force gave some hope for an early offensive action, Joffre asked Gamelin to prepare the decisive "Instruction No. 6." It called for a general attack by all armies on September 6.

The complicated story of how the German armies blundered into the Marne defeat out of the feeble hands of Moltke into the irresponsible hands of Lieutenant Colonel von Hentsch, who presided over the destiny of the German Empire from September 6 to 9, has often been told.[1] When the haggard German troops recoiled on September 9 from the menace of the advancing British Expeditionary Force and French Fifth Army, the "miracle" of the Marne raised Joffre to the stature of a legendary hero, and long after Joffre had fallen from power it shaped the career of Gamelin.

The first rewards for Gamelin's service in the Marne battle were the rank of lieutenant colonel and the post of chief of the bureau of operations. After the failure of the French offensives in the spring and summer of 1915, Gamelin urged Joffre to create a large mass of reserves to exploit future anticipated successes. The long-hoped-for and repeatedly announced "breakthrough" of the German line never materialized, but there was a mass of 40 or more French divisions available when the German attack came at Verdun. The existence of this reserve made the successful but costly defense of Verdun possible, and it enabled Joffre to think in broad terms when the British needed assistance on the Somme. But the "blood bath" of Verdun and the Allied failure at the Somme brought Joffre into eclipse. He was replaced by the eloquent, mercurial, thrusting Nivelle. As a consequence Gamelin's position on the staff became insecure and he took command of a brigade. He distinguished himself in

[1] Though the younger Moltke was head of the German field armies in 1914, the actual orders to the First and Second German armies which governed the course of the battle of the Marne from the German side were issued by Hentsch, who was Moltke's liaison officer at that time.

the stubborn fighting of the Somme, rising to the rank of brigadier general in December, 1916. From 1917 to 1918 he commanded the 9th Division.

In the critical days of 1918 Gamelin made the reputation of
being a tough, imperturbable, tenacious fighting officer. The
9th Division was thrown into the breach when the German offensive threatened to drive a wedge between the British and French
forces on March 23. For three days his division held up the advance of six German divisions. In the confused fighting he commanded a makeshift force of French and British infantry divisions and seven squadrons of cavalry. He impressed the troops
as being a cautious, economical commander who attained his
objectives with minimum losses by a meticulous regard for terrain, artillery preparation, and human factors. His philosophic
calm inspired confidence. "There is nothing to be gained by
getting angry with things," he used to say. "It is a matter of indifference to them." He seemed to agree with Haldane that
"things military must be learned not from the generals but from
the philosophers." By the time the war ended he had made a
very distinguished record as a fighting commander. He had also
taken a vital part in the staff operations early in the war. At no
stage in his well-rounded career had he committed an obvious
error in judgment. He was destined for rapid postwar promotion.

II

WHEN the German armies collapsed in November, 1918, the
prestige of the German military system collapsed with them.
Brazil, which had previously sought the services of German military missions, now asked for French officers. In 1919 Gamelin was
selected to head a French military mission there and remained
in South America from 1919 until 1925. This gave him a background of foreign travel and the international outlook essential
for a superior officer. In September of 1925 he was detailed to
the French command in Syria, where he faced the problem of
quelling a revolt of the Druses. One of his first tasks was to re-

lieve a French outpost besieged at Soueida. His manner was so
deliberate and his preparations so thorough that one correspondent wrote in a sarcastic vein: "General Gamelin now has more
troops than the entire population of Druses, men, women, and
children—when he gets reinforcements he may *perhaps* attack."
Six months of campaigning and a bombardment of Damascus
that killed 1,400 civilians brought peace to Syria. Gamelin came
back to France in 1928 as a corps commander. He was appointed
deputy chief of staff, and in 1931 he became chief of staff. His
succession to Weygand as vice-president of the Supreme War
Council and commander in chief designate in case of war was
almost automatic in 1935. He was then regarded as the most
scholarly, accomplished, and competent professional soldier on
the active list. His mastery of all the topographic features of the
French frontiers and its road systems was absolute. His acquaintance with the senior officers of the army was such that he could
name and recognize every officer with the rank of colonel or
above. He had a way of instantly putting one who met him at
ease by treating all people as if they were old acquaintances. As
Jules Romains pointed out, one always wanted to agree with a
man "whose authority contained so little that was offensive."
He could talk on European problems with the air of a super-
latively well-informed historian. His colorless personality and
complete indifference to politics made him a popular choice to
succeed Weygand.

Simultaneously with Gamelin's assumption of supreme command the German rearmament program began. Italy was already
embarked upon a program of imperialist expansion. The situation was one of increasing hazard for France. Gamelin had to
deal with rapidly changing ministries and a foreign policy as
tortuous as it was pusillanimous. In the comparative madhouse
of flux the army was the one solid national element in French
society. It alone could have brought national security back to its
rightful place as the first objective of the government. But the
voices of the soldiers had to be resolute, their vision clear. No
ancient professional prescriptions timidly administered would

suffice. If honest professional advice was repeatedly offered—
with clear warnings given as to the danger facing the state—and
were repeatedly ignored, there was always the honorable course
of resignation.

It cannot be said that Gamelin was unaware of the growing
dangers of the French military situation. German and Italian
military preparations were of such a vast and open character that
they could be and were described with fair accuracy by the
European and American press correspondents. One did not need
the services of a military attaché. Even so bookish an ambassador
to Berlin as Professor Dodd could gauge the potential menace
of nazi war preparations. Pikestaff plain, too, were the implications of doctrinal changes in the application of industry and
mechanics to war. Field trials in the Spanish Civil War were not
for the fascists alone. As a student of philosophy Gamelin should
have been among the first to see the menace inherent in the
fanatical and demonic character of the nazi system of thought.

Gamelin did, of course, take steps to meet the dangers of a
collision with the rearmed Reich. But the steps taken were dic-
tated by the military experience of 1918. He approved the completion of the Maginot line and unsuccessfully urged its extension to the sea.[2] When this advice was refused, he did not resign.
He attempted to offset the French numerical inferiority vis-à-vis
Germany by extending the period of military service from one
year to two. In simple terms this meant that he still looked at
military problems as something to be solved by numbers. He
did not see in new doctrines, individualistic training concepts,
the application of machinery to war, or new co-ordination of
air and ground forces a means of gaining equality or even
qualitative superiority over an enemy of potentially greater numbers. Lest the obvious snap-judgment observation be raised that
these are the counsels of perfection, easy to make in the clear
light of afterknowledge, it can only be said that library shelves
are well stocked with foreign and American military journals

[2] The nature of the terrain in the north did not favor the construction of deeply
anchored subterranean fortifications of the Maginot type.

that printed millions of words on these subjects—*at that time*. There is little or no evidence to show that Gamelin digested the tremendous volume of postwar German military literature. Nor did he give more than passing attention to the prophetic book of Colonel Charles de Gaulle, *Vers l'armée de métier,* which advanced the claim of mechanized forces, or to Paul Reynaud's *Le problème militaire française.* So great was his faith in the "incomparable" infantry of France (armed with almost the identical weapons of 1918) that Gamelin allowed his country to repeat Ludendorff's error of making trucks to carry the troops rather than masses of tanks and planes to give them a chance for survival after they arrived where he wanted them to fight.

The existence of the Maginot line gave Gamelin's military thinking the appearance of soundness. He took comfort in General Chauvineau's dictum that "the attack must have three times as many infantry effectives, six times as much artillery, and twelve times as much ammunition, if it hopes to dominate the defense." He did not believe that the German army had developed new and effective means of breaking through the fortifications in the west. The war that he foresaw promised to be a long-drawn-out struggle of attrition, in which the French armies and fortified positions would contain the German armies until the British blockade accomplished its mission of strangulation and exhaustion. He did not expect that Germany would collapse without a military disaster, but that progressive weakness would lead to lowered nervous resistance, which would appear at the first shock of a real defeat.

The military reorganization of 1938 in France pointed toward a preparation for this kind of a conflict. A single Committee of National Defense was set up, covering land, sea, and air forces and representing the economic and financial elements of the nation. As chief of staff to Daladier, who attempted to achieve this co-ordination, Gamelin was in a position to influence the whole range of French preparation for war. His crystal-clear academic discussions with the members of the Committee of National Defense and his orderly reports and minutes enabled him to dominate the organization. Gamelin's chief opposition in the committee came from Admiral Jean Darlan, whose salt-water language was an excellent cover for his growing political ambitions.

Gamelin's relations with General Georges, who was to serve as commander of the armies in France in event of war, soon became complicated by the top-heavy military organization set up. Gamelin was to be generalissimo of the Allied forces in France and responsible for land and air operations in all theaters. Prewar calculations envisaged him in the role of a sort of super-Foch, with Georges commanding the armies on the German frontier as Pétain had done under Foch in 1918. But because no war developed immediately on the Italian, African, or Syrian fronts, and because Poland collapsed, both Gamelin and Georges became in effect commanders in France. The separation of the French general staff into three divisions located at Meaux, La Ferté-sous-Jouarre, and Vincennes did not help matters. Rivalry between the two men was bound to develop under these circumstances.

If French military preparations for war were open to question in the realm of intellect and doctrine, there is less room for question about the inferiority of their material preparation. In the matter of light artillery the French army was supreme in the period 1914–18. But in 1939 the French field artillery, even when modernized, was out of date. The artillery ammunition situation was even more critical. Shells were scarce and a prolonged controversy over the type of fuse desired held up the production of everything heavier than the 75 mm. shell. Similar professional squabbles over the type of fuse for antiaircraft shell limited the effectiveness of this arm. It might be well to add, for whatever warning value it may have, that this intensely interesting professional debate over fuses was in fact about to be settled at the time of the armistice with Germany in June, 1940! The experiences in Spain had shown that the French 37 mm. anti-tank gun did not possess the penetration required, but the 47 mm. gun that was to replace it had virtually no stock of ammunition. French efforts to devise a perfect land mine for antitank protection failed. The improvisations resorted to proved to be just what improvisations usually prove to be in modern warfare —totally ineffective. The failure to exploit anything like the full possibilities of antitank and antipersonnel mines was just another example of the lack of military enterprise in France. It was left for the Germans to introduce both of the principal novelties of ground operations in the present war—the use of tanks in masses and the use of land mines on a prodigious scale.

The French tanks were excellent, but there was no effective organization on a basis larger than the division, and no clear-cut doctrine on their employment as such. Trucks were available to haul infantry but they were not available to service tanks. The individual fighting capacity of the French tank was higher than that of the average German tank of its own weight, but maintenance service, especially refueling, had not been worked out on the scale of continuous service which the situation soon demanded. There was certainly nothing like the preparation that enabled the German panzer divisions to keep rolling day after day from Sedan to Dunkirk. It has been reported that one excellent French tank unit in the scrambled fighting on the Somme was reduced to the "injun-fighting" tactics of covered-wagon days and forced to form an immobile, hollow circle for want of fuel in the logistic breakdown that followed the unexpected character of the war. The French military aviation, which was the most numerous in Europe in 1935, was allowed to fall to a poor fourth in 1939, well below that of Germany, Italy, and Britain.

III

WHEN Germany occupied the Rhineland on March 7, 1936, Gamelin is said to have offered to drive them out if Prime Minister Sarraut would consent to general mobilization. He was not prepared to act against the 30,000 German troops in the area without placing the whole French military machine on a war basis. He was also unwilling to risk the occupation of the Saar as a countermeasure. If World War II did not begin then, it began, according to Liddell Hart, when Italy and Germany gave active assistance to General Franco in July, 1936. The formation of the Rome-Berlin Axis on November 1, 1936, ended forever the possibility of dealing with the Reich alone. From this time on Gamelin had to count on a war of two fronts.

Gamelin strongly supported the maintenance of France's alliances, even when these were being undermined by diplomatic events over which he had no control. He preferred to fight at the time of Munich rather than see the bastion of Czechoslovakia and her 30 divisions surrendered. He is said to have urged that maximum concessions to Hitler should leave the main line of Czech fortifications, strategic railways, and armament factories in Czech hands. But the appeasers had their way. Nine months after Munich, Gamelin came to the conclusion that this surrender had tipped the balance against France, since by this time the Siegfried line had progressed to a point where it made the prospect of military pressure on the Reich unpromising. He regarded the loss of the Czech war material and armament plants as more serious than the loss of her 30 divisions. Until August 23, 1939, there was still room for hope that the vast forces of Russia might be turned at once against the Axis, but the German-Russian nonaggression pact swept that prospect aside. Poland could no longer be saved.

There should have been little mystery about German grand strategy in 1939. As early as June 20, 1939, the antifascist "Friends of Europe Information Service" in Britain published a bulletin ("No. 15") on Hitler's strategy in event of war. Its author was obviously well informed on political and military matters. He set down the assumption that Germany would turn 80 per cent of her army against Poland in an annihilating attack to be launched in three directions (from East Prussia, Silesia, and Pomerania). He pointed out that the Germans would adopt a defensive policy in the west on the assumption that the Allies would remain on the defensive. No air raids would take place on London and Paris to encourage a similar policy on the part of the Allies. An air stalemate would enable Germany to concentrate the full striking power of the Luftwaffe on Polish objectives. The Germans assumed that France and Britain would refrain from launching an attack on Italy in an effort to insure her neutrality. After the defeat of Poland, the writer of the bulletin predicted that a peace offensive would follow. Gamelin probably did not read this summary, but it was widely read in Britain and it fitted the pattern of German movements in 1939 perfectly.

Like Joffre in 1914, Gamelin gave the impression of utter confidence and serenity in the crisis of 1939. To a public alarmed at the prospect of seeing the French army bleed itself white on the Siegfried position, he gave assurance that he did not intend to begin the war with a Verdun battle. This gave the impression that he had another less costly and more promising alternative in mind. Isolated from the impending harsh realities of war in his headquarters in Paris, and later in the keep of Vincennes, surrounded by his personal staff of 15 officers adept at flattery and skilled in the ritual of idol worship, he presided over the mobilization of the French army like an "imperturbable military Buddha."

Under the hot sun of a late summer in 1939 the mobilization of the French army was completed without molestation from the enemy. The new British Expeditionary Force took up its position in France in the period of false calm and the two armies marked time while Poland was struck down in a three-week campaign by the amazingly effective co-ordinate action of the Luftwaffe and the German armored forces. The press of the Allied countries treated the uninterrupted mobilization of Franco-British forces in France as if it in itself assumed ultimate victory. Gamelin said, "All I need is a fortnight to complete my mobilization in peace."

Since it was impossible to go to the aid of Poland, many voices were raised in France urging that action should be taken to define Italy's position, and if hostile to strike her down while the Germans were still occupied in the east. Gamelin did not favor opening new fronts. He was content to perch *au balcon* at the head of the Alpine passes and await developments. When Weygand advocated the opening of a front in the Balkans, he opposed this on the grounds that German numerical superiority and interior lines would render this dangerous. He wanted to confine operations to western Europe, which would force the Germans to attack the Allied fortified lines in the west.

Because of the German air supremacy, Gamelin vetoed the British proposal to bomb German synthetic gasoline plants for fear of reprisals. He even refused to permit the RAF to bomb German troops on the march in Germany.[3] Thus the air stalemate developed along with the "Sitzkrieg" on the ground. This pleased General Vuillemin, commander of the French air force, because he had feared that the shortage of French planes would force them to use their reserve pilots, who would be shot down in two weeks. France would have to keep back its well-trained pilots until first-line planes were procured. The full force of the German air power remained a secret until the attack of May 10, a factor that worked in favor of the enemy. Boredom as thick as night fell upon the front. It was not dispelled by Gamelin's super-cautious advance into the no man's land between the Maginot and Siegfried lines toward Saarbrücken. One supremely apt picture of the situation in the west reached the press and picture magazines of the world. It showed a French poilu slumped in a chair in the midst of a wood behind the front lines, his automatic rifle on the ground in front of him, on his face the unforgettable impression of utter boredom and purposelessness. Experts were careful to point out that the shiftless appearance of the French troops, their dog-eared, untidy uniforms, and boy-scout-looking camps, their carelessly constructed barricades over which ancient Hotchkiss machine guns pointed with faint menace at the empty skies, were all marks of a veteran, competent, "cagey," battle-worthy army.

In December, 1939, Gamelin asked the well-known French writer Jules Romains, who was about to begin a tour of the front

[3] Great Britain Air Ministry, *The Bomber Command* (London, 1941), p. 45.

and a visit to Belgium, to look everything over and give him a criticism on his return. Romains visited all sections of the front and drew up a list of suggestions based on his own observations and on countless talks with officers. This list called attention to many weaknesses in the French position, from Montmédy to the sea, such as the absence of bombproof shelters, the shortage of concrete blockhouses, the weakness of antitank provisions, the narrow belts of wire, and the limited firing capacity of the main Maginot forts. Although Gamelin was on very friendly terms with Romains, he did not acknowledge the report or call him in to discuss it. As was his custom with unpleasant papers, he probably immediately put it away in a drawer and forgot it. An important memorandum of General de Gaulle on the dangers of the French strategy of waiting and the weakness of the Maginot line in the face of German equipment and methods was similarly ignored. General Georges is said to have made the following marginal note on it: "Interesting but the constructive aspect is less valuable than the critical—For examination."

Gamelin was not apparently disturbed or impressed by the rapid collapse of Poland. The social and military weaknesses of the Polish state in his opinion made it impossible to draw useful military lessons from her defeat. A single small pamphlet on German tactics in the Polish campaign was circulated in the French army, but it was not backed by action on the part of the high command. The Norwegian disaster, however, focused criticism on Gamelin since he obviously misjudged the speed and weight of the German stroke in that theater. Daladier, his chief supporter, was replaced by Reynaud as prime minister, and Reynaud was not so easily impressed with Gamelin's facile academic explanation of Allied strategy.[4] In fact, Reynaud became so suspicious of Gamelin's leadership early in May that he was preparing to replace him by either Giraud, Weygand, or Huntziger when the German blow fell in the west. There was no time after Norway to apply the lessons of the campaign or to restudy the

---

[4] Daladier continued in the cabinet until May 18 as minister of defense, in which position he continued to support Gamelin until after the Sedan disaster.

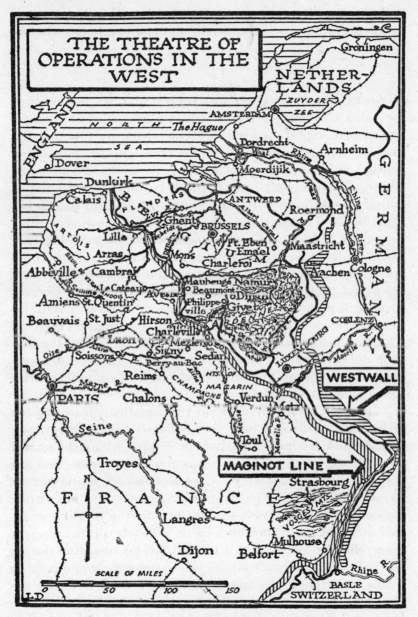

The Western Front

Polish disaster from the standpoint of new tactics. The German assault in the west had to be faced with the concepts and weapons of 1918.

IV

As THE decisive battle in the west drew nearer, the fundamental anomalies of French strategy became apparent. The Maginot line was the logical outcome of French defensive concepts, but since it did not extend to the sea, the French northern flank was exposed to a German attack through Holland and Belgium. This made it necessary to supplement the Maginot defenses by military action *outside* France. From 1937 onward the French high command accepted the idea of waging a defensive campaign behind the Maginot line and an offensive campaign in Belgium. This half-defensive, half-offensive program was based on certain unchallenged assumptions. One was that the forest of the Ardennes would prove to be an impenetrable barrier to a German advance. Another was that despite the lack of direct liaison between staffs, joint Anglo-French-Belgian operations on the Dyle River line were possible. Finally it was assumed that if the Germans did penetrate the Ardennes and the Belgian fortifications, the Allied armies in the north would be in a position to strike a fatal blow at their flanks.

Thus the French plan of war in 1940 entailed a basic division of doctrine (defensive in France, offensive in Belgium) and divided the army into two parts (one covered with concrete, the other thrust far beyond the protection of casements and the operational range of reserves). Captain E. Bauer, writing in the *Revue militaire suisse* for September, 1942, said: "France was not defeated so completely in 1940 because the frontiers of Alsace and Lorraine were encased in concrete or because the Franco-Belgian frontier was neglected, but because, after the job was finished, the French armies were arranged on one hand as if this masterpiece of engineering (the Maginot line) did not exist at all, and on the other hand as if it extended all the way to Dunkirk." That Gamelin with all his philosophical and metaphysical gifts did not see or violently object to these inherent offenses against logic is difficult to explain.

As early as December 16, 1939, Gamelin predicted that the Germans would attack via Holland and Belgium. In the following month because they showed no inclination to accept an Allied offer of joint military action, he warned Belgium and Holland that it might be impossible to send French troops far into neutral territory—although this plan remained the basis for French strategy. By February, 1940, it was practically decided that the Allied armies would act upon the "Dyle hypothesis"; namely, that they would send 30-odd divisions into Belgium to operate on the Dyle River line. The Dutch made it clear that they would need the support of French troops inside Holland, and part of General Giraud's force was earmarked for that task. As the spring of 1940 passed in inaction, Gamelin explained his policy of "watchful waiting" by comparing armies to "fleets in being," costly to maintain, "to be kept intact as long as possible and risked only for decisive action." "Both sides," he said, "are under armor; the first to stick his head out will be destroyed."

Then, in a magnificent but fatal non-sequitur to this logic, he proceeded to invite the disaster which he forecast. Possibly because he knew that Premier Reynaud had criticized him for want of energy and daring, Gamelin met the German assault in the west with more than his customary swiftness and energy. His order of the day unwittingly provided the most damaging material for a future criticism of his own policies by asserting that "the blow which we have been expecting since October has at last fallen." This informed the world that his sole aim during all the months of military reverses had been to force the Germans to attack in the west. On the morning of May 10, Gamelin felt that he was on the eve of a complete vindication of his military program. With the swift, impetuous stroke of a chess player whose opponent makes a long-expected move, Gamelin sent an Allied force of 30 divisions racing northward into Belgium and Holland. At the end of the second day motorized forces of General Giraud reached Breda.

The Allied divisions, moving with great swiftness and precision northward, were curiously free from air attacks.[5] This in itself should have aroused the suspicion of Gamelin. It might have told him that the Germans were eager to have him do just what he was attempting. The long Allied columns were ignored by the Luftwaffe, which concentrated its attack on rear areas, airfields, and communications. The confusion existing in Belgium and Holland, and the penetration of the Belgian and Dutch lines on the second day of assault, should have made it clear to Gamelin that the five-day estimate of the German push through the Ardennes was no longer valid. Either Gamelin was not fully informed of the situation in the north or he was seized with one of his fits of academic indecision. He did not take the heroic step necessary to save the northern force from what was an obvious trap. A terrible, face-destroying decision to withdraw the whole northern force, at the end of the first or second day of action, alone could have prevented the disaster of Flanders.

It took Gamelin five days (the time he calculated the Belgian lines would be able to hold the Germans) to grasp the full significance of the developments in the north. By that time the Germans had pushed the Belgian forces back from the Albert Canal line, and Holland had succumbed to a bewildering attack of three dimensions. Swarms of Stukas and highly trained small-combat squads cut Corap's ill-fated Ninth Army at Sedan to shreds. The mighty armored forces of the enemy were ready to pour through the gap. Why reserves were not available to support this poorly trained and indifferently commanded force at the hinge of the Maginot line has never been revealed. The Germans had always shown a marked tendency to strike at points where Allied armies joined or at other natural lines of cleavage. Corap has been cleared of the early charges of gross neglect in failing to destroy the Meuse bridges, but the impression of slackness in the Ninth Army remains. It served no purpose to replace

[5] General Giraud's Seventh Army racing toward Breda was the exception. It was heavily attacked by German aircraft on May 10. P. Tissier, *The Riom Trial* (London, 1942), p. 148.

Corap on May 15 with the thrusting General Giraud, since the confusion of the Ninth Army was so great that Giraud was never able to collect its staff and wandered into the enemy lines.

The Battle of Flanders and the Battle of France

It was at this tragic hour that the division of the French general staff into three parts proved fatal. Its ponderous machinery could not keep pace with the lightning character of developments. Gamelin was not in touch with armies in the north. He was not correctly informed of the situation at Sedan. In a subdued but confident mood he appeared before the members of the Committee of National Defense in the afternoon of May 15 and assured them that the situation was not beyond repair. But when he reached the castle of Vincennes and conferred with his staff, the full force of the impending tragedy broke over him. His quick academic mind told him that all was lost. Like a nervous chess player, who sees a sudden checkmate looming where he thought to win a coup himself, Gamelin figuratively swept the pieces off the board in an impatient gesture of surrender. He called Daladier on the phone and admitted that the situation was indescribably grave.

Daladier, who had been deceived by the confident attitude of Gamelin up to that time, was thunderstruck. When Gamelin admitted that he did not have a single army corps at his disposal between Laon and Paris, Daladier is said to have observed: "Then it means the destruction of the French army." According to William Bullitt, who was present during this phone conversation, Gamelin replied: "Yes, it means the destruction of the French army." [6] In spite of this admission, Reynaud could not obtain cabinet approval of Gamelin's dismissal until May 19 when Weygand replaced him.

Two decisive acts remained to Gamelin before he lost power. After spending a hectic day in uncertainty (and without consulting Reynaud), he issued his famous order of May 17 which carried the stirring "conquer or die" words of the Marne order of 1914. But the magic did not work this time. There was not the slightest change in the Allied strategic position to warrant it, and in view of the colossal concentration of German armored and infantry strength rolling toward the sea in the Somme area there was not the remotest hope of its fulfillment. The message was utterly meaningless. Even if all the French troops in that area had obeyed the order literally and died fighting with their puny weapons against the terrifying team of the dive bomber and the tank, the situation would not have been materially al-

6 A. Gérard (Pertinax), *Les Fossoyeurs* (New York, 1943), vol. I, pp. 91–92.

tered. Morale sagged immediately and irretrievably. France was lost!

The final act of Gamelin in the fearful drama of Flanders also bore the faint remembrance of happier days at the Marne in 1914. Five hours before he was replaced on May 19 he ordered General Billotte, commanding the Allied forces in Flanders, to launch a counterattack against the Somme gap. Before this could be undertaken, Weygand assumed supreme command. His first question to Gamelin was: "Where are the French and British forces in the north?" So great was the confusion and breakdown of French intelligence that Gamelin could not give Weygand a clear picture of the situation in Flanders. The order for the counterattack was postponed and Weygand was forced to undertake personal air reconnaissance in order to judge the situation.

It becomes clear that Gamelin's eleventh-hour order for a counterattack by the northern armies was a leap in the dark. It would be unfair to suggest, as some have done, that he made this move in order to forestall his dismissal, since it would have been difficult for Reynaud to remove him while the only possible measure for the relief of the entrapped northern forces was under way. Nor does it seem fair to compare Gamelin's dismissal on May 19 with a hypothetical removal of Joffre after the Battle of Charleroi in 1914 and say: "In this case there would have been no victory at the Marne." Joffre at least knew where his own forces were. He developed a plan possible of achievement. Gamelin was acting in the absence of information.

V

ONE IS forced to admire Gamelin's composure in this moment of personal and national disaster. There were no heroics or melodrama. The mask of academic serenity was never lifted to reveal the extent to which he considered himself personally responsible for the fall of France. On May 23 he was found trimming the roses in the back yard of his apartment at No. 55 Avenue Foch in Paris. He assured his friends that he could and would defend his military policy and program. When the final collapse came he submitted to arrest and imprisonment at Riom with dignity and silence. Along with others he was sentenced to life imprisonment by Pétain in advance of the trial.

It is obviously too early to pass anything like final judgment on Gamelin. Some of the French archives were destroyed in the evacuation of Paris. Full documentary evidence may never be available. The Riom trial was stopped by the Vichy regime when the testimony of the defendants began to embarrass Pétain and the nazis, but enough was revealed to show that French military resources were not fully used to defend France in 1940 and that treason had its role in the defeat of France. Gamelin steadfastly refused to testify at the hearings. The whole matter of Gamelin's responsibility for the French military position on May 19 is bound up with the supreme question of the Weygand-Pétain decision on June 16 that the whole war was lost and that Britain could not possibly prevail against Germany and Italy. Thus the full truth about the first stages of the war in the west may be hidden for years. But because of the immense warning value they contain, certain conclusions can and must be drawn.

Along with many others, Gamelin completely misjudged the character of the social and military revolution that was taking place in the Reich during the years of his power. He compromised with the politicians instead of forcing them to provide for the security of the state. He was blind to the tactical innovations that the Germans had prepared in peace and had practiced in Poland and Norway. He staked his whole concept of a defensive war on the Maginot line despite World War I teachings as to the strength of positions in depth. He abandoned his cautious program of static defense in favor of a bold stroke as far north as Holland. He took no warning from the immunity that the Allied relief columns enjoyed from German air attack. He did not interpret the events of the first two days' fighting in Holland and Belgium as invalidating previous concepts as to time and disposition of forces. He spent five vital days in arriving at a correct estimate of the German plan of attack. It was then too late to withdraw the northern forces. By the time he turned over control to Weygand he had lost touch with the French armies in the field and had no clear grasp of the military situation. He showed little or no appreciation of the potentialities or proper use of air power or tanks in modern war.

As evidence of the complete breakdown of the French war machine and the atmosphere of unreality with which it went to its doom, the Germans report that when their advance column rolled into Abbeville on May 20, the local French garrison was on the parade ground going through its ancient and elaborate evolutions in close-order drill.[7]

The question may well be raised: how could a professional soldier of Gamelin's attainments perform with such incredible maladroitness in a crisis which he admitted he foresaw since the start of hostilities? A complete answer (if it were possible) would be of immense importance to professional soldiers everywhere. A partial answer might be that Gamelin was an academic soldier. Viscount Gort said flatly: "He was not a fighter." In the isolation of high office Gamelin retired more and more into the ivory tower of philosophic reflections on past military events and paid insufficient attention to the practical aspects of war. Combat officers visiting his headquarters at Vincennes found no opportunity in the erudite discussions of philosophy and art to comment on their front-line experience. According to André Géraud, Gamelin's ideas "came ready-made—he ceased to examine whether they were still valid. He felt that he had foreseen everything, calculated everything, arranged everything, and that he had nothing more to do." When the crisis of May smashed his little academic world to bits, he was incapable of elasticity of mind or resolute action. "He was a cold light."

Lord Tweedsmuir, writing about another soldier, summed up with amazing exactness the tragedy of Gamelin. He said:

He was first and foremost a highly competent professional soldier. Now, a soldier's professionalism differs from that of other crafts. He acquires a body of knowledge which may be varied and enlarged by new conditions,

[7] *Deutsche Wehr*, February 28, 1941, p. 139.

such as new weapons and new modes of transport, but which in essence is a closed technique.—A powerful mind might work brilliantly inside its limits with little impulse to alter fundamentals. Change and expansion were consequently in the nature of a revelation, and were brought about either by a great genius, or slowly and grudgingly by some cataclysmic pressure. Hence the more competent and better trained the soldier was, the more averse he would be to alter his traditional creed until its failure had been proven with utter finality.

Because of the utter finality with which the career of Gamelin set the seal of failure on his methods and concepts, it may well mark the end of one military epoch and the beginning of another. Certainly any soldier after Gamelin who permits himself to enjoy the luxury of complacency and the comfort to be found in the maintenance of old concepts, who does not subject himself and his thinking to repeated and vigorous examination, whose mind is closed to the almost limitless application of science to the "new face of war," courts similar disaster for himself and for his country.

DE GAULLE

☆

"He was the spokesman of unconquerable France."

ON THE morning of June 18, 1940, an RAF bomber landed at Croydon airfield carrying among its passengers a six-foot French major general: Charles de Gaulle. He arrived at the darkest hour in France's history. Marshal Pétain had just acknowledged the triumph of Germany by asking for an armistice under conditions that precluded a retreat to new lines in southern France, a continuation of the war from Africa, or an acceptance of Churchill's offer to unite the empires. The tall French general brought with him from the chaos of Bordeaux only a family photograph, an extra pair of trousers, and a few shirts. Since it was no longer possible to fight in metropolitan France, General de Gaulle determined to carry on the battle from a new base. That night in a second class London hotel he set forth a new objective for France and himself. He would (*a*) continue the war at the side of Britain, (*b*) protect the French Colonial Empire and use it as a military base against the Axis, and (*c*) work for the final deliverance of France. He announced these resolutions by radio to the people of France.

At first sight there was something supremely quixotic and presumptuous about this program. General de Gaulle was a penniless exile, a junior general whose oak leaves were barely 34 days old. True, he had held a post as undersecretary of war in the Reynaud ministry, but Pétain had swept this government aside to make "a soldier's peace." That a junior general—above all, that a junior who had been right in most of his views on the war —should question the armistice decision of "great" military leaders such as Weygand and Pétain, was a shocking example of bad military manners. Who did this upstart think he was? Few men had ever heard his name.

Even before Frenchmen learned the humiliating terms of the armistice, they again heard the passionate voice of General de Gaulle urging them to repudiate the surrender. His appeal rang out in sharp contrast to the mumbling armistice message of Pétain. He said:

Is all hope gone? Is the defeat final? No! Believe me, for I speak to you with full knowledge of what I say.—The very same means that conquered us can one day give us victory.

France is not alone! She is not alone. She is not alone. She has a vast empire behind her. She can form a coalition with the British Empire, which holds the seas and is continuing the struggle. She can, like England, have limitless access to the immense industrial powers of the United States.

This war is not limited to the territory of our unhappy land. . . . This is a world war. All our mistakes, all our delays, all our suffering do not alter the fact that there exist in the world all the means needed to crush our enemies some day. Although we are today crushed by mechanized force, we can in the future conquer through superior mechanized force. Therein lies the destiny of the world. . . .

In Africa we must refuse to carry out the terms of the enemy—. We must not allow the panic which has gripped Bordeaux to spread overseas.

Having warned against the mechanized phase of the continental war, De Gaulle now pointed to the second or global phase of the war.

His challenge was lost on the government of France which put its trust in the judgment of "senior" officers who had once shared in great military events but who had not kept abreast of progress in the conduct of war. The train of events begun at Bordeaux had its tragic culmination in the armistice car at Compiègne. De Gaulle was stripped of his commission and placed under arrest by decree. This closed one phase of his career that began in 1911 when he entered St. Cyr as an officer candidate.

II

CHARLES ANDRÉ MARIE DE GAULLE was born at Lille on November 22, 1890, the son of a distinguished professor of philosophy. His spare frame, towering height, gaunt face, and swaying gait

DE GAULLE

gave an impression of peasant origin. Classmates at St. Cyr called him "the asparagus stalk." He showed "a fierce energy," excelled in his studies, and upon commissioning, chose service in the 33rd infantry regiment commanded by a painstaking student of infantry tactics named Colonel Henri Philippe Pétain. Here began a curious relationship between De Gaulle and Pétain which was to span two wars, to see France at the height of her military power and in the depths of defeat.

Lieutenant de Gaulle served with his regiment on the Belgian frontier in 1914 where he was wounded in action. He won a captaincy, three citations, and another wound stripe in 1915. He served on the Verdun front in 1916 where he was again wounded and taken captive. The remainder of the war he spent in various German prison camps. After five attempts to escape were frustrated, De Gaulle reconciled himself to the task of studying his captors. He wrote a description of the weaknesses and elements of dissension in the German army.[1]

After the war he served a brief term as instructor in military history at St. Cyr, joined Weygand in the defense of Warsaw in 1921, and entered the École de Guerre in 1924. His strong independence of mind annoyed some of his instructors, but it won the approval of Marshal Pétain, the commandant. The divergence of view arose over the then popular device of luring the enemy into a disastrous attack on positions especially prepared for defense. De Gaulle denied the universal application of this theory, holding that mobility and striking power were the only real assurances of success in battle. Pétain, then still vigorous in mind, may have recalled the discouragements he encountered in trying to improve infantry tactics in earlier days. At the conclusion of the course in 1926, he placed De Gaulle on his personal staff.

Between 1927 and 1932 De Gaulle served on the staff of the army of occupation at Trier, held command of a chasseur battalion, and went on missions to Egypt, Iran, and Iraq. In 1932 he was appointed secretary of the National Defense Council where,

[1] *La discorde chez l'ennemi* (Paris, 1924).

for the first time, he dealt with military problems on a national level. As he examined the military position of France in the light of possible future developments, he found considerable reason for alarm.

The potentialities of the internal combustion engine and the technical perfection of the highly trained Reichswehr, which Seeckt built up within the limits of the Versailles treaty, appealed to De Gaulle's imagination. If the supertrained Reichswehr obtained the machines of modern war, tanks and planes, it would have tremendous advantages over the mass army of the French Republic. New power concepts such as fascism were arising in Europe; they disturbed the previous tempo of political and military change. New methods of transport and warfare constantly widened the gap between the French army and the military requirements of France's foreign policy. French military leaders might have unshakable confidence in the doctrines and weapons of 1918, but this did not halt the steady deterioration of her military position.

Fully matured and with a varied experience behind him, De Gaulle now set down his military ideas in three provocative books: *Au fil de l'épée* ("At the Point of the Sword"), 1932, a study in the philosophy of command, *Vers l'armée de métier* ("Towards a Professional Army," published in this country as *The Army of the Future*), 1934, and *La France et son armée* ("France and her Army"), 1938. He argued strongly against the prevailing tendency to regard military leadership as a set-piece technique. The conduct of war could not be reduced to a formula. A nation could build up a strong defensive position, try to force the enemy to attack it under conditions that assured his defeat, but there was no assurance the enemy would do so. Such a program, he held, staked the safety of France on the stupidity of the enemy and restricted the French army's freedom of action. Millions might be spent on protective walls of concrete and steel, but these walls were immobile. Everything immobile could be destroyed or by-passed. Surprise and change were the essential features of war. Only the development of individual initiative, a high degree of self-reliance and enterprise in the French officer corps, could adequately safeguard the nation against future trials and dangers. To use De Gaulle's words, the philosophy of training leaders should aim at inducing them to exercise "imagination, judgment, and decision, not in a certain direction, but for their own sake and with no other aim than to make them strong and free." He felt that "those who have the germ of military leadership" should extend their interests beyond the limits of military studies. The breadth of vision, the mental resiliency, and the audacity required for the superior direction of modern war could not be developed except on the broadest cultural foundations.

In his *Army of the Future* De Gaulle analyzed the impact of technological advancements on the French military position and set forth his concepts of a mechanized elite army. In a style at once brilliant and somber he described the military perils of France's position.

As looking at a portrait suggests the impression of the subject's destiny to the observer, so the map of France tells our own fortune. The body of the country has in its centre a citadel, a forbidding mass of age-old mountains, flanked by the tablelands of Provence, Limousin, and Burgundy; and, all around, vast slopes for the most part difficult of access to anyone attacking them from the outside and split by the gorges of the Saône, the Rhone and Garonne, barred by the walls of the Jura Alps and the Pyrenees or else plunging in the distance into the English Channel, the Atlantic, or the Mediterranean; but in the Northeast, there is a terrible breach between the essential basins of the Seine and the Loire and German territory. The Rhine, which nature meant the Gauls to have as their boundary and their protection, has hardly touched France before it leaves her and lays her open to attack.

To his mind the natural barriers to an invasion of France by Germany such as the rampart of the Vosges, the slopes of the Moselle and the Meuse, formed "appreciable but not very deep obstacles, which a slight error, surprise, or neglect would be sufficient to lose." Should the enemy penetrate any of the bulwarks of French defense, the whole system would be destroyed. The valleys of the Sambre, the Scheldt, the Scarpe, and the Lys were like "railways eager to guide the enemy." The 125 miles from the frontier to Paris could be covered in six hours by a motor car, one hour by plane. He had no illusions about successful resistance if Paris fell, recalling that every time Paris had been taken by the enemy in the past century, it broke the resistance of France.

The machine era which had eliminated the old security of distance also intensified France's comparative industrial and economic weaknesses. Not only was Germany supplied with war industries and resources on an immensely greater scale, but those that France had were concentrated in dangerously exposed areas. The machine not only reduced distances, it also altered military concepts of time. If Germany should penetrate the Ardennes barrier, France not only would lose vital industrial resources but would be deprived of space and time in which to improvise counteraction.

De Gaulle saw, through the oratory of the pacifists and the confusion of the collective-security advocates, the bald fact that the greatness or downfall of France always depended directly on the fortunes of battle. Since the loss of a single battle in the era of the machine might be irretrievable, an army that did not permit her instantaneously to counter a mechanized attack was useless, however large it might be. This hard fact might be distasteful to French idealists and politicians, but it was basic to French security. De Gaulle criticized the limited depth of the Maginot line, and the fact that it left the whole French northern flank exposed. Above all, he opposed the doctrine of static warfare that underlay it. Any attempt to impose immobility on a battlefield by mere weight of concrete or steel was to deny the efficiency of the machine.

"Machines control our destiny." This refrain recurs continually throughout De Gaulle's writings. Machines eased man's burdens, made it possible for him to span great distances, move masses, increased his potentialities for destruction a hundredfold, but they also imposed new demands on men. It was no

longer sufficient for a soldier merely to be able to work the bolt
of a rifle and carry a pack. Complicated machines required well-
trained operators. This led De Gaulle into a field of thinking
which caused many to reject all his views and to suspect him of
antidemocratic purposes. He frankly advocated a small, long-
term professional force of elite troops to counter the highly
trained Reichswehr.

As the British writer Major E. W. Sheppard pointed out, De
Gaulle's enthusiasm for the elite army may have caused his
sounder, less objectionable ideas on the make-up and function
of a mechanized force to be ignored by political and military
leaders who otherwise might have supported him. Parties of the
left regarded the proposed elite army as a veiled attempt to prepare for a dictatorship and destroy the republic.

It did not increase De Gaulle's popularity to point out, as he
did in pitiless fashion, the great gap between the existing French
army and the military requirements of French policy. This criticism reflected upon nearly every ministry that had held office
since 1919. Conservatism bred of the victory in 1918 led the
French high command to accept the impossible task of defending
France with "an army slow in formation and motion, when the
geographical, political, economic, and moral conditions peculiar
to her position deprived them of any margin of safety or any
allowance for delay."

To De Gaulle's way of thinking, the one chance of securing
France's military and political position lay in a mechanized
professional army. "The tank not only revived the art of surprise
and maneuver but added to it the relentlessness of machinery."
The army of the future, he prophesied, would move entirely on
treads. Once the decision was made to discard the wheel and the
marching men in favor of caterpillar-borne guns and men, revolutionary mobility would follow. No longer would the zone and
tempo of advance be limited to the extreme range of artillery or
the pace of the foot soldier.

De Gaulle believed that an army of six mechanized divisions

would permit France to face the future with safety. In *The Army of the Future* he described the composition and operation of these forces as follows:

A heavily armoured brigade, moving across country as fast as a horse at the gallop, armed with 500 guns of medium calibre, 400 smaller pieces, and 600 machine-guns. . . . This brigade of two regiments, one of heavy tanks, the other of medium tanks, with a reconnaissance battalion of very fast light machines, provided with improved equipment for liaison, observation and field work, will constitute the principal echelon of the larger unit.

A brigade of infantry consisting of two regiments of infantry and one battalion of riflemen, armed with 40 auxiliary pieces, the same number of antitank guns, 600 light and heavy machine-guns, provided with special tools for quickly digging trenches and shelters, equipped, as to clothes, painted sheets, trellises, etc., in such a way as to offer to the sight, and thus to attacks, only unrecognizable objects, will be devoted to the task of occupying, mopping up and organizing the territory which the terrible but temporary power of the tanks will have virtually secured. The mobile, but on the whole haphazard, short-range fire which will be operated in concert by the tanks and the infantry, must be covered, from as far away as possible, by another much more accurate system of fire. This is the task of the artillery. . . . Two artillery regiments, one consisting of heavy, short guns, the other of lighter long-range pieces, will form another strong unit, completed by an antiaircraft group, and capable of discharging 100 tons of projectiles in a quarter of an hour, to a depth of six miles beyond the battlefront.

The division, consisting of three complementary brigades, reinforced by a battalion of engineers to deal with crossings and a battalion of communication troops, will have at its disposal a reconnaissance group for scouting purposes. This latter will be composed of very fast whippet tanks, of troops brought up in their train for fighting on foot, and of light vehicles for distant liaison; the whole designed to get in touch with the enemy, to hold a front temporarily, to cover a flank for the time being, to cover a retreat.

Aerial units, not intended for casual tasks at anyone's behest, but having a definite mission of keeping a single specific general constantly informed and always supporting the same comrades in battle and lengthening the effective range of familiar artillery will be the eyes of the main unit. . . . Each division will possess a camouflage battalion. . . .

A light division will be attached to the ensemble formed by the six divisions of the line, for scouting purposes and to prevent surprise; this will be of the same general type as the others, but provided with faster, more lightly armoured machines, light artillery, and with more mobile infantry. . . . Finally, there will be the general reserves consisting of a brigade of very heavy tanks capable of attacking permanent fortifications, a brigade of artillery of very heavy calibre, a regiment of engineers, a regiment of signallers, a camouflage regiment, a regiment of reconnaissance aircraft, a regiment of riflemen and the usual supply services. These will complete the army of shock-troops.[2]

Such a mechanized army would have three times the fire power of six divisions of 1914; it would have 10 times the speed and range as well as infinitely greater defensive strength. De Gaulle thought that 100,000 men would be sufficient to operate six mechanized divisions and carry out his system of "fire, shock, speed, and camouflage." Air power was to be linked with the army of caterpillars. Planes would be used for reconnaissance and signaling, for concealing tanks with smoke screens and noise. Above all, the air force would provide super-long-range artillery to reach deep into the enemy's rear. In his view, planes would play a central role in war since the tank gave these long-range weapons a ground complement hitherto lacking. The combination of the plane and the tank would enable a mechanized force to strike in Schlieffen fashion deep at the flanks and rear of the enemy.

It would not be correct to assume on the basis of these books, as some have done, that De Gaulle foresaw the character of the coming war with Germany with entire clarity, or that he was the only prophet of mechanized war. General J. F. C. Fuller, his British contemporary, covered the same field and in many respects more thoroughly. De Gaulle seemed to think that tanks could reduce forts or ride roughshod over them. He did not envisage the extremely important role of combat engineers in preparing break-through gaps for tanks. One gets the impression that De Gaulle looked upon engineers in the old sense of bridge builders and road menders. Neither Fuller nor De Gaulle clearly foresaw the development of the combat team and task force system which was such an essential element of German military practice in 1939–40. None of the exponents of the elite army

[2] Quoted from *The Army of the Future* (J. B. Lippincott Co., Philadelphia, 1941) with the permission of the publisher.

was aware of the vital role that mass armies—as today on the Russian front or on the far-flung Pacific battle front—would play in exploiting the success of aerial and mechanized forces. To say, as some have done, that France was conquered by an elite corps of 50,000 tankers, engineers, pilots, and bombardiers is to ignore the massive weight of some 100 infantry divisions which alone gave finality to their accomplishments.

There is a vagueness in De Gaulle's writings about the course of battle once the mechanized army was launched. He showed no appreciation for the potentialities of paratroops or air-borne infantry. De Gaulle apparently envisaged only the operations of a mechanized army against a nonmechanized force. He speaks of "attacking the enemy position" or "the enemy camp." There is no clash of mechanized forces, no tank plus antitank against tank engagements which have characterized mechanized war in North Africa. The word antitank appears only twice in *The Army of the Future*. He did not foresee the role of the antitank mine, the dive bomber, or the ground-strafing plane in modern war.

Though De Gaulle's ideas got some support in French political circles, notably from Paul Reynaud, who wrote his own book on "The French Military Problem" in 1934, opposition to the elite principle was overwhelming. "France cannot entrust her fate to a professional army of 100,000 men" was a popular expression. Marshal Pétain, who had supported De Gaulle in earlier years, now broke with his former protégé. He described *The Army of the Future* as a pack of "witticisms." Others lamented its "mischievous" influence on military thought. The French army decided to form three light mechanized divisions in 1934, but their tables of equipment and the doctrines governing their employment in war ruled out the realization of De Gaulle's basic ideas. For better or for worse, France continued to base her military policy upon a system of alliances that was already showing signs of crumbling, upon the Maginot line, and upon her traditional muscle-moved citizens' army. She spent the enormous sum of 372,000,000,000 francs on her armed forces from 1919 to 1939, yet her army was not powerful enough to steel her politicians against international blackmail in 1936, 1938, and 1939. It was too weak to save her from disaster in 1940.

As is often the case with innovators in the military field, De Gaulle's ideas received greater attention abroad than they did at home. In Austria, Britain, and particularly in Germany, De Gaulle's books were carefully studied. Philippe Barrès, on a visit to Berlin in 1934, was embarrassed to find that nazi military and diplomatic officials knew all about De Gaulle's ideas while he, a Frenchman, had never heard of them. General Heinz Guderian, the foremost nazi theorist of mechanized warfare, frankly acknowledged indebtedness to De Gaulle in his *Achtung Panzers!*

As war drew near in 1939, the French army hastily decided to form four heavy armored divisions to augment the three light mechanized divisions of 1934. Only two of the heavy armored divisions were actually ready when the Germans struck in May, 1940. Two were in the process of organization and had to be rushed into battle with equipment and personnel incomplete. Mere numbers, however, meant little. It was not a question in May–June, 1940, of five French armored divisions against 10 German panzer divisions. The nazi technique of mass employment of tanks, and co-ordination of infantry, engineers, tanks, and planes, including dive bombers, so outmoded French tactics as to make numbers of little account. French tank doctrines did not envisage their employment in masses but tied them to infantry and artillery.

Colonel de Gaulle saw in the victorious sweep of the Wehrmacht through Poland a vindication of his ideas and a final warning to France. He was profoundly disturbed at the course of the war during the "Sitzkrieg" period. On January 26, 1940, four months before the German blow in the west, he wrote a long memorandum on the military situation to Gamelin, Weygand, Daladier, and Reynaud.

This memorandum contained some of his most acute observations in the field of military thought. There was no longer any time for fine academic discussions of military policy in the traditional manner. Disaster was impending. The stakes on the board were nothing less than the life of France. Condemning the official doctrine of war, De Gaulle pointed out the moral and military consequences of "sinking the entire fortune of France in cement." He warned that the Maginot line, "however reinforced, however much infantry and artillery occupy it, or rest on it," could be crossed! The only effective counter to a mechanized army, he held, was a mechanized army. This was impossible without a complete reform of the French military system.

He urged that France enlarge her manufacturing program and exploit the full possibilities of American production, ordering tanks and bombers on a grand scale. Yet it would not be enough merely to turn out vast numbers of tanks and planes to support and complement existing military formations. Mechanical forces should be separate from other organizations and designed for their own action. Finally he dealt with the larger aspects of the war.

From this combination of modern elements on land and sea and in the air, a new strategy must come, wide enough in space and rapid enough in time to be on the scale of what modern invention allows. This extension of the field of action and of force would, no doubt, bring a vast extension of the theater of war and profound changes in the political conduct of the conflict. Mechanized war, going hand in hand with that of economic warfare, will start into activity parts of the world which now look on. That is an inevitable consequence of evolution. The important thing is to get the benefit of this modern strength for our side instead of leaving it to the enemy. The French people must on no account yield to the delusion that the present military immobility is necessarily a characteristic of war. The contrary is the truth. The gasoline engine confers on modern destructive weapons a power, a pace, a range, such that this present conflict must—sooner or later—be marked by movements, surprise, irruptions, pursuits of which the scale and rapidity will infinitely surpass even the most overwhelming past events.

This was the first clear statement of any Allied military leader that envisaged extension of the war to new theaters and pointed out the revolutionary character of the struggle. Elsewhere efforts were made to evaluate the military disaster in Poland with the measuring stick of 1918. The desire of the French high command to confine the war to the Franco-German frontier was merely their final attempt to impose outworn doctrines on "the new face of war." It was their last delusion as to the nature of the coming battle. That General Gamelin could send the First French Army racing northward into a German trap on May 10, 1940, with the exultant cry, "I shall now repeat the maneuver of Austerlitz," reveals the completeness of his confusion.

On May 15, the day after the German panzer army broke through the French line at Sedan, De Gaulle was raised to the rank of general of division and given command of the 4th (heavy) Armored Division. The three excellent light mechanized divisions which had been rushed northward into Belgium were in the process of being cut off. When General de Gaulle reported to General Doumenc's headquarters at Montry, he learned that one heavy French armored division, operating without adequate reconnaissance and provision for refueling, was surprised by German tanks at Dinant and cut to pieces. Another had been frittered away at Verviers. His new command, the 4th Division, was made up of two battalions of 30 model B-2, 30-ton tanks each; two battalions of 40 12-ton tanks each; two artillery units of 16 75 mm. guns each; plus a battalion of chasseurs in trucks. The division lacked its normal complement of antiaircraft guns and supporting planes. General de Gaulle was ordered to delay the Germans near Laon despite the fact that his command had never operated together and some of the tank crews had never fired their guns.

The 4th Division went into action on May 18 south of Laon. A considerable advance was made in one sector before massed Stuka attacks and failure of supporting units compelled withdrawal. Then the 4th Division was sent to attack the enemy bridgehead south of Abbeville on May 30 and 31. Here General de Gaulle's unit scored the outstanding French tank success of the war. It advanced nearly 10 miles and captured many prisoners and much matériel. But minor victories could not stem the tidal wave of defeat sweeping over France. On June 5 the great Anglo-French army, which had been sent northward into Belgium on May 10, ceased to exist as a military force. The tide of battle then moved southward. In a last minute attempt to improve the situation, Premier Reynaud made General de Gaulle undersecretary of war on June 7, 1940. All that De Gaulle could do then was to urge a fight to the end. If no stand was possible in France proper, the government should move to North Africa. "Even if we were temporarily reduced to possessing only half of Morocco," he said, "we should still carry on. . . . Time will swing the balance of mechanized superiority to our side. . . . American aid will give us victory." It was to no avail; confusion mounted; defeatism increased. On June 18 he left Bordeaux for London.

III

AFTER De Gaulle had set up his headquarters in Britain he waged an incessant war of words not only against the Germans but against the defeatists of Bordeaux and the collaborationists of Vichy. Savagely he attacked the senile Pétain:

Marshal, yesterday I heard your voice—I listened to what you said to the French people to justify what you have done.

You first depicted the military inferiority which caused our defeat. . . . Next you declared there were only two alternatives . . . accept the conditions imposed by the enemy or take refuge in the Empire and continue the war. You thought it was your duty to stay. . . . In truth our military inferiority has been terrible. But what was the source of that inferiority? You who were at the head of our military organization after the war of 1914–1918, you who were generalissimo up to 1932, you who were minister for war in 1935 . . . did you ever support, urge, or demand that the necessary changes be made in this bad system?

We didn't need you, Marshal, to obtain and accept such conditions of slavery. We didn't need the Conquerer of Verdun. Anybody would have done as well!

On June 28, 1940, the British government recognized the Free French movement of General de Gaulle. As the symbol of his movement he adopted the double cross of Lorraine and the proud motto of 1871 *"Not Forever."* Frenchmen of all descriptions flocked to his banner; a new army was recruited and trained; a Free French navy carried on the war at sea. Then General de Gaulle prepared to push the colonial phase of the war. If the Axis was to be defeated, its forces had to be stretched thin. This involved a long war and the opening of new theaters and bases.

When Russia and the United States were drawn into the struggle, the conditions essential for a United Nations victory were at hand. It was now possible to foresee a realization of De Gaulle's promise that Germany, which defeated France through superior mechanized force, would, in turn, be overwhelmed by superior mechanized force.

Africa always bulked large in his mind. "Africa," he used to say after the collapse of June, "that's where we should have made preparations for the next battle. From the very moment we felt that things were going wrong, as early as May 16, we should have made this great decision and begun to carry it out."

His first efforts to gain control of French territory in Africa followed the British attack on French warships at Oran. Despite the heartburnings caused by this event, De Gaulle's organization was able to rally the Chad, the Gabon and the Cameroons to the Free French side by the end of August, 1940. Then came his abortive attack on Dakar in September, which caused many men to doubt his military as well as his political gifts.

Yet General de Gaulle survived this fiasco, and from that time on co-ordinated the military effort of the Free French movement closely with that of Britain. A force under General Catroux took a prominent part in the occupation of Syria in July, 1941. Other units co-operated in the conquest of Eritrea, distinguishing themselves in the hard fighting at Cheren. A Fighting French force of all arms under General Koenig made a magnificent defense at Bir Hacheim in May, 1942, against the most powerful units of the Afrika Korps. General Koenig and General de Larminat led Fighting French units in the battle of El Alamein; and when the British Eighth Army advanced into Tripolitania,

Fighting French forces from Lake Chad under General Leclerc, after a spectacular desert operation, fought their way into Tripoli and joined the Eighth Army. They co-operated with General Freyberg in his flanking operation toward El Hamma, which turned the Mareth line.

With the Allied invasion of North Africa, General de Gaulle's program for the liberation of France through an invasion of Europe seemed assured of ultimate realization. Yet his position with reference to that program underwent considerable change. Never officially supported by more than a fraction of the French colonial population, De Gaulle's movement now was called upon to co-operate with General Giraud, who controlled Morocco, Algeria, and Senegal.

From this co-operation General de Gaulle ultimately emerged as the acknowledged leader of the French National Committee of Liberation. After the close of the Tunisian campaign, the French army in North Africa, which had signalized its rebirth by fighting alongside the Allies and which captured 48,000 prisoners in the final operation in Tunisia, was rearmed with British and American equipment and trained for the liberation of France. This army took part in the occupation of Corsica, and in December, 1943, fought with the Fifth Army in Italy.

General de Gaulle's prestige and influence in the French underground movement may permit him to render yet another great service to his country and to the cause of the United Nations. But disregarding these prospects for the moment, and judging his career solely in terms of his military contribution to France, it seems safe to say that De Gaulle has earned a place among the great theoretical soldiers of that country. He was the one French military leader who had a fairly clear idea of the military problems of his day. He warned repeatedly against a static defense and emphasized the potentialities of mechanized attack. When the continental phase of the war was terminated by the collapse of France, he showed an early appreciation of the expanding character of the global war. In particular, he foresaw the supremely important part that Africa would play in the future strategy of the anti-Axis powers. He kept the spark of French resistance burning.

The final appraisal of the French people and of history will not dwell on the personal idiosyncrasies of General de Gaulle but will acknowledge the greatness of his military and moral gifts, his burning love of country. It will recall that when other voices were silent or counseled abject surrender, he was the spokesman of unconquerable France.

WAVELL

☆

*"The ideal officer should be afraid of nothing—
not even of a new idea."*

AS THE clouds of war hung over Europe in the summer of
1939, two generals were inspecting troops in Syria. News camera-
men caught them riding in a gleaming black Renault past
regiments of colorful French colonials and picturesque camel
troops. One of the soldiers was world famous. He was small,
sharp-eyed, trim-mustached, 69-year-old Maxime Weygand, former collaborator with Foch, covictor with Pilsudski at the
Battle of Warsaw in 1920, and former vice-president of the
Supreme War Council in France. The other man in the car was
a comparatively unknown, one-eyed, compact British general of
medium stature with a bull-dog chin. He was General Sir Archi-
bald Percival Wavell, the British chief of the Middle East command. All eyes and cameras followed Weygand, who was expected to play the leading role if the war should spread to the
Mediterranean. Wavell was the forgotten man in the hurly-burly
of military publicity that attended the outbreak of war. Veteran
newsmen in Cairo could not dig up enough about him in the
files to make a respectable column. All they could say was that
he was a student of the great Allenby, and that he was taciturn
to the point of using words as if they cost a guinea each.

If relatively unknown, Wavell began the war with certain
real advantages over better-known British soldiers, such as Gort
(commander of the BEF in France) and Ironside (chief of the
imperial general staff). He did not have a reputation to lose!
This was true, of course, only as far as the British public was
concerned. Wavell was well known in the army for his service in
World War I, for his knowledge of Russian and Middle Eastern

International News Photo

WAVELL and AUCHINLECK

problems, for his scholarly volume on the campaign in Palestine in 1917–18,[1] and for his Lees Knowles lectures on generalship at Cambridge University. He had put in years of work on a biography of Lord Allenby.[2] These evidences of scholarship and erudition, however, were forgiven by his brother officers because Wavell was not equally articulate in speech.

Wavell came from a military family. His father and grandfather were both professional soldiers. He was born in Essex where his father's regiment was quartered in May, 1883. As proper to a prospective officer, he was schooled at Winchester and Sandhurst and took a commission in the Black Watch Regiment in time to see service in the Boer War. At the close of this war he was transferred to India. He served on the Western front (where he suffered the loss of his left eye) from 1914 to 1916, and spent one year as British military observer in the Caucasus. In 1917 he was sent as War Office liaison officer to the Egyptian Expeditionary Force, then under the command of General Allenby. This gave him an opportunity to observe this gifted and imaginative soldier at close range. In 1918 he took an active part in the Palestine campaign as chief of staff of the XX Corps under General Sir Philip Chetwode. During the two years in Palestine, Wavell learned many of Allenby's tricks of command, his skill in handling the polyglot British army that defeated the Turks in 1918, his brutal but effective way of maintaining discipline and morale. Above all, he saw a military mind of real magnitude—freed from the shackles of trench warfare—resort to ancient stratagems of war and deceive and destroy an enemy whose intrepid and tenacious fighting had hitherto held British armies in check. It was an experience no officer could forget.

In the period of retrenchment that followed the end of World War I, Wavell went back to England to command first a brigade and then a division at Aldershot. He was the principal author of *Field Service Regulations, 1935,* the last prewar edition of that official manual. To demonstrate the obsolete character of former

[1] *The Palestine Campaign* (London, 1928).
[2] *Allenby: A Study in Greatness* (London and New York, 1940–41).

official regulations, he once put his division on the road at Alder-shot with every single item of equipment called for in the field-service regulations. The 15-mile-long column of Wavell's division jammed the roads and broke up the plans for the maneuvers. The War Office did not appreciate this kind of humor, and doubtless was relieved to send him off to Russia in 1936 and to Palestine and Transjordania in 1937. It discounted Wavell's en-thusiasm for parachute troops which he had seen at the Russian maneuvers of 1936. Bright young men were not welcomed by the stuffy overlords of Britain's military machine at this stage.

In the year he served as commander in Palestine and Trans-jordania, Wavell had to deal with repeated anti-Jewish out-breaks of the Arab population. In this difficult and thankless post he demonstrated ironhanded firmness coupled with velvet-handed diplomacy, and gained fresh information about the theater in which he was to serve in World War II. When the reform of the British army was undertaken by Hore-Belisha in 1937–38, Wavell was called back to England to head the southern and finally the command at Aldershot. This indicated that he was being groomed for a vital command in case of war. As ten-sion mounted in the summer of 1939, he was made commander in chief of the Middle East, a command that included Egypt, the Sudan, Kenya, British Somaliland, Palestine, Cyprus, and Transjordania.

Before departing for Cairo in 1939, Wavell delivered three lectures on generalship at Cambridge University which were distinguished for their urbanity, humor, and insight into human factors in war. Since these lectures serve to throw light on his subsequent career in North Africa, certain points in them are worth reviewing at some length. Wavell felt that the strategy and tactics imposed on the BEF by conditions in France from 1914 to 1918 left no chance for the "imaginative planning, boldness in execution, and relentlessness in pursuit" that characterized great British military exploits of the past. "We must get the last of the Flanders mud out of our minds," he said. He did not think that the stationary war of trenches would be permanent, but felt that new developments would bring mobility back to the battle-field. Equipment and tactics were certain to change, but some essentials for a commanding officer were timeless.

To his mind, a good general should be able to measure up to the Socratic standard. Namely:

> He must know how to get his men their rations and every other kind of store needed for war. He must have imagination to originate plans, practical sense and energy to carry them through. He must be observant, untiring, shrewd, kindly and cruel; simple and crafty, a watchman and a robber; lavish and miserly; generous and stingy, rash and conservative. He should also, as a matter of course, know his tactics; for a disorderly mob is no more an army than a heap of building stone is a house.

Wavell stressed physical fitness and hardihood as primary essentials of a successful commander. Officers as well as weapons should be able to survive unnatural tests and carry on. The general should have a touch of the gambler and be willing to run risks in order to win great gains. According to Wavell, sound topographic knowledge and the ability to prepare for moving and supplying troops over the terrain involved are the real marks of military understanding. He extended the indispensable requirement of personal courage to cover fear of new ideas as well as enemy bullets. As far as the technical side of soldiering is concerned, a modern commander should know a great deal more than the ancients. He should be familiar with aircraft and their performance, tanks and their capacities, armored cars, wireless, smoke, chemical-warfare equipment, camouflage, propaganda, and military engineering. Above all, he must understand men.

Wavell's relationship with Allenby taught him that a commander could get the most out of his subordinates if he gave them freedom of action to the limit of their abilities. He stressed the necessity of taking every precaution for the comfort and safety of troops. The common soldier would tolerate, even admire, a tough and ironhanded leader, if he knew that the rigorous action was taken in his own interest. The kind of discipline Wavell wanted was the kind that insured that "where two or three men gathered together in battle there should be courage and enterprise in them." The ideal foot soldier should combine the qualities of a game stalker, a petty sneak, and a ruthless gunman. Individual resourcefulness and battle cunning in the common soldier should be sought by every means within the general's power. Moving men into battle in long waves, as Haig did at the Somme, was merely to sanction mass butchery. With an army toughened and trained for war the general could afford to drive the heart out of it, if necessary in order to save lives and insure victory. He likened the relationship between the general and the army to that between a horse and a rider. "The horse (the army) should be cared for (training and maintenance) in the stable as if he were worth £500. But he should be ridden in the field as if he were not worth half a crown."

It was a mistake, Wavell felt, for the British army to spend all its time studying the characteristics of foreign soldiers. In his opinion it would do well to analyze the national characteristics and aptitudes of Britishers and adapt them to the most formidable war methods which it could devise. He did not care to see a British army formed in German or French molds. Wavell's lectures demonstrated that he was competent to analyze the craft of a military commander; it remained to be seen whether or not he could practice it successfully, for he had never exercised an independent command in the field.

II

SINCE Italy did not enter the war in 1939 there was no immediate fighting in the eastern Mediterranean. General Wavell's command in September, 1939, consisted of some 30,000 British and colonial troops stationed in Egypt, Palestine, and Transjordania. They were equipped with a fair number of armored cars and Bren gun carriers, but were allotted only the planes deemed obsolete for action in France. As the war went on, Wavell received reinforcements from India, Australia, South Africa, and Canada, which increased the size of his army by the time Italy

entered the war. Wavell used the period of relative inactivity
that preceded this event to train his troops in desert operations
and to harden them by long marches. From his headquarters in
Cairo he supervised the billeting and rationing of an army that
embraced at least a dozen races and nationalities. He built up
the strong morale and discipline required for sustained offensive
operations.

Wavell's position in Egypt was delicate and complicated. The
Egyptian government, never too reliable, hesitated to be drawn
into the war. Cairo was a nest of Axis intrigue with spies as
thick at the bar of the fashionable Mena House as flies around
a mess-hall door. He had to keep happy troops and officers of
widely different interests and nationalities, maintain friendly
if distant relations with the Egyptians, and administer the immense military district under his command. Wavell followed
Allenby's habit of spending as much time as possible with his
troops, covering his vast domain by plane. His frequent trips
were sometimes intended to throw Axis informers off the track.
He lunched, swam, and hunted with King Farouk, often making
a point of doing so just before some military stroke. He seldom
risked a speech to the troops, but has shown that he could turn
off an appealing order of the day when he had to. Like Allenby,
he maintained distant relations with the troops, but they re-
spected him and had complete confidence in his leadership.
Even the monocle he wore in his right eye seemed natural and
lacking in affectation to the otherwise scurrilous Australians:
they knew he had only one eye! In the heat and confusion of
Cairo his coolness and collected manner inspired confidence.

When Italy entered the war on June 10, 1940, the Egyptian
theater entered the zone of active operations. The collapse of
France destroyed all joint Allied plans for the protection of the
eastern Mediterranean. Weygand had been called back to France,
and the tortuous policy of his successor, General Henri Dentz,
made it clear that the French army in Syria could not be counted
upon to defend even that area against Axis penetration. An Ital-

ian army of nearly 290,000 men was based in Libya under Wavell's old professional friend, Marshal Rudolf Graziani. It possessed 1,900 cannon, 779 tanks, 15,000 machine guns, and 10,000 trucks. This army had formerly faced the possible menace of a French advance from Tunisia. Now it could concentrate its full force against the frontiers of Egypt. In Italian East Africa (Eritrea, Italian Somaliland, and Ethiopia) was another fascist force of 120,000 white and native troops under the duke of Aosta, the ablest of the sons of the House of Savoy. This force threatened Kenya, the Sudan, and British Somaliland. Graziani's army, however, was considered the real menace to Egypt. His well-known aggressive tendencies (he had conducted the rapid advance from Italian Somaliland into Ethiopia in 1936) suggested that an invasion of Egypt would soon follow Italy's entrance into the war.

III

GENERAL WAVELL's adversaries drew first blood in the battle of the Middle East. On August 5, 1940, three columns of white and native troops under the duke of Aosta invaded British Somaliland. Since Wavell's plans for the defense of this area had been made on the assumption of support by forces in French Somaliland, the blow could not be parried. The small Somaliland camel corps under Lieutenant Colonel Arthur Chater (500 British and 500 native troops) put up a delaying action but was withdrawn by sea to Aden. The fascist forces entered Berbera on August 19. When the news arrived in Cairo, General Wavell did not break off his daily swim at the Mena House pool. Patience and imperturbability were qualities he also had included in his sketch of the ideal commander.

Against his main adversary in the west, Wavell adopted a policy of bluff and bluster. A few sharp engagements on the frontier convinced Graziani that Wavell had large forces at his disposal and was trying to lure the Italian army into a trap.

Finally in the first week in September, Graziani's army was ready to move. It left its bases at Bardia and Fort Capuzzo on September 12 and swept into Egypt through Halfaya Pass. Covered by Italian aviation, light Fiat tanks and armored cars raced forward to Sidi Barrani. They covered the distance of 100 miles in five days. Here the Italian forces stopped to entrench, dig the necessary wells, and perfect communications. Water supply was a decisive factor, for the desert between Sidi Barrani and Mersa Matruh was waterless. Pipe lines were extended from Libya, which supplied the Sidi Barrani garrison with 335,000 liters of water daily. Roads were constructed which occupied the Italians until December, 1940. The 1st and 2nd (Libyan) divisions and the 3rd Black Shirt Division were stationed in Sidi Barrani and in its outlying defenses at Maktila. In support positions were the Catanzaro and Cirene divisions, while the armored division of General Maletti was stationed in two camps to the south.

As General Wavell studied the Italian dispositions at Sidi Barrani, he came to the conclusion that they were faulty and could be attacked by surprise. He called General Wilson into his office and sketched out a plan of attack by a British force half as strong as the enemy. He asked if the plan seemed feasible. General Wilson (who was to have executive charge of the operations) agreed that, given surprise, there was a prospect of overwhelming the enemy. Minute plans were then drawn for the attack on Sidi Barrani.

The operations that followed were made possible by a number of apparently unrelated occurrences. First, Admiral Cunningham's torpedo bombers crippled the Italian fleet at Taranto on November 11, cutting Graziani's sea communications; and Winston Churchill, with rare courage and foresight, sent first-line fighter planes and medium tanks from Britain in the face of a threatened German invasion. These reinforcements arrived in time to provide General Wavell with the equipment necessary to command the air over the desert and to put into action the 7th Armored Division which was superior in quality to the

Italian armored force.[3] Numbers were heavily on the Italian side; no less than 60,000 men were concentrated in the vicinity of Sidi Barrani. Many more troops were in support at Sollum and Fort Capuzzo. The striking force of British and imperial troops numbered less than 40,000, and there was only one tank division. But the morale of the men of the British army was extremely high; they were confident of their weapons, training, and leadership.

In the view of many military critics it was impossible to surprise an adversary on the sun-baked desert coastal plain. Armored cars and reconnaissance columns could be spotted from the air miles away. The waterless rocky plain leading to Alexandria and stretching into Libya was regarded by both sides as an enemy to be overcome, rather than an ally to be used. Wavell was the first to see that the desert could be used like the sea to convey men and supplies to the decisive point if only the mechanical equipment were available and absolute mastery of the air obtained. The problem of supply, particularly water, was rendered simpler by the presence of the British fleet. It was an additional advantage that Mersa Matruh enjoyed rail connections with Alexandria.

For the first time in the history of World War II the full force of British power was to be thrown at the enemy in one area simultaneously. The fleet was to bombard Italian positions from the sea and co-operate with the land forces. The air force was to prepare the way for infantry and tanks by neutralizing the enemy air force, and by bombing and machine-gunning enemy troop concentrations. An elaborate feint on the model of Allenby's Gaza maneuver of November, 1917, was prepared. Dummy implacements, a fake airdrome, and a big artificial tank park con-

---

[3] The now famous 7th Armored Division fought in nearly every important engagement of the British armies in North Africa from 1940 to 1943. In 1940 it was hardly more than an armored brigade. General Michael O'Moore Creagh was in command of the British armor in the first Libyan campaign but tactical control of the whole force was in the hands of Lieutenant General Richard Nugent O'Connor, field commander of the army of the Nile. General Creagh fell ill just before the battle and General Caunter led the 7th Armored Division.

structed east of Maktila caused the Italians to expect a conventional British frontal attack on Sidi Barrani by way of Maktila. The attention of the Italian staff was fastened on the eastern approaches to their position. Meanwhile a real tank depot was hidden in the desert southwest of Mersa Matruh. In it, through the night of December 8–9, the 7th Armored Division was concentrated. Winston Churchill sent an encouraging wire to General Wavell, quoting the scriptural phrase: "Seek and ye shall find, knock and it shall be opened unto you." Wavell's own order to the troops was a masterly appeal to their spirit and morale. He said: "In everything but numbers we are superior to the enemy. We are more highly trained; we shoot straighter; we have better weapons and equipment. Above all, we have stouter hearts and greater traditions, and we are fighting in a worthier cause—."

Throughout the bitter cold night of December 8–9 British troops and tank crews in the desert slept beside their arms and machines. A half-moon hid the approach of the British columns and sandstorms bit into the faces of the men. As the first streaks of dawn lighted the east, British bombers roared over the Italian positions protected by fleets of fighter planes. On the flying fields at Sidi Barrani, Sollum, Fort Capuzzo, and Bardia hundreds of Italian planes were destroyed on the ground. Sweeping back, the planes took new bomb loads and returned to attack the Italian positions at Sidi Barrani. Ships of the Royal Navy appeared offshore and blasted Italian artillery parks. With Italian attention drawn to their coastal and eastern flank, the 7th Armored Division rolled northwestward out of the desert. The Italians had placed minefields on their eastern and southern flanks but had only a wire barrier on the west. Through it the 7th Armored Division crashed, catching the Italians with their armor still in parks. Many of the Italian tanks never fired a gun or moved a tread. General Maletti was killed by machine-gun fire as he valiantly attempted to put his division into action. British armored cars raced toward the sea at Buq Buq, and by nightfall the Italian garrison at Sidi Barrani was surrounded.

Two days later it surrendered. Forty thousand prisoners and an immense store of military booty fell into British hands.

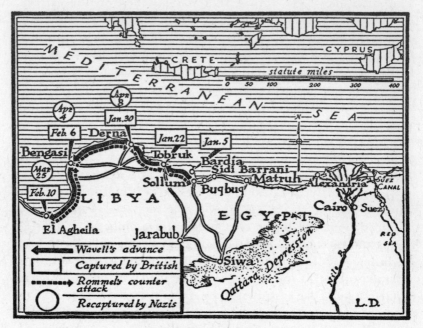

The Libyan Campaign

As soon as General O'Connor saw that the work of the 7th Armored Division had been completed he turned it westward. The Italian Catanzaro Division marching hopefully toward the sound of battle ran into the British tanks—and being helpless in that situation surrendered.

The most amazing thing about the success was the surprise attained. British intelligence had spread the impression that an advance by Graziani was expected in the near future. Axis newspapers had stated pontifically that surprise was impossible in the desert theater. Newsmen in Cairo were kept completely in the dark until Wavell called them into his office at ten o'clock in the morning of December 9 and informed them that the attack had been launched. Not a single correspondent (and they have

proved remarkably effective in smelling out zones of impending
action) had the slightest idea that a British offensive was contemplated.

The extent of the success at Sidi Barrani was frankly a surprise
to Wavell. He had purposely worded the first announcements
of the battle in modest terms, thinking that it would enable him
to break off the operation without loss of morale in case of
failure. In the preparatory stages of the operation the troops
engaged had been informed that they were to undertake a routine training march. Once he saw the low state of Italian morale,
and studied the remaining Italian positions in Cyrenaica and
Libya, Wavell decided that the situation justified a tremendous
gamble. Since British losses were extremely light, he decided to
throw his small striking force against the retreating fascists with
the aim of capturing or destroying the whole Italian army in
Cyrenaica. He even decided to pull out the 4th Indian Division
and send it to General Platt for operations in Eritrea. He knew
that relentless pursuit of a beaten foe called forth the greatest
qualities in an army. Troops were naturally inclined to relax
after the first victory. But Wavell decided "to ride the horse as
if it were not worth a half a crown." He gave orders for an immediate continuation of operations.

From this point on, Wavell's great victories of December,
January, and February took on the form of magnificent improvisations. There was no time to prepare each new movement
with the care and detail of the Sidi Barrani operation. So, favored
with the terrain involved and command of the air, Wavell repeated an encircling maneuver at Fort Capuzzo, Bardia, Tobruk,
and Bengasi. Graziani proved helpful by acting on the World
War I doctrine of fighting battles for territory. As a result, parts
of his army were captured or destroyed in each defended area.
This system of isolated fortress positions failed completely. The
most daring stroke of the whole campaign was Wavell's decision
to send the 7th Armored Division cross country to cut off the
retreat of General Tellera's forces some 50 miles south of Bengasi. They caught this column of 112 tanks, 216 guns, 1,500

trucks and 20,000 men on the open road and bluffed and fought it into surrender. It was one of the most audacious and brilliant operations of the war.

The rate of Wavell's advance into Libya did not equal the speed of German blitz campaigns elsewhere, but for a British advance it was rapid. Bardia was taken on January 5, Tobruk on January 22, Derna on January 30, Bengasi on February 6, and El Agheila on February 10. By that time 134,000 Italian soldiers had been killed or captured and an immense quantity of arms had fallen into British hands. Most welcome of all was the fact that the victories were accomplished with British losses of less than 3,000 men. The only reinforcements received by the striking force after taking Sidi Barrani were in infantry and artillery. The main brunt of the advance fell on the 7th Armored Division which, after fighting over 500 miles of rough terrain, was due for an overhaul. Wavell's victories were celebrated around the world, and he suddenly became "the most famous British general." Even the Germans spoke of his ability with respect.

According to Alexander Clifford, a British observer who covered the entire war in North Africa, "Wavell's army won because it was superior in the only two spheres where it could be superior: in quality of leadership and quality of individual fighting troops. Victory came through nonmaterial, impalpable things, largely qualities of the mind: through a disciplined audacity, an intuitive awareness of when and where risks could be taken—." It took Graziani, who had never before been on the receiving end of mechanized war, eight weeks to learn that it was futile to fight for "places." By the time he learned this lesson his army had dissolved and he was replaced by a German leader, General Erwin Rommel.

When Wavell's forces reached Bengasi, many expected that the advance would continue into Tripoli. These hopes were based on an ignorance of the real situation in Libya. The public had little knowledge of the relative weakness of Wavell's striking force. Almost unnoticed was an occurrence in the straits of Pantelleria on January 10 which changed the whole character of the war in Libya. On that day a British convoy, passing through the straits under protection of cruisers and the aircraft carrier *Illustrious,* was attacked by nazi dive bombers operating from Catania in Sicily. Despite heavy losses from antiaircraft fire, the German pilots attacked with such desperate resolution that the British cruiser *Southampton* and the destroyer *Gallant* were sunk. The *Illustrious* was severely damaged. After that, the surface forces of the British navy ceased to operate in this theater. With immunity from surface attack, German mechanized equipment was shipped to Tripoli. In February and March a mechanized force headed by General Rommel was concentrated west of Bengasi. Luftwaffe squadrons appeared on the Libyan front. General Rommel soon possessed superiority in both mechanized and air strength. The swiftness of this transport performance on the part of the enemy was ominous. General Wavell's advanced positions could no longer be held. The African force of General Rommel (who kept the Italian General Gariboldi at his headquarters as concession to Italian pride) struck at El Agheila on March 25, forcing the British to retreat. The British and the neutral press played it up as a mere fluctuation in the battle; but, when the same force took Bengasi on April 4, the strength of Axis forces in this area could no longer be concealed.

General Rommel was a commander of long experience, tough and resourceful. He served throughout World War I, and in the Polish, Flanders, and French campaigns. His sweeps into Cyrenaica were bold and extremely well organized. On the night of April 8 a small detachment of his motorcycle troops armed with tommy guns cut off a British convoy. In the confusion they captured three of General Wavell's most valuable assistants, General O'Connor, General Philip Neame, and General Michael Gambier-Parry. It was a heavy blow to the Middle East command.[4] On April 14 General Rommel's forces, which had passed

---

[4] Churchill's witty attempt to explain this surprise could not conceal its importance. In describing the event he used the hackneyed phrase of the Air Ministry, "From these operations three of our generals failed to return." Generals O'Connor and Neame escaped from captivity in the confusion following Italy's withdrawal from the war in September, 1943.

up Tobruk, moved across the Egyptian border at Sollum.

The British public watched with dismay the loss of the territory occupied in Libya, but it did not lose confidence in Wavell. Unlike Graziani, who lost the same territory, Wavell saved his army from destruction or capture. Leaving a strong garrison at Tobruk, he withdrew to his old positions at Sidi Barrani and Mersa Matruh and awaited the Axis thrust. It should be remembered that while Wavell was being driven out of Libya he was at the same time carrying out the conquest of Italian Somaliland, Eritrea, closing in on the Italian forces in Ethiopia, and preparing to aid Greece against an impending invasion by the nazis.

IV

THOUGH fighting of an indecisive character broke out on the frontiers of Egypt and Kenya as soon as Italy entered the war, Wavell did not begin his program for the conquest of Italian East Africa until his Libyan drive had reached its crest at Bengasi. There were far-reaching political as well as military reasons for the campaign. South African leaders (particularly General Smuts) were eager for a conquest of Italian possessions in Africa. The British occupation of the entire Red Sea littoral, the shores of the Gulf of Aden, and the approaches to the Indian Ocean might encourage the United States to remove this area from the combat zone and thus facilitate shipment of arms and munitions to the Middle East. The military motives for the conquest were not so pressing. The duke of Aosta was isolated from Italy and, like a cut flower, was certain to fade with the gradual exhaustion of his supplies. As long as his army was in being it constituted a menace to the security of the Sudan, but he lacked strength sufficient to operate alone against Egypt. The task of destroying his forces and occupying his territory involved moving troops across immense distances and extremely difficult terrain.

The British forces available for these movements were very small indeed: they numbered less than 50,000 men. Only a

limited number of tanks and Bren gun carriers could be allotted
to the forces, and air support in all the southern operations depended on the small South African air force. In general, the
troops and weapons employed were merely those that could be
spared from other more vital theaters in the Middle East. When
the conquest was practically over, one British wit (paraphrasing
Churchill's splendid tribute to the RAF) quipped: "Never have
so many been defeated by so few."

The attack on the duke of Aosta's forces began from four directions in February, 1941. One British column advanced from
Moyale in Kenya toward Mega and Neghelli in Ethiopia. A
second column from Kenya (commanded by General Sir Alan
Cunningham) crossed into Italian Somaliland, bridged the Juba
River, and advanced on Mogadiscio. The main Italian resistance
in this colony was broken in the battle over Mogadiscio in which
10,000 Italian prisoners were taken. General Cunningham's
column then moved northwest along Graziani's old route into
Ethiopia, capturing Gabredarre and Jijiga. After the latter
strong point was captured, part of Cunningham's column turned
to the northeast to assist a British force which had landed at
Berbera on March 17 to reconquer British Somaliland. The remainder of Cunningham's column pushed on to Harar and Dire-
dawa, where it cut the Addis Ababa-Djibouti railway on March
30. A third British column advanced from the Sudan in the
direction of Burye, Debra Markos, and Addis Ababa, which was
occupied on April 6. Here this column made a junction with
General Cunningham's force and turned northward to attack
the Italian garrison at Dessye. A fourth British column, operating out of Kassala in the north, invaded Eritrea and captured
Agordat on February 2. The main Italian resistance in this colony was encountered at Cheren, where the fascists put up their
most stubborn and intrepid fighting of the campaign. Here the
added strength of the 4th Indian Division which Wavell sent to
General Platt after his victory at Sidi Barrani may have turned
the balance in favor of the British. This mountain stronghold
was not taken by the British until March 28. Its fall enabled the

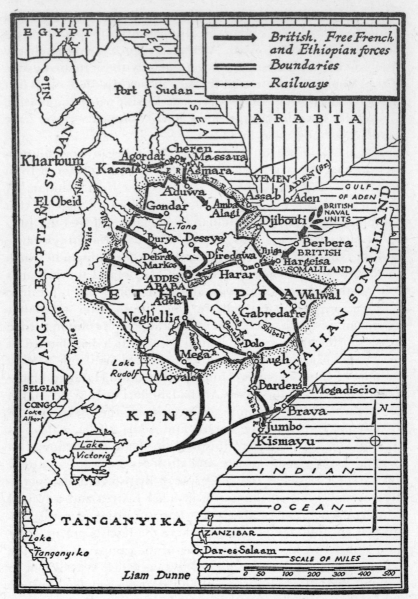

The Ethiopian Campaign

British to divide their forces in Eritrea. One half of the column
moved northward to occupy Massaua and Assab; the other half
drove southward to hem in the duke of Aosta at Amba Alagi.
Here, on May 19, the Italian viceroy surrendered the fragments
of his army. Scattered bands of Italian and native troops continued to resist, but the conquest of the Italian East African
Empire had been completed in seven months.

These victories revealed the hollowness of Italian military
pretenses. Fascist troops in some cases were found to be equipped
with artillery which had been used in the Tripolitan war in
1912. The duke of Aosta repeated Graziani's error of fighting
for places and his army was reduced piecemeal. In general, the
morale and fighting spirit of the troops in Italian East Africa
was higher than that shown by Graziani's army in Libya. The
British campaign was carried out methodically and, considering
the distances, terrain, and forces involved, it was a rapid conquest. General Wavell was successful in co-ordinating the movements of four widely separated columns and in keeping the wild
tribesmen of Haile Selassie from butchering helpless Italian
colonists. The seven-month conquest of three Italian colonies
ranks with the greatest British colonial campaigns.

V

A GREAT soldier is not to be judged by his victories alone. Defeat
and frustrations are often required to bring out the truly superior
qualities of a military leader. Wavell was to have his share of
disaster. The vastness of his military domain presented problems
and vexations great enough to tax the strongest mind. Axis plans
for the spring of 1941 brought him into conflict with a formidable
German army in the Balkans. Here his forces were called upon
to face blitzkrieg as practiced by the masters of that craft.

The Italian army had blundered into defeat in Albania and
required early rescue. Throughout the winter of 1940–41 and
in the early spring German penetration of the Danubian and
Balkan countries went on. Hungary, Rumania, and finally Bul-

garia submitted to nazi military occupation. These steps were preliminary to a German stroke at Greece. To the surprise of all, including the nazis, Jugoslavia refused to join the Axis camp. This upset in German plans seemed to offer the prospect of a joint Jugoslav-Greek-British front against the Axis in the Balkans. If Jugoslavia fought, the Allies could count on a paper force of 1,300,000 men. Churchill took the great risks involved in a Balkan campaign for political and prestige reasons. He ordered a British force to Greece. An expeditionary army of 60,000 British troops and approximately 100 fighter planes (commanded by General Sir Henry Maitland Wilson) began to land in Greece in March. There were hopes that this force would stiffen Greek and Jugoslav resistance and have an encouraging effect on Turkey.

An Allied victory over a large nazi force of 33 divisions (including six armored divisions) and two fleets of the Luftwaffe was hardly to be expected, but a prolonged resistance was anticipated which would use up German men and matériel. The terrain involved seemed favorable for defense against a mechanized attack. The Greeks had recently shown and the Serbs had frequently proved their high military qualities. But there were many factors that operated against a successful collaboration by the Allies. By preserving a "correct" attitude toward the Axis up to the last minute, Jugoslavia had refused to take part in British and Greek staff conversations. As a consequence the Allies were forced to fight without adequate liaison.

The bold and brilliantly executed German attack on April 6 soon shattered all hopes of a prolonged Allied resistance. German air power again proved decisive. Blitzkrieg tactics confused the Jugoslav army and cut it into helpless parts in seven days. With their left flank exposed by the sudden collapse of Jugoslav resistance, the British and Greek forces were driven into retreat to escape encirclement. So rapid was the German advance in the north that Greek armies in Albania were cut off and forced to surrender on April 23. Australian forces under General Sir Thomas Blamey made a heroic stand at Thermopylae in order to safeguard the evacuation of the main British forces. Despite savage bombing from the air, 45,000 of the 60,000 British troops were successfully withdrawn from Greek ports by the end of April.

As at Dunkirk, the BEF had to abandon most of its heavy equipment, and the haggard men who reached the security of Egypt and Crete spoke in bitter terms about the lack of air support. The Balkan disaster was rendered endurable only by the escape of the major part of the British army. The Australian troops bore the brunt of the fighting; and, to still the rising criticism in that country, General Blamey was appointed to the post of second in command to General Wavell. Unfortunately, numbers of the Australian troops evacuated from Greece were sent to Crete for "rest and refit," where they soon found them-selves for the second time victims of German air superiority.

The Greek disaster, like most other disasters in war, did not come singly. General Wavell at the same time had to face a dangerous rebellion in Iraq which was inspired by nazi intrigue and which aimed at disrupting the Allied oil supply in the east-ern Mediterranean. It also threatened to open the back door to Palestine and the Suez to Axis penetration. The problem of sup-pressing the revolt was particularly difficult because of the dangers inherent in the Arab situation in the Middle East and because of the distances involved. By a remarkably speedy trans-port performance, tanks and armored cars landed at Basra were able to occupy Bagdad on May 31 and put an end to the revolt. By this time, however, a new disaster had befallen General Wavell's forces in Crete.

The British had been in occupation of Crete for eight months. Suda Bay provided the navy with an excellent deepwater harbor in which heavy and light craft could be based. Its flying fields permitted British bombers to menace Axis lines of communica-tion in Libya. It was a strategic prize of the first importance and should have been defended with all the resources available. A shortage of antiaircraft artillery, however, prevented adequate protection of the three principal flying fields. The garrison of

50,000 British and Greek troops possessed the normal equipment of tanks and artillery but it was lacking in modern automatic weapons. The defenses erected were designed primarily to repel a traditional landing from the sea. Beaches were wired and mined. Pillboxes and machine-gun nests guarded the strategic points. The defense of the island was entrusted to General Bernard Freyberg, V.C., a New Zealand veteran of World War I known for his personal courage and enterprise.

On May 20, 1941, after a savage 10-day bombing attack, German parachute and glider troops were dropped from fleets of transport planes that followed close upon the heels of German bombers. So rapidly were these troops reinforced from the air, and so perfect were their equipment and organization that the Greek and British infantry were gradually pushed from their defensive positions around the airports and Suda Bay. It was the strangest battle of the war. German troops were supported by the air but had no tanks or artillery. British fighter planes withdrew after the first day of attack because their flying fields could not be defended. This left the Greek and British defenders without air support. In the end superior German direction, unremitting air support, and constant reinforcement by additional parachute troops and infantry carried in transport planes (many of which deliberately made crash landings) proved decisive. There was not time to reinforce the British garrison from Alexandria before the crisis was reached and, even had there been time, the forces that arrived would have been engulfed in the growing confusion in Crete. General Wavell was forced to make the distasteful decision to cut his losses and evacuate the island. Fifteen thousand dazed and beaten men reached Egypt on June 1. Like the men evacuated from Greece, they spoke (when they spoke at all) about the savage power of the German air force. For the second time it became painfully clear that the British armies in the Middle East could not be expected to meet the German Wehrmacht with any prospect of success until approximate equality in the air had been attained.

There was a strong outburst of criticism in Britain and Australia over the Greek and Crete disasters. The public took little comfort from the fact that the Iraq rebellion had been crushed at the same time. In both campaigns the Australian troops seemed to have been left "holding the bag." Though there was no official protest by the Australian government, it was widely felt that "a fresh mind might prove to be useful in the Middle East command." British commentators were forced to praise the brilliance and execution of the German attacks on Greece and Crete. It was pointed out that one of the alleged reasons for inadequate British air support in the Greek campaign was shortage of suitable flying fields. Yet, after being in possession of the same Greek flying fields for less than three weeks, the Luftwaffe used them to mount one of the heaviest and most sustained air offensives of the war. The air operations of the Middle East command seemed to be lacking in other particulars than a mere shortage of planes. Critics pointed to the unrelated series of pinprick bombing operations which were carried out by the RAF all over the eastern Mediterranean from Bengasi to Rhodes. Against an adversary waging total war they did not make much sense.

The public accepted the validity of Churchill's explanation that the fighter plane squadrons had to be withdrawn from Crete because of the lack of adequate antiaircraft guns to protect their flying fields. They could not understand, however, why these fields had not been rendered useless for the Luftwaffe. It was felt that eight months could have been used by the British forces in Crete to pour a lot of concrete and take other measures to increase the defenses of the island. One must conclude that, had the roles of the two armies and their equipment been reversed, the British would have encountered far greater difficulty in overcoming a German garrison of equal size.

The fact that German planes had used French airports in Syria to support the Iraq rebellion seemed to point in the direction of a nazi penetration of that country at the close of the Crete campaign. There were rumors that German armored cars and mechanized equipment had been landed at the port of Latakia. The obvious dangers to the British position in the Middle East made it necessary to forestall this step by military action. Accordingly, on June 8, a small force of British and Free French troops under General Wilson moved into Syria. The announced aim was "occupation," not invasion. At first the advance was slow and every effort was made to win over the Vichy forces by propaganda. Peaceful penetration failed, however, and serious fighting delayed the advance of British and Free French columns. American newsmen who witnessed the Allied advance in Syria described the armies as "lacking in modern equipment." The pace of the Allied advance was therefore disappointingly slow. The capture of Damascus on June 21 was almost lost sight of in view of the startling German declaration of war on Russia on the following day. The Syrian campaign did little to enhance British military prestige in the Middle East.

General Wavell supervised one more important military movement before his career as commander in the Middle East was suddenly terminated. On June 15 he sent forward strong armored forces supported by infantry to test the strength of the German-Italian position at Sollum. The aim was something more than a reconnaissance in force, for an attempt was made to encircle the Afrika Korps at Halfaya Pass. Indian troops skilled in hill fighting attacked the German and Italian outposts with great resolution, but the German organization for support of the advance posts was too effective. The attack bogged down. Meantime General Rommel met the British encirclement maneuver by tanks with an encirclement of his own. A tank battle on a considerable scale followed, in which the British forces withdrew after very heavy losses. "There had been miscalculations and mistakes," said one British reporter. "One battalion of tanks was left for ten minutes exposed to the enemy's antitank gunfire while the commander hesitated what to do next. In the last analysis the British had simply been outfought. It was a moment of appalling seriousness."

VI

IT WAS under these rather depressing circumstances, and after the German war on Russia was a week old, that General Wavell was suddenly transferred to the command of India. Judging his performance solely on the basis of his two-year tenure as commander in the Middle East, one can safely draw the following conclusions. Wavell was the first British soldier in World War II to grasp the full lessons of the German campaigns in Poland and France and apply them to the conditions of desert fighting. He was the first British soldier in this war to co-ordinate effectively the full power of British sea, land, and air forces in a single campaign. His success in handling the many races and nationalities making up the Allied armies in the Middle East was conspicuous. The Libyan victories were the cheapest triumphs ever won by a British force against a European adversary—if not the cheapest in all British military history. Even though the territorial gains in Libya were quickly lost to General Rommel, Wavell still had to his credit the destruction of Graziani's army and the conquest of Eritrea, Italian Somaliland, and Ethiopia. These and Syria were the only British conquests of the war. His victories cheered and inspired the whole British Empire and the neutral world at a time when the Axis powers seemed invincible. Italian military prestige suffered blows from his hand that were almost fatal. When he left Cairo there was no part of the British Mediterranean Empire in Axis hands.

To newsmen in India, Wavell admitted the mistakes of his period of command in the Middle East with admirable candor. He said that he had miscalculated the speed with which the Germans were able to pour troops into North Africa. In this circumstance he described his plan to hold Cyrenaica with partly trained and partly equipped troops as a "mistake."

Wavell's position in India assumed new significance when Japan entered the war on December 7, 1941. The balance of power was so heavily weighted against the United Nations in the Pacific that Wavell was forced to stand helplessly by while Japan overran Malaya, the Dutch East Indies, the Philippines, and Burma. He was able to protect the Indian frontier, and behind this wall he energetically built up Indian military strength for a final reckoning with Japan.

On June 18, 1943, Field Marshal Wavell was raised to the peerage and appointed viceroy and governor general of India to succeed the Marquis of Linlithgow. He chose Viscount Wavell of Cyrenaica and Winchester as his new title. This sudden elevation to an important political post was accompanied by a change in the Indian command, General Sir Claude Auchinleck replacing Wavell as commander in chief in India. On August 25, 1943, a Southeast Asian command was established under Vice-Admiral Lord Louis Mountbatten to direct operations against Japan in this theater. These events put an end to Wavell's military career and opened before him an opportunity to make a reputation in one of the most difficult of all roles, that of the soldier-statesman.

Looking back on the extreme perils through which Britain has passed in the present war and seeing the dangers that menace her in the future, Wavell urged his countrymen to fall back upon their ancient sources of strength. In the introduction to his recently published second volume of the life of Allenby he wrote:

There were dangers ahead even before the disaster of the present war shook us from complacency and ignoble ease. Country life had given place to town life; courage and toughness seemed rated lower than of old; cleverness was being reckoned of more account than character; leadership was gained by caution rather than by daring; pleasure and personal advantage were being set before duty. The dangers and hardships of today are helping to bring back the old standards of courage, self-sacrifice and hard work. These qualities will be very necessary in the great task before us of rebuilding a shaken world.

ROMMEL

☆

"His subordinates called him the publicity Napoleon."

SINCE German policy does not allow individual soldiers to overshadow the Führer, no German general has arisen in the present war with anything like the legendary stature of Hindenburg in 1914–18. Rommel has been the single notable exception, and he was not fighting in Russia, the graveyard of military reputations, but had an independent command in North Africa where his formidable reputation was of political as well as military usefulness.

When he landed in Tripoli to help Graziani in February, 1941, Rommel was virtually unknown outside Germany. Within a year, however, he became the most publicized of German commanders. Gallup polls showed that until November, 1942, the British people considered Rommel the ablest commander produced by the war.

Born in Heidenheim, Württemberg, on November 15, 1891, he was christened Erwin Johannes Rommel. He seems to have come from middle-class parents, although his father has been listed by different writers as a bricklayer, a blacksmith, a teacher of mathematics, a butcher, and a professor at Munich. Lord Strabolgi gave currency in 1942 to the erroneous belief that Rommel rose from the ranks by stating that "if Rommel had been in the British army he *might* have risen to the rank of sergeant." Strabolgi was basing his ironical observation on the false assumption that Rommel was a ranker, whose personality, unconventionality, and vigor would have been a bar to progress in the British army. The fact is that Rommel entered the German army as a *Fahnenjunker* or cadet captain in the 124th infantry regiment in 1910. This in itself indicates that his family background was above average.

Rommel was a lieutenant when the war broke out in 1914, went immediately to the Western front, was wounded in northern France, and acted as battalion adjutant in the Argonne battle of 1915. When the opportunity offered, he transferred to a Württemberg mountain battalion and saw service in the southern Carpathians and on the Italian front. Fighting against the French, Rommel had a hard time of it, but against the less formidable Rumanians and Italians he had brilliant successes. He distinguished himself in battles on the Isonzo front in 1917. In a series of operations at Kolovrat Ridge, Kuk, Luico, and Matajur, Rommel's battalion defeated five fresh Italian regiments in 28 hours, capturing 150 officers and 9,000 men. These exploits brought him the coveted order Pour le Mérite, but he narrowly escaped capture a few days later at Pirago. Early in 1918 he was promoted to captain and served as an assistant staff officer in France till the end of the war.

As a leader of a small unit in 1914–18, Rommel proved himself to be an aggressive and versatile commander. He had a highly developed capacity of utilizing terrain. His men were trained to take cover when possible in movement and to dig in whenever they stopped. Rommel was tireless in reconnaissance and attributed many of his successes to the fact that he possessed better information about the enemy than they did about him. Information was shared with junior officers, noncoms, and even private soldiers. Into every battle plan and maneuver Rommel tried to introduce some element of deception and surprise. He instinctively sought out the weakest element in the enemy position and worked out a plan of attack designed to exploit that weakness and confuse the enemy as to his real intentions. He took great pains to insure proper fire plans and used his machine gun and hand grenades in 1916–18 with the same skill that he used his 88's in 1941–42. Rommel was never afraid of changing plans or disobeying an order if he had better local information than his superior officer. He seems to have had a distinct flair for determining the psychological moment when the cracking enemy should be attacked with every man at his dis-

posal. If necessary he would order his men into the zone of a
German barrage in order to give the enemy no respite in flight.
In January, 1917, he bluffed a Rumanian detachment at Ga-
gesti into surrender by blandly assuring their commander that
the war was over. He used the same trick on the Italians in
1917–18, just as he lied to his own troops in November, 1941
(saying that Moscow had fallen), in order to get them to make a
supreme effort against General Ritchie's offensive.

Reports on Rommel's postwar career present a veritable
jungle of fantasy. What he actually did was to stay in the army
during the Reichswehr period. The official *Rangliste des Deutschen Reichsheeres* lists him as a captain of infantry from 1920
on. Widely circulated stories say that he left the army after the
war and studied at the University of Tübingen, where the
Deutsches Kolonialinstitut specialized in African problems.
Claims that he was an early convert to the Nazi party, an SA
leader in Württemberg, and a bodyguard to Hitler seem equally
unfounded. Certain sensational sheets in Britain commonly refer
to Rommel as the "killer of Coburg," an obvious distortion of a
relatively unimportant incident in the early history of the Nazi
party. Someone apparently invented the story, now widely circulated, that he used to sleep in front of Hitler's bedroom door
where the late Reinhard Heydrich is supposed to have broken
two of his ribs stumbling over him in the dark. As far as I have
been able to discover this is utter nonsense. Reichswehr officers
were simply too busy to engage in extracurricular activities of
this sort. The bodyguard legend may have had its origin during
the Polish campaign in 1939 when Rommel organized an elite
guard to protect Hitler at the front. His real relations with the
Nazi party are hard to trace, but a careful study of German newspapers, periodicals, and radio broadcasts seems to indicate that
Rommel was labeled as a 100 per cent nazi *only* when he was
retreating or his army in trouble. The fact that many Germans
once thought of him as the only man who could lead the army
or part of it *against* Hitler seems to argue against any real connection between Rommel and the fanatical nazi elements.

Rommel did not come to the United States to study our Civil War campaigns as is often reported. This particular rumor confuses him with General von Schell or General von Boetticher, former German military attaché to the United States.

During the period when all this was supposed to be happening, Rommel was following out a conventional career as a Reichswehr officer. From 1920 to 1925 he was a captain attached to the staff of the 1st battalion of the 13th infantry regiment. When Hitler came to power in 1933, Rommel was a major teaching infantry tactics at the Dresden Military Academy. In the year 1935 he published a small training manual for platoon and company officers called "Problems for the Platoon and Company" (*Aufgaben für Zug und Kompanie*). He dealt with his experiences with the Württemberg mountain battalion in his "Infantry Attacks" (*Infanterie Greift An*), published when he was a lieutenant colonel in 1937. Both books were based on his experiences from 1914 to 1918 and were written along the pattern of the small battle picture, a technique widely used at the Infantry School at Fort Benning, Georgia, where German officers such as Adolf von Schell studied. Neither of Rommel's books made much of an impression at the time; they were given only brief and perfunctory reviews in the German as well as American military periodicals. After he became famous in 1941, these books were resurrected and restudied. *Infanterie Greift An* was reported in its twelfth edition in the summer of 1942. Had Allied commanders been familiar with this book they might have been better prepared to deal with Rommel in North Africa.[1] It was Montgomery who finally penetrated the fog of legend surrounding Rommel and observed that his one great weakness was that he tended to repeat his tactics.

Up to the year 1940, when he was made commander of the 7th Panzer Division, Rommel was an infantry specialist. What experience he gained with mechanized equipment arose from

---

[1] An English translation of *Infanterie Greift An* ("Infantry Attacks") has recently been published by the *Infantry Journal*.

his contacts with the motor transport corps of the Reichswehr.

His relations with the Nazi party are hard to define. Rommel did not cut certain Jewish veterans of his old mountain battalion, and yet the nazis considered him "safe" enough to entrust with academic posts at Dresden and Wiener-Neustadt. Contrary to the common report, he was not appointed director of the Kriegs-akademie in 1937. His first direct contact with large-scale military movement came as commander of Hitler's personal headquarters on the marches into Vienna, the Sudetenland, Prague, and Warsaw. Other names captured the headlines in the Polish campaign; the honors went to Blaskowitz, List, Kluge, Reichenau, and Kuchler. Rommel was still an unknown.

II

IT WAS as commander of the 7th Panzer Division in the attack against France that Rommel's star rose. The 7th (the Ghost) Division was the first to break through the Ardennes and cross the Meuse in May, 1940. It was the first to reach the sea at Abbeville. Rommel was cited as one of the most successful armored division commanders of the Wehrmacht, promoted to the rank of lieutenant general, and awarded the Knights Cross of the Iron Cross. Though his exploits were temporarily lost sight of in the shower of marshals' batons that followed Hitler's triumph over France, tales of his activity soon flooded the Reich. In the approved nazi style of battle narrative, one of his officers, Lieutenant Tschimpke, wrote about the crossing of the Meuse at Houx on May 13:

> In the midst of this infernal noise—at the very decisive moment in this desperate situation, the figure of the general [Rommel] suddenly appeared. Leaping and crawling over fences and bushes . . . he squirmed up to a new bridge which the pioneers had built under the cover of darkness. "We can't go on," they said to the general. He was not dismayed. The word "Impossible" does not exist for him. . . . He speaks only one word, "Tanks." Under protection of smoke they deploy into position behind the river banks.

By massing his tanks on the river bank and using them as artillery Rommel blasted the machine-gun emplacements that held up the river crossing.

Newspapers repeated his alleged remarks in taking over command of the 7th Panzer Division: "Gentlemen, don't think I am crazy. Trust me! To the right there is nothing. To the left there is nothing. To the rear there is nothing. Rommel is in front!" These heroics, reminiscent of General Pope's famous and ill-starred remark, seem only to have increased Rommel's reputation among the Germans. Even the *Militärwissenschaftliche Rundschau* (November, 1940) carried a story of how Rommel bluffed off a French tank attack in the mist by firing Very pistol flares at them to simulate antitank guns.

Early in the year 1941, Rommel was placed in command of the Afrika Korps, a body of elite troops trained for the conquest of Lebensraum in Africa. He was reported to have made a thorough study of North Africa as a "tourist" and lectured before the Geographical Society at Cairo on the terrain of the Western Desert in 1936. These stories like the claims about Rommel's early participation in the training camps for the Afrika Korps cannot be verified.

The record of Rommel's activity in Africa from February 12, 1941, to late September, 1942, is fairly clear. His name first appeared in the headlines on March 31, when elements of the 15th German Panzer Division and the 5th Light Motorized Division surprised and defeated Wavell's advance force at El Agheila. For a time the Germans were willing to pretend that General Italo Gariboldi, who succeeded Graziani, was in command; but after this temporary sop to Italian pride, Rommel took charge of Axis affairs in North Africa.

By the time of the German victory at El Agheila, Wavell's force had already been weakened by transfers to Greece and by the assumption of British operations against Italian East Africa. The single British armored division, which had borne the brunt of the fighting since December 9, 1940, was far inferior to Rommel's 15th Panzer Division. As a consequence, the British ad-

vance positions became untenable and a retreat, facetiously
called the "Bengasi Handicap," began. Rommel's advance was
rapid and unorthodox. Motorcycle patrols and armored-car detachments swept deep into British positions, disrupting communications, and, on one occasion, captured a staff car carrying
Generals Neame and O'Connor. This was a serious blow to General Wavell because O'Connor was one of the best field officers
in the British army. Leaving a British garrison at Tobruk, General Wavell withdrew the bulk of his forces to the strong frontier
position at Sollum-Halfaya Pass. Rommel began the invest-
ment of Tobruk on April 7, 1941, but a tenacious defense of
that fortified port was maintained until it was relieved by the
British autumn offensive.

Rommel soon made his vigorous personality felt in the Afrika
Korps, and tales of his eccentricities were spread by the newspapers of the world. He was an ardent Leica fan, snapped pictures constantly from the top of his command car, bawled out
orders, and raced from place to place with apparently limitless
vigor. When not traveling by staff car, he covered the battle
front in a Feisler-Storch observation plane. As in 1914–18 he
wanted to see everything himself and was proud to be called
the "general of the highway." His eccentricities seemed to en-
dear him to the men of the Afrika Korps, although his outbursts
of temper were not pleasant. He had frequent quarrels with his
subordinates. His controversies with Field Marshal Kesselring,
commander of the Luftwaffe in the Mediterranean area, were
bitter. One German officer admitted that "there were times when
Rommel drove his commanders to exasperation by changing his
decisions." Some officers who were taken prisoner said that Rommel "was a great soldier but often petty, childish, and indecisive."

Rommel took little pains to conceal his disdain for the Italian
troops who served under him. Tact is not one of his qualities.
When his overbearing manner became pronounced, the Italian
commander in North Africa ironically awarded him the "Silver
Medal for Valor" on February 15, 1942. Rommel repaid the

left-handed compliment by invariably referring to the Italian king as "Emperor of Ethiopia" long after the British had conquered this empire. Perhaps it was the charge that Rommel deliberately sacrificed Italian units in North Africa in order to save German troops which made it desirable for Hitler to transfer him from Italy to the anti-invasion command late in 1943.

He had a kind of irrepressible arrogance which led him to harangue prisoners, comment on British leadership, and promise victory while the issue was still in doubt. His coarse speech and broad humor appealed to his troops. "Today," he would say, "we kick the Englishman in the belly. Tomorrow we kick him in the chest. The day after we kick his hind-end. He cannot stand it! His leaders cannot meet new situations." The fact that Rommel will lecture to anybody at the drop of the hat probably accounts for one of the nicknames, "the Professor," which his own troops gave him.

Harold Denny, an American correspondent captured by the Afrika Korps in 1941, tells how, as the column of prisoners marched to the rear, German soldiers stopped to photograph them. Just then "Rommel drove up in a staff car—burly, unshaven, wearing a dirty greatcoat, and looking almost as disreputable as the prisoners." A short, round-faced, red-haired bundle of energy, he rebuked the soldiers for stopping to photograph the prisoners but proceeded to photograph them himself. "Then, leaning one elbow on the windshield, supporting his chin with his fist and looking militantly over the desert, he struck an effective pose and let the soldiers photograph him." He was often referred to by subordinate German officers or the "general staff clique" as the "publicity Napoleon."

Rommel took pride in his ability to stand the hardships of desert fighting, though after two years of campaigning his health failed. He escaped death in November, 1941, when a commando party raided his villa outside Tobruk, only because he was absent at the time. A group of marauding British tanks nearly cut him off a few weeks later. When asked by German reporters why he risked death or capture in exposed areas, Rommel sensibly

replied that he had to be at the front because split-second decisions are supremely important in desert fighting.

III

ROMMEL'S first real test as a leader came in the British offensive
of November, 1941. General Cunningham's plan called for a
holding attack on the Halfaya–Sidi Omar defenses by the 4th
Indian Division, while the 1st New Zealand Division was to
move northward around Sheferzen toward Fort Capuzzo and
Bardia. The 4th, 7th and 22nd armored brigades were to sweep
around the Axis' right flank toward El Gobi, Sidi Rezegh, and
Tobruk. It was hoped that Rommel's infantry and armored
forces would be encircled and destroyed. In the matter of special
competence, the Afrika Korps then had an advantage over the
British Eighth Army. Rommel had some of the best specialists
in the German army working for him: General Cruewell, his
second in command, a tank-plane man; General Bismarck, expert on motorized infantry; and General Nehring, antitank
specialist.

The British general, Sir Alan Cunningham, had conducted a
brilliant campaign in Ethiopia but it was against an adversary
lacking in resource and determination. He had no experience in
handling large numbers of tanks. General Gott, his corps commander, was an infantryman. Major General Frank Messervy
commanding the 4th Indian Division was a cavalryman, so was
Lieutenant General Willoughby Norrie, commanding the 7th
Armored Division. To use the words of a British officer, "they
all had experience in armored warfare and in the desert—yet
one would hesitate to term any of them fully tank-minded or
experts in mechanical fighting." [2] Brigadier Jock Campbell
(commanding the 7th Support Group), who showed great capacity at Sidi Rezegh for directing the kind of chaos involved in
tank fighting, died in an automobile accident before his talents
could be fully utilized.

[2] Major E. W. Sheppard, "The Libyan Defeat" in *Fighting Forces*, p. 21 (August,
1942).

The first stages of the British attack progressed favorably, indicating that Rommel was caught by surprise. He was, in fact, preparing an attack on Tobruk. One can only speculate on what effect General Cunningham's attack might have had if it had come after Rommel had committed the bulk of his forces against

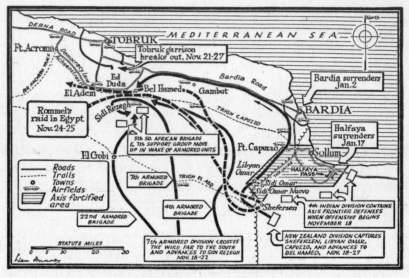

Sidi Rezegh—Tobruk

Tobruk. The holding attack of the 4th and 7th Indian divisions pinned down a large Axis force on the frontier. The 22nd armored brigade had a tough fight with the Ariette Division at El Gobi in which both forces lost heavily. The New Zealanders advanced according to plan and the 7th Armored Division reached the Axis airfield at Sidi Rezegh on November 20, destroying many parked planes. The 7th Support Group and the 5th South African brigade dug in at this point.

Instead of avoiding battle at Sidi Rezegh, Rommel sought it, and by concentrating the bulk of his 21st and 15th Armored divisions against the British 4th armored brigade he inflicted heavy losses on it. As the battle at Sidi Rezegh took on an extremely chaotic character, and the British commander lost immediate control of events, Rommel threw his armor against three British armored brigades in turn. So confused was the situation at Sidi Rezegh that the disposition of British and German units "looked like an eight-decker rainbow cake" on the map. British intelligence officers threw down their pencils in disgust and no longer attempted to chart the course of the battle.

By November 23 Rommel had cut down British tank forces considerably and had driven the 5th South African brigade from its entrenched position. Then, on November 24, Rommel sent the Ariette Division and a German tank brigade on a sweep across the Egyptian frontier to disorganize the enemy. Though this bold move had no permanent effect, it disrupted British supply lines and gave the British command a few bad days. It would appear from Major Peter Rainier's frank memoirs that Rommel's tanks actually chased Cunningham away from and back to the original battlefield.[3] But this may be a distortion of what actually happened. The New Zealand Division made fleeting contact with the garrison at Tobruk on November 27, but it was apparent that the British offensive had slowed down. General Cunningham was replaced on the following day by General Neil Ritchie. By this time Rommel had regrouped his armor and recaptured Sidi Rezegh and Bell Hamed but did not have strength enough to exploit this success. General Auchinleck's decision to continue the offensive and his policy of harassing Rommel by small-scale raids on his rear and communications had their result.

On December 5 Rommel retreated toward Gazala, making the relief of Tobruk real for the first time. Rommel held the line Gazala–Alem Hamza until December 16, and retreated via Derna and Bengasi (occupied by the British on December 25) to El Agheila on January 7. There he halted to receive reinforce-

[3] Major Peter W. Rainier, *Pipeline to Battle: An Engineer's Adventures with the British Eighth Army* (New York, 1944), pp. 128–129.

ments while the British slowly advanced and built up supply depots. Meantime, Rommel's forces encircled at Halfaya-Sollum-Bardia were squeezed out by the British.

Rommel's drive back into Cyrenaica in January and February, 1942, which forced a British withdrawal to the line Gazala–Bir Hacheim, won the praise of Air Marshal Sir Edward Ellington. He wrote: "Rommel, without attempting to deprive the British of air superiority, and with little air support, inflicted a severe reverse on the British forces. . . . If the explanation is that General Rommel concentrated superior forces at the decisive point . . . sufficiently superior to counter his enemy's air superiority, it argues a superiority of generalship which, to say the least of it, is disturbing." [4]

The skill with which he exploited British weaknesses showed that Rommel was a resourceful soldier with a remarkable facility for keeping his armor concentrated in the fluctuations of desert fighting. The British tendency at that time to commit their tanks into battle in driblets made him look all the better. "What difference does it make if you have more tanks than I if you present them to me a brigade at a time?" Rommel once asked a captured British tank officer.

IV

ROMMEL's turn at the offensive came on May 26, 1942, when he attacked the British and Fighting French on the line Gazala–Bir Hacheim. He showed a disregard for the conventional rules of desert warfare by attacking during the "impossible" heat months. The offensive was strongly supported by dive-bombing attacks on Allied strong points. The objective was to shorten his communications by taking Tobruk and at the same time destroy as much of the Eighth Army as possible.

His first move was to throw elements of his two armored divisions around the Allied flank at Bir Hacheim while the Ariette

[4] Air Marshal Sir E. Ellington, "The War in the Air" in the *Army Quarterly,* p. 63 (April, 1942).

and Trieste divisions attacked the southern end of the minefields at Bir Hacheim. This attack struck the British and their
allies at a disadvantage, for the two German armored divisions
encountered only the British 4th armored brigade, some units
of the 22nd armored brigade, and a motorized infantry brigade.
By co-ordinated action of infantry and engineers, a 10-mile gap
was cut in the Allied minefield and the French garrison at Bir
Hacheim isolated. This gap was widened and made it possible
for Rommel to supply his forces east of the minefield. Of this
bold maneuver, in which Rommel risked the loss of part of his
armor in the early stage of the operation, General Sir R. Gordon-
Finlayson wrote: "That any opposing general should have dared
to take such a decision is almost as humiliating as the fact that
he not only carried it out, apparently without difficulty, but also
that a few days later, with still less difficulty he was able to increase the gap." [5] This left General Ritchie with the choice of

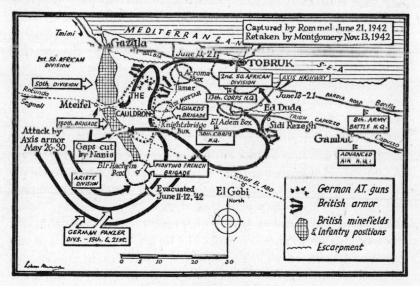

Knightsbridge—Tobruk

[5] General Sir R. Gordon-Finlayson, "The War on Land: The Middle East" in
the *Army Quarterly*, p. 190 (August, 1942).

withdrawing from Cyrenaica or fighting Rommel's antitank guns and armor at a disadvantage. He chose the braver but in this case the more disastrous course.

On June 13 Rommel ambushed the main body of British tanks at Knightsbridge by decoying them into a mass of antitank guns and artillery. By Churchill's admission the British lost nearly 250 tanks on that day. The speed with which the trap was set and sprung as well as the speed with which Rommel exploited the success left his adversaries confused as well as beaten. How the Germans were able to conceal this gigantic trap from British air observation is difficult to understand, but reports indicate that the gun positions were dug in and well concealed.

Fantastic stories arose about Rommel's "secret" antitank gun which was nothing but the old dual-purpose 88 mm. gun which had been doing yeoman service in the German army since the Spanish Civil War. One American magazine assured its readers on "high sources" that Rommel lured the British into this trap by broadcasting fake radio messages *en clair* indicating that the German position at Knightsbridge was desperate, thus inviting the British attack. Aside from being too simple an explanation of the British disaster, this account credits the British Intelligence Service with excessive naïveté.

Rommel did broadcast instructions *en clair* by radio during this battle, but it was to control his own forces, not to deceive the British. American reporters at an advanced British radio station heard his cool voice directing the operations of all arms in concert. It was an impressive performance. Until late in the North African campaign Rommel had the advantage of directing his forces by a map reference device known as the "thrust line." This was simply a line drawn on a tactical map from one known position to another. Since the location of the daily thrust line was known to all his subordinates but not to the enemy, Rommel could broadcast direct battle instructions *en clair* without fear of revealing his plans to the opposing commander.

The loss of British armor on June 13 was decisive and made retirement inevitable. Part of the British forces retired on To-

bruk and the rest made for the Egyptian frontier. More than
30,000 troops managed to take up their position in Tobruk in
the seven days that followed, but they were too weak to man the
27-mile perimeter of the fortress. Rommel allowed them no time
to consolidate their position, but moved up his armor and artillery. On June 20 he mounted an attack of great intensity and
power on the eastern approaches to the town after feinting an
advance toward Gambut. The attack itself was in the nature of a
surprise. It was prepared on the World War I model. After
heavy and sustained artillery fire, infantry and tank forces moved
forward on the heels of the barrage. When it lifted, they broke
through the Tobruk defenses. German troops reached the harbor that afternoon compelling the surrender of the British garrison.

Without wasting time in Tobruk, Rommel drove his armored
and motorized divisions forward to Matruh. Seven days after
the fall of Tobruk he captured Matruh along with its garrison
of 8,000 men. They had been left to gain time for a retirement
of the main British army. General Auchinleck took personal
command of the Eighth Army, relieving General Ritchie, and a
defensive position from El Alamein to the Qattara Depression
was finally held. At the end of June, Rommel was within 65 miles
of Alexandria.

The brilliant campaign of May and June, 1942, brought Rommel a new burst of publicity. He was raised to the rank of General Field Marshal and awarded the Oak Leaf with Swords to
the Knights Cross of the Iron Cross. On a trip to Berlin in September to receive his marshal's baton, he boasted to newsmen
that the Afrika Korps would soon push on to Alexandria and
Cairo.

As the German offensive on the Stalingrad front bogged down,
the German press and radio used its massed facilities for "building up" Rommel. They splashed colored pictures of him in
nearly every German magazine. They coined a new word "rom-
meln" to fit his shifty disconcerting tactics. According to German press and radio reports Rommel was everywhere at once

while directing battle. He personally designated where the engineers should make a breach in the enemy minefields; he gave the artillery their targets, and he led the infantry attacks in his staff car, miraculously escaping the hail of enemy shrapnel and high-explosive shells. While occasionally reminding nazi readers that the Führer directs *all* military operations, the nazi press made it clear that Rommel was the most resourceful soldier produced by the war.

As it turned out, Rommel never knew how close he was to a decisive victory in June, 1942. The British position at El Alamein was unfinished and the Eighth Army had suffered extremely heavy losses. His own troops were tired and faced grave supply problems, yet an all-out effort by the Afrika Korps in the first week of June might have brought him to Alexandria. But Rommel grew cautious. He tried a feeler attack on El Alamein on July 1 under cover of a dust storm, but the British massed their remaining tanks and drove him out. A sharp British counterattack on the following day captured 2,000 German prisoners and 30 guns. Local British attacks on July 4, 10, 18, 22, and 27 must have convinced him that the front was strongly held. He made no further large-scale effort until the end of August—then it was too late.

Under cover of a waning moon on the night of August 30 Rommel threw his armor and motorized infantry at the southern sector of the Alamein front. It encountered a solid resistance of artillery fire and failed with the loss of 100 tanks and 2,000 men. The British did not follow up the repulse with a counterattack; they were husbanding their armor for something more important. American observers report that in this operation Rommel made all the mistakes that the British committed in the earlier fighting in North Africa. He did not employ his tanks in maximum force; he failed to provide adequate reconnaissance and ran into minefields and rough ground. When the British refused to be "sucked into" making tank attacks against his antitank guns and artillery, Rommel had no recourse but to retreat.

Associated Press Photo

ROMMEL

From September 5 onward the Afrika Korps was observed to be digging in and fortifying its position. Lanes of mines 6,000 yards deep covered the Axis front; gun positions and command posts were blasted out of solid rock. While the army worked, Rommel took time out to visit Berlin, leaving Generals von Stumme and Thoma in charge of operations. He appeared as the guest of honor at Hitler's Sportspalast speech on September 30 and received a tremendous ovation. In the presence of Goebbels he held a press conference for the foreign and German journalists at which his boastfulness and lack of taste made a distinctly bad impression. At a time when the British newspapers were singing his praises, Rommel belittled the British Eighth Army and declared that the "British were *cowardly* and fought *dishonorably*." According to Arvid Fredborg, correspondent for the *Svenska Dagbladet,* "the respect which the correspondents in Berlin held for the field marshal was cancelled by that one interview. 'He is a great soldier,' they thought, 'but certainly not a great man.' " In this case Rommel merely acted on the level of his previous performance. In 1937 (23 years after 1914) he wrote that in an engagement during which his company was roughly handled, the gallant French army had deliberately killed wounded Germans.[6]

Major General J. F. C. Fuller asserted that Rommel's decision to hold the thin strong line at El Alamein showed that he failed to comprehend the necessity for a defense in very great depth against a modern mechanized attack in a desert area—despite all his experience. After his capture, General Thoma charged Rommel with two serious tactical errors in preparing for the defense of El Alamein. He insisted that Rommel's orders to mass the German armor in the north close to the front line caused unnecessarily heavy losses from British artillery fire. He also complained that Rommel's location of the German minefields was

[6] While the *Infantry Journal's* edition of "Infantry Attacks" was being prepared for publication, I edited this item out of the text because I felt that nothing would be gained by reprinting stories of this kind. Yet it is significant that Rommel would stoop to this kind of vilification in 1937.

faulty. Many sections were not under direct observation by German artillery and therefore could be "lifted" by the British without undue losses.

At the battle of El Alamein (October 23–November 12) General Montgomery outmaneuvered and outfought the Afrika Korps. With the Anglo-American invasion of North Africa from the west, the whole strategic situation in the Mediterranean changed overnight. Rommel arrived posthaste from Berlin to conduct the long retreat of his battered forces into Tunisia. It was one of the longest and fastest retreats in history. Although he sacrificed large numbers of Italian infantry in order to escape with German elements, he did save a battle-worthy remnant of the Afrika Korps for operations in Tunisia. It was a notable military achievement.

New mechanized equipment poured into Tunisian ports, and in February the 21st Panzer Division was again in shape to do battle. Abandoning Tripoli, Rommel took up a defensive position in the Mareth line, while General von Arnim with the 10th and 15th Panzer divisions and constantly reinforced German and Italian infantry forces held the northern sector of the Tunisian front.

The frantic efforts of the German press and radio to convince the German and Italian people that Rommel's retreat from El Alamein to Tunisia was one of the greatest feats in military history did not detract in the least from General Montgomery's equally brilliant feat of bringing the Eighth Army into Tunisia on his heels in a condition to crack the Mareth line. Praise of Rommel's skill as a tactician and administrator could not conceal the inherent weaknesses of the Axis position in Tunisia. The operations of Rommel and Arnim seemed designed primarily to gain time and to delay a United Nations invasion of Europe as long as possible.

Singling out the American forces on the Central front, Rommel launched a series of savage attacks in February to test them out and to disorganize General Eisenhower's plans. Concentrating elements of the 21st and the 10th Panzer divisions, Rommel struck the American forces at Faïd Pass and Sidi-bou-Zid on February 14, 1943. Preceded by intense dive-bombing attacks, German tanks rolled over the American position, surged forward through Kasserine Pass and menaced the supply bases at Tebessa and Thala.

For a week the hard-pressed American forces retreated; then on February 25 they counterattacked and slowly drove Rommel's forces backward. Shifting his forces back to the Mareth line, Rommel tried the same kind of smashing assault on a sector of the Eighth Army front. This time he apparently moved without proper reconnaissance, for his tank attack was stopped dead in its tracks by British antitank guns and artillery. Rommel is reported to have told his troops in an order of the day that if they failed to dislodge the Eighth Army at Medenine "the days of the Axis forces in North Africa are numbered."

Ironically enough this was the last operation Rommel directed in North Africa, for he was called home by the Führer immediately afterward. A special communiqué of the German high command released on May 11 reported that Rommel's health, already overstrained in the fall of 1942, gave way after he had reached Gabes on his retreat from the Mareth line. Hitler called him back for medical treatment and to award him the Oak Leaves with Swords and Diamonds to the Knights Cross of the Iron Cross for "the unique merit of his two years' campaign in Africa." There is some basis for the stories of Rommel's ill health. He admits that for the first three months of World War I he suffered severely from a stomach disorder brought on by eating greasy food and freshly baked bread.

His successor, Colonel General von Arnim, attempted to defend the line Enfidaville–Pont-du-Fahs–Medjez-el-bab–Sedjenane. Here the final defense of Tunisia began on April 24. It ended suddenly and dramatically on May 7 with a British and American break-through to Tunis and Bizerte. In six hectic days the whole Axis war machine in North Africa collapsed. By May

13 all organized resistance in Tunisia was at an end. Some 252,000 Axis prisoners, including General von Arnim, fell into Allied hands.

V

ROMMEL is unquestionably a tactician and military organizer of real ability. His conduct of operations both in advance and retreat has been marked by sound organization and bold improvisation. Each of his major battles up to the autumn of 1942 revealed some new feature though, as General Montgomery pointed out, he had a tendency to repeat his major tactical operations. He attained impressive victories with limited forces, but these victories did not lead to decisive results. In time he taught his adversaries the tricks of desert fighting. Until he met up with Generals Montgomery and Alexander, no British leader opposed him with land and air power concentrated effectively at the decisive point. Until the autumn of 1942 Rommel always enjoyed qualitative superiority in tank and antitank equipment. This often enabled him to offset British superiority in the air.

Alan Moorehead, who followed the fortunes of the British Eighth Army from August, 1941, to August, 1942, believes that Rommel revealed little of the genius for which he was given credit in this period. The Afrika Korps was a better fighting organization at that stage than the Eighth Army; it had a better and tighter system of control. Rommel's habit of close front-line control of operations was a factor in its success, but "Rommel was merely an expression of that abler German army." By the fall of 1942 the British Eighth Army was a better fighting force than the Afrika Korps, and Rommel's days of triumph in North Africa were over.

The Führer kept his promise that when Rommel's health was restored he would be given a new assignment worthy of his talents. When the Italian situation became critical in September, 1943, Rommel was sent to northern Italy and Jugoslavia where he supervised operations until December. Then it was announced that he had been appointed inspector general of the German anti-invasion forces in western Europe.

Thus the fortunes of war may bring Rommel into final battle with his old adversaries: Montgomery, Tedder, Coningham, and Eisenhower. In such an event Rommel can be expected to show his old-time cunning, energy, and audacity, but he will be dealing with men who know his methods. It will not be enough merely "to repeat his tactics." In desperate battles for survival, character is often a greater asset to a general than cunning.

MONTGOMERY

☆

"A Cromwellian figure, austere, severe, accomplished and tireless."

ONE afternoon early in August, 1942, two Messerschmitt 109's were returning from a raid behind the British lines on the El Alamein front. By a malicious turn of fate one of the pilots happened to spot a lumbering RAF Bombay transport plane scudding along under a low ceiling. Dipping his wings to attract the attention of his companion, the leading fighter swept down on the hapless transport with blazing machine guns. The pilot of the Bombay maneuvered his slow plane in a desperate effort to escape. He finally dove toward the ground, lowered his landing gear, and attempted to land in order to save his passengers. The second Messerschmitt swept down like a hawk. Just as the wheels of the Bombay touched the ground, a long burst of incendiaries ripped through the plane. The transport burst into flames, careened wildly over the rough ground, tipped upside down, broke up, and burned furiously. Among the seven British officers who perished in the blaze was Lieutenant General W. H. E. (Strafer) Gott, who had just been chosen to command the British Eighth Army. He had left the front that afternoon for a well-deserved rest in Cairo before taking up his new post.

The "best desert fighter" in the British army, Gott's tragic death was just another example of the fantastic string of misfortune that followed the Eighth Army after Wavell's transfer to India. Gott's death was a tremendous loss to the British Empire but, as is sometimes the case when the hand of fate topples the carefully laid plans of men, it made possible one of the most amazing careers in the annals of the British army. It led to the appointment of General Bernard Law Montgomery to the command of the Eighth Army.

The circumstances of Montgomery's appointment are worth setting down at some length, since they give us a standard by which to judge the results of his command. General Neil Ritchie had commanded the British Eighth Army from the time that Cunningham lost control of the battle of Sidi Rezegh in November, 1941, until late in June, 1942. During his command he drove Rommel to El Agheila in December, 1941, but was forced back with heavy tank losses to the line Gazala–Bir Hacheim. When Rommel assumed the offensive in May, 1942, Ritchie had been unable to relieve the gallant Fighting French garrison at Bir Hacheim, had stumbled into Rommel's tank trap at Knightsbridge on June 13, and was unable to provide an effective defense of Tobruk, which fell on June 20 with a loss of 30,000 men. When the battered remnants of the Eighth Army retreated from Mersa Matruh, General Auchinleck relieved Ritchie and took personal charge of the final British defense position at El Alamein. There, after heavy fighting in July and August, the two tired armies lapsed into positional warfare.

Auchinleck never quite "clicked" as a commander in the Middle East despite his capacity as an organizer. He possessed real courage, ruthlessly sacked his friends when they failed, and did a brilliant job of deepening and holding the El Alamein line, but the army never quite appreciated him. Neither did the correspondents or the staff at Cairo who wistfully recalled the splendid openhanded manner of Wavell. When Auchinleck attempted to "vitalize" the high command by moving the staff out of Cairo into tents on the fringe of the desert, scurrilous troops sardonically referred to GHQ as "the short-range desert force." Though large-scale reinforcements were on the way to Egypt in July, Rommel was still at the gates of Alexandria. The British fleet based at Alexandria had steamed into hiding, and Cairo was openly preparing to receive the Afrika Korps. New blood was needed to restore the situation in the Middle East. Churchill decided to place Alexander in command and give the Eighth Army to General Gott who had come through two years of fighting in the Western Desert with a brilliant reputation.

No other commander seemed equally qualified to restore the morale and fighting power of the army.

Not that the Eighth Army had lacked promising officers—but most of them had been lost by enemy action or accident. O'Connor, the brilliant field commander, had been captured early in 1941; Russell and Pope were killed in a plane crash; Jock Campbell, the magnetic and audacious leader of the 7th Support Group, was killed when his car overturned on a narrow road; Gatehouse, Briggs, and Lumsden were wounded by the bombs of a Stuka; rising young officers like Garmoyle and Coombes were gone; and now Gott was dead. Surely the Eighth Army lived under an unlucky star. The troops felt this and often sang a plaintive song which some nameless musical wag originated on Wavell's first retreat:

> Oh, Sidi Barrani!
> Oh, Mersa Matruh!
> The Eyties will get there,
> Then what will we do?

Now the "Eyties" were at El Alamein and the fate of the whole Middle East hung in the balance. The choice of the right command for the Eighth Army was a matter of inestimable importance. Churchill picked Montgomery.

II

MEN remembered that Alexander had been the last man off the beach at Dunkirk, but that was an evil memory. He had commanded the last stages of the Burma campaign but that also was a campaign without glory. As for Montgomery—he was frankly an unknown. No one noticed him when he registered at Shepheard's Hotel in Cairo. They noticed him the next morning, however, when he left for his first inspection at the front at 0500 hours. Something new had been added to nervous, defeatist Cairo! His first order to the troops read: "We will fight the enemy where we

MONTGOMERY and ALEXANDER

now stand; there will be no withdrawal and no surrender." From that moment on the Eighth Army never looked back.

After they had time to look up his record and size up the new commander in the flesh, the Eighth Army found that it had a somewhat astonishing person at its head. Slightly above average height, Montgomery was a slender, hard, hawk-like energetic man, with piercing blue eyes, long nose, and sparse, sandy hair. His habits were frankly disturbing. He neither smoked nor drank, but quoted scripture; prayed regularly; detested unnecessary noise; set aside two-minute periods before conferences for coughing; demanded utmost punctiliousness of his officers and men; conducted violent, whirlwind inspection trips; showed a weakness for bizarre headgear; wore fantastic combinations of clothes; painted his nickname "Monty" on his personal reconnaissance tank; and insisted on lecturing his officers at odd and inconvenient hours. Montgomery had "character" and an innate sense of the dramatic. Within a few weeks he was known to every man in the Eighth Army. After Mr. Willkie spent a few hours in the Western Desert and a few minutes with the correspondents at Cairo, Montgomery became known to the world. This was on September 5, 1942.

Montgomery, the son of an Episcopalian bishop, was born at Moville, County Donegal, Ireland, on November 17, 1887. After graduating from Sandhurst he entered the Royal Warwickshire Regiment, was twice wounded in France during World War I, and served with occupation troops in Germany and Ireland. In 1934 he was a colonel instructing at the Staff College in Quetta, India. He commanded the 9th infantry brigade at Portsmouth in 1937 and led a division in Palestine during the disorders of 1938–39.

When World War II broke out Montgomery commanded the 3rd Division in France and brought it through the hell of Dunkirk. After the evacuation he commanded the V Corps for a time before taking over the southeastern command. He apparently did not study war to the exclusion of all other things until after the death of his wife (Betty Carver) in 1937. "My wife and I used to do things together," he once told newsmen, "now—I like birds!" He apparently not only studied military history but also investigated the psychology of command in large armies because he was able to do in a few weeks what Auchinleck had notably failed to do in many months—he made a lasting impression on every man in the Eighth Army. This was no mean feat; that army was one of the strangest racial mixtures ever placed on a single battlefield. It was composed of Britons, South Africans, Australians, New Zealanders, Indians, Greeks, and Frenchmen.

Up to the time he proved himself in victorious battle against the Afrika Korps at El Alamein, all Montgomery had to work on was his sense of the dramatic, his drive, and his unmistakable concern for the welfare and preparation of his troops. His trips of inspection were endless; his regime of violent exercise and realistic training was so severe that the men looked forward to the prospect of battle with a sense of relief. He is said to have invited a small group of officers to a Spartan meal, lectured them for two hours, and then remarked in bidding them farewell: "I trust that you are militarily revitalized!" Back in England in 1941 he made all the officers in command up to the rank of brigadier do a seven-mile run once a week. In Africa his regime was even more exacting. As one American officer said: "Montgomery put an army that was already supposed to be veteran through a physical-conditioning program equal to that of the commandos. After that the Germans could not stop the Eighth Army. There were other factors but this was the only new one."

Everywhere he spoke to the troops and officers. "We have got to get a spirit into every man in the Eighth Army that burns like a flame!" He described his plans to the officers with utmost frankness. "War is a simple thing. The ABC of modern combat is common sense!" He made every man in the army a partner in his project—the defeat of Rommel and the destruction of his army. He told the plan of El Alamein to the whole army so that every man understood the part he was to play. All Montgomery's major orders to his corps commanders from El Alamein to Tripoli were oral. He had no use for elaborate paper plans. A superior commander should not sit up nights wrestling with paper work and files. It would be better, he said, to go to bed or read a good book. He kept a picture of Rommel in his headquarters to remind him constantly of his mission. Morale in the army soared like an ascending rocket. The effect of Montgomery's assumption of command was described by Churchill as nothing short of "electrifying."

Though it does not detract in the least from Montgomery's magnificent achievement in raising the effectiveness of the Eighth Army to the pitch of fighting efficiency shown in October, it should be said that for the first time the Eighth Army was really getting the equipment required for modern combat—and getting it on an ample scale. Ritchie had to fight German tanks with two-pound antitank guns. He had to meet German Mark III and Mark IV tanks with inferior British and early American models. He never had enough of the excellent 25-pound field guns to make up for his other deficiencies, and above all he had no self-propelled guns. Major General Daniel Peinaar, commander of the South African Division, used to say: "Give me a good self-propelled assault gun—never mind the armor—and I'll drive Rommel out of Libya." While Rommel was beating Ritchie in May and June of 1942, large-scale reinforcements of men and equipment were being sent from Britain and the United States. Three well-trained British divisions—the 44th, 50th, and 51st—left England for Egypt during these months. Large numbers of British six-pound antitank guns arrived to augment the less effective two-pounders. Enough 25-pound field guns were sent to provide one gun for every 23 yards of front. American planes swelled the superiority that the RAF already held in the air. Finally, brand-new American Mark IV (General Sherman) tanks and 105 mm. self-propelled assault guns arrived in numbers to give the Eighth Army superiority in the quality as well as in the quantity of its armored equipment. The Mark IV tanks and 105 mm. assault guns were to be General Montgomery's tactical surprises. After the battle of El Alamein, General Alexander told American officers that the American Mark III (General

Grant) tanks saved the Eighth Army from disaster in June and July, 1942, and that the Mark IV tank made the victory at El Alamein possible.

Montgomery also had "brains" at the top of all parts of the Eighth Army. His intelligence officer was Lieutenant Colonel E. T. Williams, a former Oxford don. With Lindsell in charge of supplies, Gatehouse and Lumsden in command of his tanks, and with Freyberg, Moreshead, and Wimperley in command of his infantry divisions, Montgomery had the best subordinate commanders any leader could have wished for. He insisted on the best staff and rear establishment possible on the ground that "an army commander's administration in the rear should be on a scale commensurate with what he hoped to achieve at the front." Officers who did not meet his high standards were dealt with frankly. "You are a good officer," he would say, "but you are not good enough for me."

The position that Montgomery took over extended from the Qattara Depression northward to El Alamein from which it took its name. It was a 40-mile line which ran through Himeimat, Deir El Munassib, Ruweisat Ridge, past the Hill of Jesus toward Thompson's Post and the sea. There were some concrete pill-boxes on the British side but mostly well-concealed artillery and infantry positions in great depth covered by extensive wire entanglements and minefields. Land mines had become a major factor in fighting and they were used on a prodigal scale by both sides.

Severe fighting raged intermittently throughout July and August with both sides mounting offensives but lacking the strength for a break-through. Rommel launched a particularly heavy assault on the southern sector of the line on August 30 under the cover of a waning moon, but the attack collapsed under massed British artillery fire when the German tanks blundered into rough ground and British minefields. Rommel was hoping that the British would attack his armor and antitank guns with tanks so that he might repeat his triumph of June 13 at Knightsbridge, but this time the ruse failed to work. When the fighting died down on September 6 it was clear that the Germans did not have strength enough to break the British line. This was the time that Mr. Willkie made his famous statement that Egypt was safe and that the Africa Korps had suffered a real setback. Montgomery could now plan for his attempt to crush the Afrika Korps.

III

THE FORCES available in the Eighth Army consisted of the X Armored Corps (two armored divisions plus the 2nd New Zealand Division), two armored brigades, and six infantry divisions: 9th Australian, 4th Indian, 1st South African, 51st (Highland), 44th and 50th British; together with Fighting French and Greek detachments. Montgomery turned his newly arrived British divisions into veterans by training them alongside the battle-tried units that survived the retreat to El Alamein. The exact strength of the RAF under Air Marshal Coningham is not known, but it was sufficiently powerful to attack Axis supply lines with at least 700 bombers prior to the infantry assault and then pin the enemy aviation to the ground.

The Axis forces on the Alamein front in October, 1942, consisted of two German panzer divisions (the 15th and 21st), the German 90th Light (Motorized) Infantry Division, the German 164th Light Infantry Division (flown from Crete), two Italian armored divisions (the Ariette and Littorio), and the Trieste Motorized Infantry Division which made up the XX Mobile Corps, plus the Trento, Brescia, Pavia, Bologna, and Folgore Infantry divisions. The effective strength of this force on October 23 may be estimated at 90,000 men, 600 tanks, 400 guns, 900 antitank guns (including 88 mm. dual-purpose guns), and 600 planes.

The directive which Mr. Churchill gave to Generals Alexander and Montgomery was simple and brief. It read: "Your prime and main duty will be to take, or destroy, at the earliest opportunity, the German-Italian army commanded by Field Marshal Rommel, together with all its supplies and establishments in Egypt and Libya."

General Montgomery's plans for carrying it out were also simple. He had observed that whenever Ritchie waged a battle of confusion against Rommel, the Eighth Army took a beating. This time he was to make sure that the British plan was simple enough to carry out in spite of enemy interference. Once action was joined the initiative should never be surrendered to the enemy. This would prevent the kind of disorganization that had canceled British advantages in earlier battles. He replaced Rommel's radio technique of directing battles by a policy of making every man in the Eighth Army understand the whole plan of battle.

In order that he might have entire freedom to carry out his preparatory steps, Montgomery built up a "reserve army" in the back areas out of odds and ends. This secured his bases against an unexpected enemy attack. Then he pulled out two armored divisions and the 2nd New Zealand (the Ball of Fire) Division and formed them into a special assault corps called the X Armored Corps. This force was equipped with newly arrived American tanks and self-propelled assault guns and put through a vigorous training program for its break-through mission in the coming battle.

General Montgomery's plan of battle sought to achieve maximum surprise and deception. Feints were to be made by the 4th Indian Division at Ruweisat Ridge, by the 50th and 44th divisions north and south of Deir El Munassib, and by the 7th Armored Division south of Himeimat. The 9th Australian Division was to pin down the 164th, 90th, and Trieste divisions along the coast. The real attack was to come in the north at Tel El Eisa where the X Armored Corps was to use a break-through gap to be prepared by engineers and infantry. The sector chosen for the break-through was the strongest part of the German front. The point of attack apparently expected by the Germans was at Ruweisat Ridge farther south. Adopting a modification of

Allenby's Gaza deception of 1917, Montgomery formed a truck park in the rear of the break-through point. Each day German reconnaissance planes watched the training area of the X Armored Corps far behind the lines, but each night squadrons of Mark IV tanks disguised as trucks were moved into the truck park and an equal number of trucks were withdrawn. As the preparatory stages of the infantry assault and mine-lifting operations at Tel El Eisa proceeded, the whole force of the X Corps was in position to strike.

Far from suspecting a decisive British attack, so it appears, Marshal Rommel took time out in September for a trip to Berlin, leaving General von Stumme in command of the Afrika Korps. At Hitler's Sportspalast speech on September 30, he appeared as a guest of honor. There was no lack of confidence as he talked to German newsmen. "We hold the gateway of Egypt with full intentions to act. We did not fight our way forward in order to be thrown back. You can depend on it that we shall hold fast to what we have taken."

Montgomery's prebattle dispositions not only deceived the Germans as to time of the British attack, but caused General von Stumme to divide his armor. He sent the 21st and Ariette divisions south to meet the threatening British concentration in that area and held the 15th and Littorio divisions in the north. If the British attack came where General von Stumme expected it would, at Ruweisat Ridge, he hoped to crush the British penetration by bringing his armor together like the jaws of a pincer. After the battle joined, his successor found that it was too late to effect a junction in full strength. The Afrika Korps thus prepared for its own defeat.

General Montgomery's order of the day on the eve of battle read: "When I assumed command of the Eighth Army I said that the mandate was to destroy Rommel and his army, and that it would be done as soon as we were ready. We are ready now. The battle which is now about to begin will be one of the decisive battles of history. It will be the turning point of the war."

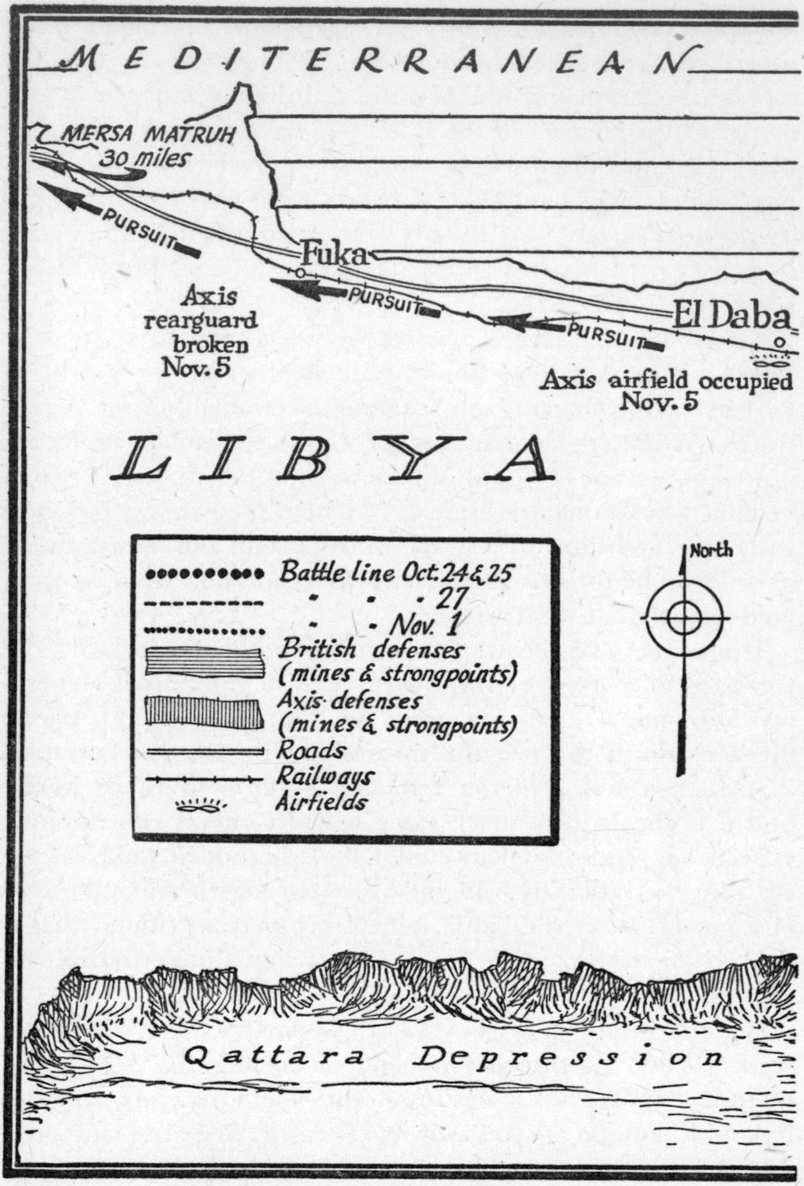

MEDITERRANEAN

MERSA MATRUH
30 miles

PURSUIT

Fuka

PURSUIT

El Daba

PURSUIT

Axis
rearguard
broken
Nov. 5

Axis airfield occupied
Nov. 5

LIBYA

●●●●●●●●● Battle line Oct. 24 & 25
– – – – " " " 27
–●–●– " " Nov. 1
British defenses
(mines & strongpoints)
Axis defenses
(mines & strongpoints)
Roads
Railways
Airfields

North

Qattara Depression

The Battle of El Alamein

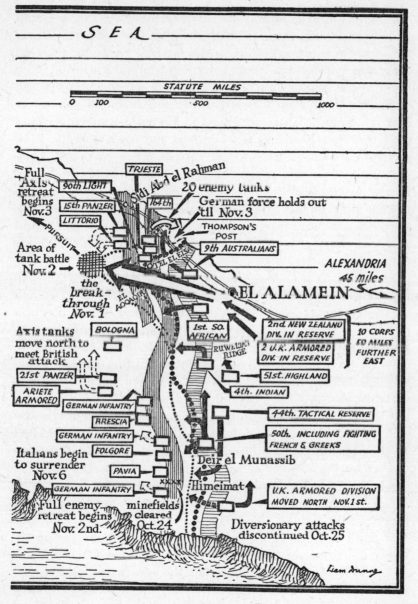

SEA

STATUTE MILES

0   100   500   1000

Full Axis retreat begins Nov. 3

TRIESTE

90th LIGHT

15th PANZER

LITTORIO

Sidi Abd el Rahman

164th

20 enemy tanks
German force holds out 'til Nov. 3

THOMPSON'S POST

9th AUSTRALIANS

COTEL EL EISA

PURSUIT

Area of tank battle Nov. 2 →

the break-through Nov. 1

EL AQQAQIR

ALEXANDRIA
45 miles

EL ALAMEIN

Axis tanks move north to meet British attack

BOLOGNA

1st. SO. AFRICAN

RUWEISAT RIDGE

2nd. NEW ZEALAND DIV. IN RESERVE

2 U.K. ARMORED DIV. IN RESERVE

10 CORPS
50 MILES
FURTHER EAST

21st PANZER

ARIETE ARMORED

GERMAN INFANTRY

BRESCIA

51st. HIGHLAND

4th. INDIAN

44th. TACTICAL RESERVE

GERMAN INFANTRY

FOLGORE

50th. INCLUDING FIGHTING FRENCH & GREEKS

Italians begin to surrender Nov. 6

PAVIA

Deir el Munassib

GERMAN INFANTRY

XXXX

Himeimat

U.K. ARMORED DIVISION MOVED NORTH NOV. 1st.

Full enemy retreat begins Nov. 2nd.

minefields cleared Oct. 24

Diversionary attacks discontinued Oct. 25

Liam Dunne

Promptly at 2130 hours on Friday, October 23, a tremendous British artillery barrage crashed down on Axis positions along the Alamein front. It fell upon the forward positions, battered the enemy command posts, and cut their communications. Under cover of this bombardment and of smoke screens, infantry and engineer patrols went forward to lift antitank mines and clear barriers. Then infantry advanced in strength. Ranging far and wide over Axis positions the bombers and fighters of the RAF carried out over 1,000 sorties, against enemy airfields, communications centers, troop concentrations, and supply depots. It was the heaviest and most sustained air attack launched up to that time in the Middle East. Later, when the troops advanced across the area over which the RAF operated, they found 550 Axis planes either destroyed or abandoned on enemy flying fields.

For seven days and nights the artillery-infantry action continued with engineers constantly extending the gap through the Axis minefields. General von Stumme was killed in action on October 26, and the command of the Afrika Korps passed to General Ritter von Thoma who made a desperate effort to concentrate his armor in the face of an impending British breakthrough. Finally on November 1 the 2nd New Zealand Division, with brigades from the 50th and 51st divisions (brought up from the south after feinting in that area), broke through the last Axis line at Kidney Ridge. The 51st Division had belated revenge that day for its losses at St. Valery in 1940. The stage was set for the advance of the X Armored Corps. It struck the Afrika Korps like a thunderbolt.

Never before had the British concentrated so much armor and fire power in a single mass. Hundreds of tanks rolled forward over Kidney Ridge on the morning of November 2. As one observer described the scene: "Each tank tore itself a bow wave and a wake of streaming dust that the sun caught and tipped with crimson. They spread out toward the sea and in toward the desert—a racing, roaring army of steel straining their petrol guts in rocking thunderous motion." As they reached the vicinity of El Aqqaqir, General Thoma met them with the bulk of his armored strength. It wasn't enough. Unprepared for the fire power, mobility, and armor of the new Mark IV tanks, and above all, for the hitting power of the 105 mm. assault guns and concentration of supporting British antitank guns, General Thoma lost the main body of his armor in a single day's fighting at El Aqqaqir and fell captive to General Montgomery.

According to the British official account there were two decisive stages of the El Alamein battle. "The first was the infantry break-through. The second was the great tank battle at El Aqqaqir. The first made the second possible, and the second sealed the success of the first. The first was completed in just over nine days. The second in as many hours. When it was over, El Aqqaqir was a cemetery of Axis armor, and the Battle of Egypt was in fact won. The rest was pursuit."

General Montgomery's decision to make the break-through in the north paid big dividends in the tank battle. It prevented the enemy from employing his favorite methods of armored counterattack on the flanks. Montgomery's choice of battlefields forced the Axis to make frontal assaults on the X Corps, and in the daylight hours of November 2 General Thoma's tanks were outfought by British tanks and assault guns. Losses were heavy in the X Corps but since the British remained in possession of the battlefield many disabled tanks were repairable. Every German tank that dropped out of the fight through damage or lack of fuel was a complete loss. After the battle 260 enemy tanks were counted on the field at El Aqqaqir.

That the tank battle of El Aqqaqir decided the issue was immediately indicated by German and Italian infantry action. To quote the British official account:

On November 2, the day of the tank battle, there were already signs of infantry withdrawal all along the front. On November 3 these signs became very definite. In the south the Italian divisions could not retreat far, for they were abandoned by the Germans, who commandeered all transport for their own men. Hardly a man of the six Italian infantry divisions escaped. Droves of prisoners were taken. The German 164th Light Division also lost heavily. Even though the Germans were the first to retreat after the battle was lost, they left behind over 8,000 prisoners apart from their killed and wounded. The Battle of Egypt cost the Axis 75,000 men, over 500 tanks, and over 1,000 guns.

Total British casualties to November 11 were 13,600 killed, wounded, and missing.

In the words of Mr. Churchill, the "bright gleam of victory" at El Alamein "caught the helmets of our soldiers and warmed and cheered our hearts." Combined with the magnificent victories of the Red army and the Allied landing in French North Africa, it assisted in wresting the initiative from the Axis. At last, the Eighth Army had produced leadership capable of exploiting to the full the human and material resources available. General Montgomery outwitted and outfought the Afrika Korps. British tactical methods were at last equal if not superior to those of the enemy.

The disposition and leadership of the Afrika Korps at El Alamein were faulty, a fact which Montgomery good-naturedly pointed out to captured General Thoma. He expressed regret that Thoma was not Rommel because he had always "wanted to talk over things" with the latter. He regarded Rommel as a good fighter but no superman, pointing out that he had a tendency to repeat his tactics. Whether Rommel was personally responsible for the decision to hold the El Alamein line, or whether he was acting on Hitler's orders, cannot be determined. If a British attack in great strength was anticipated, then a defense in very great depth was indicated. The mere possession of a few miles of desert might be important for Axis prestige, but it was not important from a strategic standpoint. By attempting to hold a thin strong line at El Alamein the leader of the Afrika Korps risked the destruction or capture of his main forces.

For two long years the Eighth Army had tried in vain to destroy the Afrika Korps. More than once it came close to achieving this end; but Rommel's skill in mechanized war, his capacity for keeping armor concentrated, his flair for tactical improvisation, his excellent transport and tank-repair service, and the superior quality of his armor and antitank guns turned prospective British victories into defeats. The Eighth Army learned mechanized desert warfare in the harsh school of lost battles. In previous campaigns the Eighth Army had possessed superiority in the air, but this in itself was insufficient to prevent German victories. Earlier British commanders had a tendency to commit their armor in driblets, only to have each small force destroyed by Rommel's concentrated armor. It took repeated bitter defeats to teach British tankers not to fight tanks without close antitank support. Never before Montgomery's command did the ground and air forces work in absolute unison. Co-operation was replaced by command at El Alamein. To newsmen Montgomery said: "We have just one plan, one idea in mind. There is no army on one hand and air force on the other. We work as a unit."

Under the warming influence of success, Montgomery expanded visibly. After the completion of the infantry phase of the El Alamein battle he received newsmen in his desert headquarters. He talked to them easily, balancing a fly swish deftly on the end of one finger. "I have defeated the enemy. I am now about to smash him—how do you like my hat?" He was wearing a black beret covered with the insignia of several units. Suddenly he broke off the conference, heaved himself into his reconnaissance tank, and disappeared in a cloud of dust.

When pressed for his secret of success in battle, Montgomery laid down the following requirements for a good general:

1. Have a good chief of staff.
2. Go for simplicity in everything.
3. Cut out all paper and train subordinates to work on verbal instructions and orders.
4. Keep a firm grip on basic fundamentals; the things that really matter.
5. Avoid being involved in details; leave them to your staff.
6. Study morale; it is a big thing in war. Without high morale you can achieve nothing.
7. When the issue hangs in the balance express confidence in the plans and in the operations, even if inwardly you feel not too certain of the outcome.
8. Never worry.
9. Never bellyache.

Before each battle he issued an order to the troops telling what he intended to do and why. As the campaign progressed he showed them in subsequent orders how his plans had worked out through their efforts. This practice had a cumulative effect in building up their confidence in him until nothing he asked for seemed impossible. He assured the army he would never order them into battle unless he was satisfied that the operation had a reasonable chance of success. As a result no general ever had a more devoted army under his command.[1]

IV

DESPITE all Montgomery could do, part of the Afrika Korps escaped destruction by a hasty retreat. Further heavy losses in men and equipment marked the Axis attempts to put up rearguard actions at Fuka (November 6), Matruh (November 8), and Buq Buq (November 10). Over the dusty roads to the west, bumper to bumper in an endless stream, the trucks of General Sir Wilfrid Lindsell (the Eighth Army's supply officer) rolled forward. But in spite of herculean efforts, the Eighth Army was never able to bring the remnants of the Afrika Korps to decisive battle. The retreat continued through Cyrenaica and Libya into Tripolitania. Names associated with former triumphs and defeats came into the news in succession: Halfaya Pass, Sollum, Tobruk, Derna, Bengasi, and El Agheila. Montgomery made a bold effort to cut off Rommel at El Agheila by sending the 5th and 6th New Zealand brigades across the desert behind the retreating Germans, but the line to be held at Wadi Matratin was too long and Rommel filtered through.

Thirteen weeks after he began to advance General Montgomery entered Tripoli and put an end to the fascist dream of empire in North Africa. In 13 weeks he had advanced 1,300 miles and reached objectives that had been beyond the strength

[1] Typical examples of Montgomery's orders to the Eighth Army can be found in Major Peter W. Rainer's, *Pipeline to Battle: An Engineer's Adventures with the Eighth Army* (New York, 1944), pp. 297–302.

of Wavell, Cunningham, and Ritchie. After months of desert
campaigning, Montgomery insisted that the Eighth Army appear
in spotless order in the victory parade in Tripoli. This gave
rise to the story (doubtless apocryphal) that Churchill jokingly
said to him in Tripoli: "If you keep this up, they'll say about
you, 'Montgomery, indomitable in defeat, invincible in retreat,
insufferable in victory.' " The victory parade over, Montgomery
moved his army forward toward the Mareth line guarding the
Axis flank in Tunisia.

Montgomery's victory at El Alamein and the advance to
Tripoli were parts of a larger Allied plan to drive the Axis out
of Africa. American and British troops landed in French North
Africa on November 8, 1942, but failed to take the all-important
ports of Tunis and Bizerte in their first improvised advance.
German and Italian troops were transported to Tunisia in
numbers sufficient to check this venture, and the campaign
settled into bad-weather positional warfare in which each side
built up its strength. Meantime, Rommel had withdrawn the
remnants of the Afrika Korps behind the dismantled Mareth
line and awaited the advance of the Eighth Army. Large scale
Italian infantry and tank reinforcements (later called the First
Italian Panzer Army) gave Rommel a formidable force. To
offset this somewhat, the possession of Tripoli gave Montgomery
ample harbor facilities for receiving supplies by sea from Egypt.

Taking advantage of Montgomery's slow approach to the
Mareth line, Rommel struck swiftly with part of his forces
against the American position at Gafsa on February 14, 1943.
Breaking through the thin line at Faïd and Kasserine passes, he
threatened the great Allied supply bases at Thala and Tebessa
but was turned back on February 22.

Perhaps his easy progress in the first stages of the Gafsa-Faïd-
Kasserine operation caused Rommel to become careless. Switch-
ing his forces back to the Mareth line he tried the same tactics
on Montgomery near Medenine on March 6. The almost in-
solent manner in which he handled his armor showed that he had
learned little from previous contacts with the Eighth Army.

Montgomery cleverly decoyed him on. Forward British gun crews abandoned their pieces in mock terror when the German tanks appeared. Without waiting for further reconnaissance, the German tankers swallowed the bait, closed their hatches, and roared in for the kill. Then, suddenly, Montgomery's real tank defenses were unmasked. A wall of fire blasted the leading column and stopped the advance cold. When the enemy retreated they left 52 wrecked tanks on the field. It was now the Eighth Army's turn to resume the offensive.

Allied military operations in Tunisia were co-ordinated by the reorganization of February 20, 1943, which placed General Eisenhower in over-all command of Allied forces in North Africa. Direct command of the armies in Tunisia fell to General Alexander as head of the newly formed 18th Army Group composed of the British First Army, the British Eighth Army, the United States II Corps, and the French XIX Corps. The Allied air forces in this theater were reorganized two days earlier under the supreme command of Air Marshal Tedder. This effected a division of forces into a strategic air force under Major General Doolittle, a tactical air force under Air Marshal Coningham, a coastal command force under Air Vice-Marshal Lloyd, and a photographic wing under Colonel Roosevelt. In the light of future developments it seems safe to say that these reorganizations made the overwhelming victory of May 6–13 possible.

Though the reorganization of the air forces did not materially change General Montgomery's relations with Air Marshal Coningham, with whom he had worked in closest harmony since El Alamein, it extended the benefits of the system for air-ground operations which these two men had worked out to the rest of the forces in Tunisia. General Eisenhower sanctioned the general policy that the air program in North Africa should be determined upon and carried out by the air officers but insisted upon real integration of air and ground operations. The experience of El Alamein showed that until the enemy air force had been cut down, no effective air support to ground troops was possible. Thus the main weight of Allied air power in North Africa was

MONTGOMERY

directed first at the bases of Axis air power and the lines supplying it. Then, after a working command of the air had been
attained, Allied air power was thrown into direct support of
ground operations. This arrangement enabled Air Marshal Tedder to achieve a concentration and flexibility in the use of the
air weapon which the Axis could not match.

An example of how this concept of air-ground co-operation
worked out in practice is to be found in the operations of the
Eighth Army which led to the forcing of the Mareth line. Though
the forts of this former French defense zone had been disarmed,
the position was still one of great natural strength. Finally, on
March 20 Montgomery was prepared to attack the Mareth position. Allied air forces in northern Tunisia kept German air
power under heavy attack, allowing Coningham, who virtually
lived at Montgomery's headquarters, a chance to use his tactical
air force in direct support of the Eighth Army. When the frontal
attack at Wadi Zigzaou failed, Montgomery varied his usual
frontal push and right hook; he threw the New Zealand Division
under General Freyberg around the left flank of the Mareth
line in a brilliant march over rough terrain toward El Hamma.
When this movement met with initial success, Montgomery
boldly reinforced success and sent the 1st British Armored
Division to support the flanking movement. General Messe, who
succeeded Rommel on the Southern front, hastily countered by
sending crack German and Italian armored forces and infantry
to defend El Hamma and the approaches to Gabes. On March 26
the battle for El Hamma reached a climax. Coningham threw
every plane that could carry a bomb or fire its machine guns into
the battle. A sustained air attack on the Axis position, which
featured the employment of Hurricane "tank busters," cracked
the defense wide open. Here it was that the 164th German Light
Division was caught moving on a road and cut up by fighter
bombers, paving the way for the advance of British armor and
infantry.

The victory at El Hamma undermined the Axis position on
the Mareth line and forced a withdrawal to Wadi Akarit. A

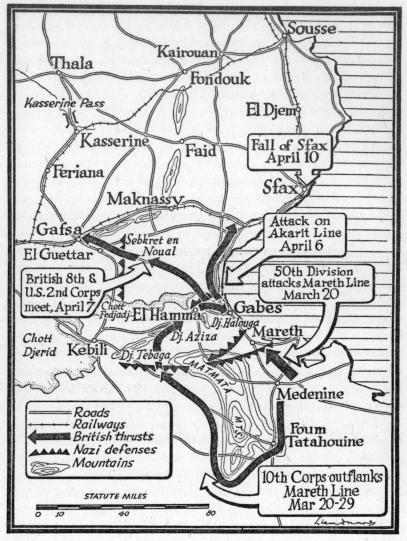

Mareth and Wadi Akarit

surprise attack on the moonless night of April 5 by the 4th
Indian Division cracked the Axis position at Wadi Akarit, driving the Afrika Korps northward to its final position at Enfidaville on April 24.[2] The Axis line then ran from that point to
Pont-du-Fahs–Medjez-el-bab to the sea west of Bizerte. Arnim
placed his strongest forces opposite the Eighth Army—a tribute
to that army and its leaders.

Banking on the legendary reputation of Montgomery, General Alexander boldly detached the 1st Armored Division from
the Eighth Army and sent it northward to reinforce Anderson's
First Army. He also sent the United States II Corps across the
lines of the British First Army to a position from which it could
menace Sedjenane and Mateur. Thus, using the threat of Montgomery's all victorious Eighth Army at Enfidaville, General
Alexander concentrated a decisive superiority against Arnim in
the north. He even transferred the 7th Armored and 4th Indian
divisions from the Eighth Army to Anderson in the last stages of
the battle.

After 10 days of savage fighting in the north, the British First
Army and the American II Corps broke through the Axis positions behind a moving carpet of bombs, crashed into Tunis and
Bizerte, and overwhelmed the Afrika Korps. By May 6 all organization in the Axis forces in the north disappeared. Mass
surrenders followed; on May 13 the campaign was over.

General Alexander is a hard man to please and General Montgomery is not an easy man to get along with, yet at the end of the
Tunisian campaign the former remarked: "When you have a
good army commander leave him alone. All I have to do is tell
Monty what I want and he goes ahead and does it. I never have
to worry about him." Together Alexander and Montgomery
made a combination whose achievement gave a new sense of
pride to British arms everywhere.

Asked by an American correspondent to sum up the lessons

---

[2] For an account of this brilliant attack led by the 2nd Gurkhas, see Lieutenant
Colonel G. R. Stevens, "The Gurkhas at Fatnassa" in the *Army Quarterly*, XLVII,
191–197, January, 1944.

of the Tunisian campaign, Montgomery replied: "First concentrate your forces; second, knit your ground and air forces together. That's it. Knit ground and air together. Knit them together absolutely."

In his opinion it was necessary to win the "air battle" before you could win the ground battle. Accordingly Montgomery urged that theater air forces be commanded by air officers guided only by the broad general directives of the theater commander. The memorandum he wrote on this subject was so impressive that much of his language was incorporated directly into Field Service Regulations FM 100–20, *Command and Employment of Air Power,* which the United States War Department issued after the Tunisian campaign. This is the first instance in modern times in which the words of a foreign officer were embodied directly in our doctrine.

V

IN JULY and August, 1943, Montgomery led the Eighth Army through some of the hardest fighting of the Sicilian campaign. For weeks his troops were held up by the strong German position at Catania. With due regard for his men, Montgomery waited until the swift flanking movement of General Patton's Seventh Army helped dislodge the enemy. He was not thirsting for additional glory to be paid for by the lives of his men.

At the close of that campaign his troops were the first to break into the fortress of Europe. On September 3, the day on which Italy signed the armistice, his troops landed at Reggio Calabria. When the United States Fifth Army and the British forces made a daring landing at Salerno, his troops finally forced the enemy to release his grip on the Allied beachhead. From that time on until December 24 he directed operations on the eastern side of the peninsula.

Montgomery's contact with the Germans in Sicily and Italy was a sobering one. He found them in many respects a tougher and more resourceful opponent than the Afrika Korps. "They

are," he said, "a professional army." They could only be conquered by an army trained to fight in all kinds of terrain and
which equaled the Germans in professional skill. To newsmen
he said "the real war is just beginning."

On Christmas, 1943, it was announced that General Montgomery would command the British ground forces under General
Eisenhower's new command. It was a task he welcomed with
scriptural phrases. Behind him lay a year in which he had built
up a defeated army, led it on an uninterrupted advance of 2,000
miles, defeated the hitherto invincible Afrika Korps, crossed a
great sea, helped conquer Sicily and materially assisted in driving
Italy out of the war. Before him lay an even greater task, that
of crushing the nazi military machine which had driven his
division off the beaches of Dunkirk in June, 1940.

No appointment could have been more popular with the
British people. They knew that it was largely Montgomery's
personality and leadership that gave the British army the skill
and spirit required to defeat the Afrika Korps. They felt that
under his leadership the British army was equal to defeating the
hard core of the Wehrmacht.

Montgomery introduced something new into British military
history—army esprit de corps. There had been regimental esprit
de corps before but not a spirit that distinguished a whole army.
In his Christmas message to the Eighth Army on taking leave
of them he said: "Wherein lies the strength of this great army?
It lies in its team spirit, in the firm determination of every man
to do his duty, and in its high morale. This army is a great family
with a spirit the like of which has seldom been seen before."

Through his leadership of the Eighth Army, Montgomery
laid the spiritual foundation for the British army's share in the
victory over Germany.

HITLER

☆

"I do not play at war. I shall not allow myself to be ordered about by commanders in chief. I shall make war. I shall determine the correct moment for attack. I shall shrink from nothing."

THE strangest and most spectacular military career in history began on August 3, 1914, when the war fever in Munich led an Austrian expatriate to petition King Ludwig III for permission to join the Bavarian army. Back of this request on the part of an unknown man lay a life of unrelieved failure and frustration. The wheels of Bavarian officialdom ground swiftly, for on the following day the young Austrian joined the 1st company of the 16th reserve infantry regiment as Private No. 148. The zealous expatriate was Adolf Hitler, and "this," he said later, "was the greatest day of my life."

Hitler was born at the Hotel zum Pommer in Braunau on April 20, 1889, the son of Alois (Schicklgrüber) Hitler, a minor customs official, and Klara Pölzl, his third wife. Reared in an atmosphere of poverty and parental bickering, he was drawn to his mother and reflected her neurotic tendencies. As a boy he was a problem to his teachers and a source of annoyance to his companions. He grew up friendless, frustrated, and without an objective in life. Twice rejected as a student at the Vienna Academy of Art, he carried away his bitterness to Munich in 1912. Though happier than he had ever been in his native land, Hitler was still without a plan or purpose until the war provided a basis for his future life and work.

With a zeal and patriotism often found in the newest converts to a cause, Hitler threw himself wholeheartedly into the German military venture of 1914. He performed the minor tasks of training and soldiery with a seriousness that provoked amusement

among his fellows. It was as if the future of all Germans depended
on the way he cleaned a rifle or ran an errand. Being a "soft
touch" for dirty work, he was made an orderly. His comrades in
arms found his lack of interest in wine and women a little
astonishing but generally regarded him as a "good soldier," a
term mercifully elastic in meaning. After one year of company
"hewing of stone and drawing of water" he was raised to his final
rank of lance corporal. Since the demand for officer material
increased tremendously in the last years of the war, but Hitler's
rank remained the same, it must be concluded that his talents
for organization and administration developed later in life.

Despite the many attempts to impugn Hitler's personal courage, his military record is clear. He took part in 48 engagements
and conducted himself with courage and fortitude. At Le Barque
on October 5, 1916, he was painfully wounded by a hand grenade.
He took part in the defensive fighting of 1917 and in the offensives of 1918. The position of his company at Montagne was
drenched with mustard gas on October 14, 1918, and Hitler,
suffering from severe burns and temporary blindness, was in-
valided to Pasewalk military hospital. Here it was in the fall of
1918, when his personal fortunes and those of his adopted land
were at their lowest ebb, amid the defeatist and communist chat-
ter of dispirited soldiers, that he saw a vision of a resurgent
Germany. In the cell-like room at Pasewalk he resolved to avenge
the defeat of the German people. He decided to become a politician.

II

EXCEPT as it bears upon the amazing grasp of military matters
which Hitler demonstrated in later years, no attempt will be
made to trace the long struggle of the National Socialist party
for political power in Germany. There can be little doubt that
a great deal of Hitler's effectiveness in the early phases of the
war can be traced to his training in the bitterly contested, street-
brawl political battles of the early days. He became schooled in
organizing meetings and timing movements, skilled in analyzing

public reaction to events and measures, expert at judging the resistance to be encountered and the force required to overcome it. His rise to power was in fact a four-year battle in which adversaries were lulled to sleep by promises of security and then ruthlessly destroyed. Ruses, traps, and tricks were employed. Real bullets were fired. Men died. It was a campaign akin to a military movement in which final victory was developed out of a limited penetration of the enemy position.

From this four-year struggle Hitler gained an accurate estimation of the power of a definite program when pitted against the status quo. He could see that words were often mightier than howitzers. He learned that nearly every political and industrial leader in the decadent society of Republican Germany had his price, and that certain sections of society would gladly undermine the security of the whole nation to achieve even a temporary continuation of their privileged position. A sense of realism indistinguishable from cynicism was the result. Against the weak ruling classes and parties of Germany (and later against his foreign enemies) Hitler was prepared to use this knowledge with fatal results.

In addition to underestimating his ability and potential menace, Hitler's adversaries also committed the fatal mistake of assuming that some other party or power would destroy him before he really became dangerous. He survived because until late in the present war his adversaries never combined against him.

For a time the moderate and conservative elements in Germany ignored him, because they were certain that the communists, under tough "Red" Thälmann would arrange for his destruction. Later they were confident that the skilled politicians, Brüning, Schleicher, and Papen, would betray him. When they failed, as did the big industrialists, many based their hopes on the Reichswehr. That the army chiefs, the historic guardians of national unity, would allow a demagogic, former Bohemian corporal to pervert the army to party and personal uses was unthinkable. First it was Hindenburg who was to put the nazi leader in his place. The octogenarian field marshal was known

JODL *(behind Hitler)*, HITLER, and BRAUCHITSCH

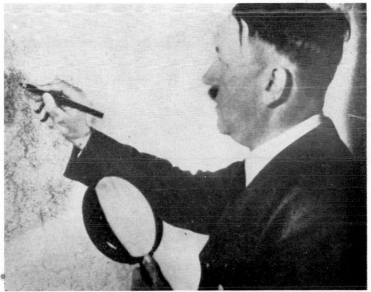

HITLER, the *Feldherr*

to despise Hitler. He was credited with the suggestion that Hitler be made minister of the Reich's post office "where he will have to lick my backside every day"—an example of broad German humor, since all German stamps then bore the portrait of Hindenburg. But Hindenburg was checked by threats of political blackmail held over the heads of his beloved Junkers in the Osthilfe scandal. In 1934 the aged field marshal died. Then it was Blomberg and Fritsch who would assert the power of the army over the new chancellor, but in 1938 they were both toppled from power.

Finally the "someone-else-will-get-him" school of thinkers were clutching at such tiny straws as the exiled Otto Strasser. By circumventing these dangers one at a time, absorbing or crushing his opponents, Hitler learned the effectiveness of the "artichoke" strategy which he applied with so much skill to the military problems of Germany in 1939–41.

The army was always first in Hitler's mind, even in the days of his struggle for political power. It is not an accident that the only paid employment he ever secured was in the Bavarian army and as a Reichswehr spy in 1919. To his mind, as to that of Heraclitus, "war is the father of all things." The economic objective of the party and the state was a *Wehrwirtschaft;* the objective of the nazi social and racial program was the creation of a warrior cult based on mythical concepts of "Blood and Soil." The 25-point nazi program of 1920 called for the creation of a national army.

Part of his success in capturing the imagination of the German people was due to his skillful exploitation of their strong military bent. He promised to release them from the humiliation of Versailles, to erase the false stain of defeat that sullied their war flags. The Jews, the defeatists, the capitalists, and the feeble leaders of the German Empire were blamed for the military defeat of 1918. The stab-in-the-back legend created by the German high command in 1918 became the spiritual basis for the re-creation of the German army.

The task of rebuilding the armed might of Germany, temporarily soft-pedaled for political and economic reasons when Hitler came to power, was the very center of his program. The skill with which he prepared for this critical step was not apparent at the time. It only became clear when placed against the background of his ultimate program. Diplomacy was used to disarm his future enemies and to insure a period of relaxed tension in which the army could be safely reconstructed. His first important diplomatic agreement was the 25-year nonaggression pact with Poland signed in 1934. Since the Polish Corridor was the most irritating territorial provision of the Versailles treaty and *Mein Kampf* made it clear that this injustice would be the first to be erased, the nonaggression pact with Poland convinced many statesmen that Hitler was a man of peace who could be dealt with by normal diplomatic means. The Polish treaty weakened the French diplomatic ring around the Reich and lulled the Poles into a false sense of security.

His second diplomatic step was even more subtle and effective. In 1935 (the year he was prepared to denounce the Versailles military restrictions) Hitler signed a naval treaty with Britain promising not to build beyond 35 per cent of the strength of the British fleet in any class of naval vessel. Concluded behind the back of France, this agreement convinced the British government that Hitler was a man of reason, that he did not contemplate a challenge to their historic command of the sea. Since it could feel secure at sea, the British government was not alarmed at the announcement of the new German military law and did not support the French desire for joint military action against the Reich. These two diplomatic agreements made it safe to launch the new military program in 1935.

On March 16, 1935, Hitler announced the "Law for the Reconstruction of the National Defense Forces." It provided for military service on a conscript basis for selected Germans of military age and set the goal of the program at 36 divisions. The Reichswehr had been limited by the Versailles treaty to a force of seven infantry and three cavalry divisions or 100,000 officers and men. The new army of some 600,000 men was to be a part of the new national defense force (the army, navy, and air force), henceforth to be called the Deutsche Wehrmacht. In October of the same year the general staff, forbidden by the treaty, was revived and placed under Colonel Ludwig Beck. The expansion of the army meant the end of Seeckt's scheme for an elite army and ended all hope of a military putsch against Hitler. When the Reichswehr was submerged in the new army the last check upon the personal authority of the chancellor disappeared.

Strange to say, many foreign military thinkers viewed Hitler's decision to abandon the Reichswehr in favor of a conscript army with unmistakable signs of relief. Professional soldiers knew how a traditional mass army would operate; they were not sure of the performance of a supertrained force like the Reichswehr. It was pointed out that Hitler could never regain the "16 lost years." The difficulties of expanding a small force into a mass army were pointed out in detail. Artillery, aircraft, tanks, and small arms could not be conjured up overnight, even by such a skillful magician as Hitler. The slow start of the new military program seemed to confirm these views. It was eight months after the announcement of the army law before a single recruit was inducted into the service. Only 26 of the projected divisions existed on paper at the end of the first year.

After 1936 the pace of German rearmament increased. The maneuvers of 1936 and 1937 were impressive not only on account of the numbers involved but also from the fact that the forces engaged showed remarkable mobility. Distances were covered in a single day which surprised foreign observers. The ominous step-by-step character of the expanding German military power became clear in 1937 when the 36 division limit (beyond which Hitler had asserted the Reich would never go) was extended to a 42 division program.

As the completely mobilized industry of Germany began to turn out modernized weapons for the Wehrmacht, those who felt that material difficulties would prevent the early completion of the military program now asserted that the shortage of trained officers would be the chief weakness of the enlarged army. Gamelin is reported to have remarked: "We have hundreds of officers who were divisional commanders in 1918; they will find that these are not easy to replace."

III

THE military techniques of national socialism must be considered as part of its revolutionary activity. Hitler more than once declared that he made the doctrines of the revolution the basis of his political and military policy. The total purpose behind the movement was the desire to increase Germany's capacity to wage war, which was held to be a permanent rather than a temporary state.

It was no ordinary war that the chancellor foresaw and planned. Even before he came to power its character was one of the favorite topics for Hitler's monologues. The military experience of 1914–18 convinced him that a war of horizontal lines, a struggle of trenches and frontal attacks, could be avoided. He looked upon the frontal attacks of infantry on prepared positions and trenches as "a degenerate form of war." Sitting on the veranda of Wachenfeld House at Obersalzburg in 1932, he outlined his military views to a group of young nazis. His ideas seemed so impossible and bizarre that some of the "bright young men" were quietly poking fun at him. They led him off on what seemed fantastic tangents, gravely discussing such themes as bacterial warfare. He rose to the bait and asserted that no method would be overlooked which gave any promise of success. Germs might be spread before the outbreak of hostilities by harmless-looking travelers. Or it might be more profitable to reserve bacterial war for the supreme crisis in order to achieve a decision by final means of disease and terror.

Above all, he promised to avoid the mistakes of 1914. Much depended on how the war was started. Such business could not be left to the generals; they were likely to be "sterile," lacking in imagination, and "imprisoned in the coils of their technical knowledge." Rudolf Hess finally brought the subject into a

favorable position for a typical Hitler broadside. He launched
into the theme:

War has been erected into a secret science and surrounded with mo-
mentous solemnity. But war is most natural, the most everyday matter.
It is eternal and universal. There is no beginning and no peace. War is
life. Any struggle is war. What is the object of war? To make your enemy
capitulate. Why should I demoralize him by military means, if I can do
so better and more cheaply in other ways?

When I wage war in the midst of peace, troops will suddenly appear,
let us say, in Paris. They will wear French uniforms. They will march
through the streets in broad daylight. No one will stop them. Everything
will be thought out in advance. They will march to the headquarters of
the general staff. They will occupy the ministries, the Chamber of Deputies.
Within a few minutes France, Poland, Austria, and Czechoslovakia will be
robbed of their leading men. An army without a general staff! The confusion
will be beyond belief! I shall have had relations with the men who will form
a new government—a government to suit me. We shall find such men; we
shall find them in every country. We shall not have to bribe them. They
will come of their own accord. Ambition and delusion, party squabbles and
self-seeking arrogance will drive them. Peace will be negotiated before
the war has been begun. The impossible is always successful. We shall have
more than enough volunteers, men like the SA (storm troops), trustworthy
and ready for any sacrifice. We shall send them across the border in peacetime. No one shall see in them anything but peaceful travelers. Today you
don't believe me, but I will accomplish it step by step. Perhaps we shall
land at their flying fields. We shall be capable of transporting not only
men but arms by air. . . . Our strategy is to destroy the enemy from within,
to conquer him through himself.[1]

This technique of breaking down an enemy by moral means
and intrigue Hitler derived from his own struggle for power and
from the Bolsheviki.

With the rambling and repetitious style common to his oral
pronouncements, Hitler continued his discussion of the new
technique of conquest. He was soon shouting to his audience as
if they were a mass meeting:

[1] This quotation and the one in the following paragraph are from Hermann
Rauschning's *The Voice of Destruction* (G. P. Putnam's Sons, New York, 1940) and
are reprinted with the permission of the publisher.

I shall never start a war without the certainty that a demoralized enemy will succumb to the first stroke of a single gigantic attack. When the enemy is demoralized from within, when he stands on the brink of revolution, when social unrest threatens—that is the right moment! A single blow must destroy him. Aerial attacks, stupendous in their mass effect, surprise, terror, sabotage, assassination from within, the murder of leading men, overwhelming attacks on all the weak points of the enemy defenses, sudden attacks, all in the same second, without regard for reserves or losses; that is the war of the future.

I do not play at war. I shall not allow myself to be ordered about by commanders in chief. I shall make war. I shall determine the correct moment for attack. . . . I shall shrink from nothing. No so-called international law, no agreements will prevent me from making use of any advantage that offers. The next war will be unbelievably bloody and grim, but the most inhuman war, one which makes no distinction between military and civilian combatants, will at the same time be the kindest, because it will be the shortest.

We shall grind down the enemy with a war of nerves. . . . We shall provoke a revolution in France. . . . The French will hail me as their deliverer. None of these people any longer want war and greatness—but I want war!

These blueprints of the coming war were laid out in the year 1932. It was small wonder that few of his lieutenants took them seriously. Rauschning considered it typical of the man that between one outburst and another he hummed familiar motifs from the *Götterdämmerung*.

No part of this discourse reached the ears of British and French professional soldiers. Had it done so, they would have regarded it as the wildest kind of folly. One can fancy them saying: "I would love to see this blatant unprofessional supervise the river crossing of a single brigade in the face of the enemy!" This type of sentence was always used as the final professional weapon to annihilate "amateur" strategists and "armchair" critics.

If the ominous and unorthodox character of Hitler's military ideas remained hidden, the outward strength of the growing German Wehrmacht could not be concealed. The march into the Rhineland in 1936 and the occupation of Austria in 1938 provided useful laboratory data on the mobility of the army.

Mechanical breakdowns, gleefully reported in the press of Britain and France, were corrected in the period before September, 1939. Since both these steps were taken against the advice of his military leaders, Hitler's personal prestige increased to a point where he could safely disregard the military hierarchy. Blomberg, Fritsch, and General Beck, the first chief of the general staff, were retired in that year. Some 20 other senior officers who were not sympathetic with the nazi regime were replaced by officers who saw in the nazi movement an opportunity for sudden and dramatic advancement, such as Reichenau, Keitel, and Brauchitsch. These men gave up the effort which had been made by Gröner, Seeckt, and Hammerstein to keep the army free from political domination by any party. They accepted the nazi movement wholeheartedly.

The "nazification" of the army was carried out in the years 1938–39. Special care was lavished on the troops. They were provided with airy, light, and attractive living quarters, supplied with excellent food, and, despite all legends to the contrary, were equipped with the most modern weapons. Nazi ideology glorified the soldier and discredited the intellectuals. It offered the army as the most promising career open to young men. Troops on maneuver were garlanded with flowers and cheered by the admiring populace. They developed a high morale and trained with a zeal which astonished foreign observers.

The nazi methods of training stressed individual initiative to a high degree. Perversely enough, the democratic countries of Europe, which lived by the doctrine of political freedom and initiative, continued to employ close-order drill, maintained the rigid formal tactics of World War I, and based their strategic concepts on the doctrine of a "continuous front"; while a regimented country like nazi Germany favored the spontaneous co-operation of small combat squads in action and trained them to take individual advantage of every terrain feature. Nazi doctrines abandoned the formalism of "fronts," stressed infiltration and deep penetration movements, and aimed at a broadened strategy of confusion. Swiftness, striking power, and resourcefulness were sought even in the smallest infantry units. Engineer and labor troops were equipped to bridge streams, blanket strong points in smoke, take pillboxes from the flank and rear, and keep motorized units moving. Cross-country work by motorized and tank units was emphasized. They were trained to go around obstacles even if wide detours were involved. Accompanying artillery consisted largely of high-angle weapons. Air support and motorized artillery were expected to keep pace with the rapid advance of mechanized troops and motorized infantry.

The armored divisions and the air force were regarded as elite troops and given concessions even greater than those extended to the other forces. Their training involved the greatest possible use of radio equipment for maintaining liaison and supplying information. No other nation made anything like the use of two-way radio communication which was the day-by-day practice of the Wehrmacht. Thirty nazi officers picked by Halder in 1936 were given a year of service with the navy and the Luftwaffe. The result was a military force of unconventional form, possessing weapons of modern design but of unknown power, and equipped to maintain a constant communication between all elements.

Behind the Wehrmacht was a second army. It was composed of all nazis from the youngest *Pimpfe* of the Hitler Youth to the armed elite of the *Schutzstaffel* or SS. No single step in the military education of German youth was neglected. If a German boy did not pass immediately from the Hitler Youth and the Reich Labor Services into the Wehrmacht, he received special training in party organizations like the Nazi Flyers Corps, the Nazi Transportation Corps, the Technical Emergency Corps (public utilities), or the Organization Todt (militarized construction corps). If he were a particularly fanatical nazi and had the right build and "blood" he might aspire to the SS. All these organizations were dedicated to preparing Germany for war.[2] In no other na-

[2] For an enlightening account of these organizations, see Alfred Vagts, *Hitler's Second Army* (Washington, 1943).

tion or time has the whole population of a country been so systematically organized for military purposes.

IV

HITLER's method of stealthy war, of conquest by demoralization
and intrigue, had its first minor trial in the annexation of Austria. The collapse of this German state was accomplished so easily
that it must be considered merely as a dress rehearsal for the
Czech crisis of September, 1938. Immediate promises by Hitler
of disinterestedness in Czech territory followed the Austrian
stroke, and, if they failed to convince the government at Prague,
they at least satisfied Britain and France.

The Sudeten crisis of September, 1938, was the first real test
of the new "white war" of nerves. It was prepared by the full
power of the nazi propaganda ministry. Göring's air force was
pictured as so dreaded a weapon that great cities like London
and Paris cowered in panic (either willfully or inadvertently increased by the actions of their own statesmen). After keeping the
nerves of Europe on edge for days and nights, Hitler cracked
the resolution of the western democracies in his famous fighting
speech of September 26. Without suffering a single military
casualty from enemy action, Hitler had undermined the bastion
of Czechoslovakia and destroyed the remnants of French diplomatic strength. It was the first successful application of the new
technique of war carried out against a non-German state thought
to be well prepared to meet the traditional forms of attack and
supported, at least on paper, by powerful allies. The subsequent
occupation of all Czech territory in the following March should
have convinced even the most reactionary political and military
minds that warfare under the aegis of national socialism would
show few similarities to the forms of 1914–18; but it did not.

As Europe slowly moved toward war in the hot summer of
1939, the western democracies had one last revelation of the
unconventional character of their adversary. On August 23 Hitler suddenly concluded a nonaggression pact with Russia aimed

at the partition of Poland. It staggered Britain and France. They had been carrying on halfhearted negotiations looking toward a military alliance with Russia to patch up the breach caused by the Munich pact.

To Hitler's mind, the Russian pact should have made a war over Danzig and the Polish Corridor unnecessary. With the Russian pact in his pocket, Hitler could go ahead with his war of nerves against Poland with perfect serenity. From a geographic and military standpoint, there was really nothing Britain and France could do to prevent the partition of Poland. According to all logic, the Poles should have capitulated gracefully, but they were too "barbaric" to fall under the spell of his "white war." Blissfully ignorant of military realities, confident of its backward army, the Polish government remained adamant. War was inevitable. But even after the German invasion began, for three days British and French statesmen were feverishly trying to arrange a new Munich.

By the careless way he brushed these cynical offers aside, it must be assumed that Hitler no longer cared if Britain and France went to war. As he judged their state of moral confusion, their lack of effective military preparations, their failure to grasp the character of the nazi military revolution, the public apathy to war in Allied countries, he was supremely confident of victory.

Foreign observers still found some cause for amusement in his egotistical announcement that he was assuming command of the armed forces of the Reich and would not take off his field gray uniform until death or victory. The idea that this pallid, nervous, prima-donna demagogue would be of any use on a modern battlefield was thrust aside as too absurd for consideration. The outbreak of actual fighting was greeted with relief by many who felt that it would put an end to Hitler's cheap victories, that he would soon be relegated to a position of Kaiserlike impotence, and that henceforth the army would rule the Reich.

V

THE character of the German attack on Poland in September, 1939, offered many surprises, but it did not open the eyes of the western democracies to the fact that this war would differ widely from the traditional pattern. The co-ordination of all German forces was impressive. Ninety nazi infantry divisions and eight armored divisions were expected to be able to advance against 60 Polish regular and reserve divisions, but the rate of advance was ominous. The fog of war and the traditional character of the military communiqués concealed for a time the nature of the German attack. It was prepared by extensive bombing raids directed at Polish telephone and telegraph exchanges and other communications equipment. These disrupted the Polish system of aircraft warning and enabled the Luftwaffe to destroy the enemy air force on the ground. Blinded by the loss of its air scouts, the Polish army was soon cut into small segments by deep penetrations of German tank columns.

All Polish efforts to establish a battle line on the pattern of 1914–18 failed. Order disappeared from the battlefield as the Polish army was reduced to little islands of resistance in the midst of an ocean of chaos. As the German strategy of confusion rendered them helpless, Polish leaders quarreled bitterly. Many felt that their army was melting away without having had a chance for a stand-up fight with the enemy. They were not the last men to experience this feeling of military frustration. With the German enemy at the gates of Warsaw, all hope was lost when the Russian army moved in from the east on September 17. The government fled in despair to Rumania, where Colonel Joseph Beck and General Smigly-Rydz set the seal of confusion on the disaster by coming to blows on the railway platform at Cernăuti.

With the final collapse of Polish resistance at Lublin on October 5, the conquest of a nation of 34,000,000 people was completed. In retrospect it seemed more impressive than while it was actually being reported in the press and by radio. The whole operation had taken slightly more than one month, the period generally required for a minor offensive in World War I. The speed with which the German columns advanced, their ability to supply advancing columns with gasoline and munitions (to say nothing of food), the skill with which they circumvented natural obstacles and prepared demolitions, the failure of the weather, the mud, and fatigue to slow down their movements, all failed to impress the outside world with the revolutionary character of the Polish campaign. Its quick success was explained away on the basis of Polish internal weakness, and on the assumption that the rashness of the Polish high command, in making a stand in their forward positions, played into the German hands. Optimism still remained high in Allied circles. Men looked forward to the day when the German legions would have to deal with the "incomparable" army of France.

The German propaganda service left no doubt in the public mind that Hitler was with the army in the east during these spectacular triumphs. When the Polish capital refused to surrender on September 17, he personally ordered the bombing and bombardment of the city. The heavy loss inflicted on civilians in the 10-day bombardment was afterward described as an "act of mercy," since it cut short a hopeless resistance.

The effectiveness of Hitler's leadership of the German war effort continued to be scoffed at in Allied circles until after the Norwegian campaign. The hand of Hitler was apparent in the political and diplomatic machinations which undermined Poland, but the military movements were credited to the German high command. The Norwegian campaign was an entirely different matter. It seemed at first sight to be so completely unrelated to the major war effort, so filled with military and naval hazards, that no German staff officer could have planned it. It had all the marks of "nazi amateur strategy." The methods employed were so foreign to the traditional methods of the German army that Hitler did not have to claim the campaign as his own. It fitted perfectly the description of war as he outlined it at Obersalzburg in 1932. And it succeeded just as easily as he predicted it would. Hitler set the major pattern of the campaign and the efficient general staff worked out the details.

A "peaceful" conquest of Denmark could be expected. It was virtually a prisoner of nazi Germany. But an attack on Norway was another matter. It involved the transport of forces by sea in the face of a superior British fleet. Like other sailors, Admiral Raeder was steeped in the tradition of maintaining the fleet in being. He could hardly be expected to support a plan which called for the protection of sea communications hundreds of miles long.[3] Soldiers trained in the traditional concepts of war were certain to be hesitant about landing operations in the face of unknown factors. Hitler, on the other hand, regarded naval vessels as being in the same category as any other piece of war equipment, built to be expended in action. After he convinced the high command and the admiralty that the wooden-horse attack on southern Norwegian bases would succeed under the protection of the Luftwaffe, he found them unable to agree to an attack on Narvik. They argued that it was impossible to supply even the small force that could be landed. Hitler insisted on the Narvik attack and is said to have offered to take personal command of the expedition. This is said to have shamed the soldiers into agreement.

A dress rehearsal for nazi total war was revealed on April 9, 1940, when small forces of German troops were landed at all principal Norwegian ports from the holds of apparently peaceful merchant ships. The Luftwaffe cowed the capital at Oslo. Planes landed men and equipment at Norwegian airports. Faked orders were issued to garrisons, batteries, and naval vessels. With only minor upsets to their plans, a small German force marched into Oslo led by the municipal police force and a regimental band. The greatest act of treachery in modern history delivered the principal cities of the country to the nazis within a single day.

After that it was merely a question of whether German re-

[3] The advantages and disadvantages of a German invasion of the Scandinavian countries in event of a general European war was discussed quite frankly in German military and naval periodicals prior to the war.

inforcements could reach the small garrisons before Norwegian and Allied action could drive them out. Here the shore-based Luftwaffe asserted its superiority. British naval efforts to cut the sea communications failed. Except at Narvik, British naval action was conducted on a hit-or-miss basis; it did not succeed in sinking a single heavy German naval unit. The tardily dispatched, makeshift Allied expeditionary force was soon forced out of its position in the hills around Trondheim by savage bombing attacks and by the breath-taking advances of German armored forces from Oslo through the mountain valleys. Even the small force of Germans at Narvik could not be defeated, since they received supplies and assistance from the air. The success of the German campaign in Norway seemed all the more startling because it was prematurely described as suicidal and fantastic by Allied leaders.

Like the Polish campaign, the conquest of Norway appeared more impressive in the full light of afterknowledge than it did at the time of occurrence. The amazing performance of the German armored columns in the mountainous valleys and the ability of air power to nullify sea power and to transport men and equipment were the chief novelties of the campaign.

Hitler's willingness to lose cruisers and planes showed that he did not regard war as a problem in mathematics to be reckoned in terms of ships sunk, men killed, or planes destroyed. He aimed at conquest. His chief political adversaries (Reynaud in France and Chamberlain in Britain, who retained the countinghouse concept of war) were both subjected to intense criticism because of the Allied failures in Norway. From the standpoint of the grand strategy of the war, the German domination of Norway prepared new difficulties for the British navy by extending the hostile coastline as far north as the Arctic Circle. It should have warned the other neutrals that Hitler planned no orthodox war against the Allies, but aimed at the military domination of Europe.

VI

HITLER regarded the Polish campaign as the "most successful" and the Norwegian campaign as the "boldest" in German military annals. Yet they were but preludes to the destruction of French military power. France was the principal enemy. If her great field armies could be destroyed, Britain could be expected to see the wisdom of accepting a "negotiated peace." The German general staff had plans at the outset of war for an attack on the Maginot line. Engineers and shock troops were equipped and trained to break through fortified positions, but the cost was expected to be high. As Gamelin asserted: "Both Germany and France are under armor. The first to stick his head out will be destroyed." A cheaper way of getting at the vitals of France was to be found in the north.

Unlike Ludendorff, who allowed his enemies time to recover between blows in 1918, Hitler timed his stroke in the west to follow immediately upon the close of the Norwegian victory. Possibly he intended the Norwegian venture primarily as a gigantic feint to raise the Allied center of military gravity northward. If he hoped to draw large Allied forces into a fruitless campaign in Norway, he was disappointed by their inability to send a large force to this theater. Events, however, proved this diversion was not necessary. He had more strength than was necessary for the stroke in the west, even with the full strength of the Allied armies massed in France.

In the spring of 1940 Hitler had at his disposal a force of approximately 150 divisions. This gave him a slight numerical advantage over the total Allied forces to be engaged. Since operations in the north would involve Holland and Belgium, their combined force of 30 divisions had to be added to the French (95 divisions) and the British (10 divisions) in France. Under the traditional military concepts of 1914–18, no military leader could launch an attack against opponents of almost equal strength with any prospect of success. A threefold superiority in manpower, a fivefold superiority in planes and munitions were deemed essential for a decisive success. The German Wehrmacht possessed no such superiority in May, 1940. It made up for its relative quantitative inferiority by revolutionary methods of war and by evolving a plan of attack which was bold, unconventional, and brilliant.

The possibility of an Allied relief force going to the aid of Holland and Belgium in case of a German attack was foreseen. In fact, the German plan, which Hitler claimed as his own, counted on this development. It was to be exploited as offering an opening for the destruction of the armies of France. To quote from his Reichstag speech of July 19, 1940:

> I therefore acquainted the German forces with the possibility of such a development and gave them instructions. . . . The basic idea for these operations was the total destruction of the Anglo-French armies. . . . In contradiction to the Schlieffen plan of 1914, I arranged for the operations to bear mainly on the left wing of the front, where the break-through was to be made, though ostensibly retaining the principles of the opposite plan. . . . A blow directed at the right wing of the Anglo-French motorized army corps must, in these circumstances, lead to its complete destruction and breaking up, in fact probably to the surrounding of the enemy forces. As a second operation, I had planned to aim for the Seine and Le Havre and also secure a position on the Somme and Aisne, from which a third attack could be launched, this attack being intended to advance across the plateau of Langres toward the Swiss frontier with the heaviest forces. At the conclusion of the operations, it was intended to reach the coast south of Bordeaux.

In plainer language, the German attack on Holland and Belgium would bring large-scale Allied aid hurrying to the north. After they arrived, a decisive German break through the Maginot extension at Sedan, followed by an advance to the channel, would cut off these forces from the main body of the French army. They would be destroyed in detail, and with them all the Dutch and Belgian forces. Then, from a line on the Somme and Aisne, a force of 150 German divisions would fall on approximately 55 French divisions. When the penetration behind the Maginot line reached the Swiss frontier (and Italy came in for the kill), France would capitulate.

The sequences of the plan were deceptive, the timing of the blows was perfect, and the execution was so methodical that one must conclude that Hitler was not merely making up an explanation in July for unexpected good luck encountered on the battlefield in May and June. The pieces of the tragic jigsaw picture fit together too perfectly. Though Hitler (who despite legends to the contrary seldom reads a book) was not acquainted with Colonel Charles de Gaulle's now famous work, the plan he evolved in conjunction with the general staff exploited the very weaknesses which De Gaulle outlined in the French military position in 1934.

The downfall of the Low Countries was prepared by frequent war scares, which were followed by periods of relaxed tension. Fifth-column agents and parachute troops collaborating with armored columns and, if necessary, savage bombings of civilian areas were to bring about a quick capitulation. It was the Obersalzburg technique applied with a few new variations on the theme of terror. The downfall of France was to be accelerated by the political confusion that would follow the crushing defeats in the north. Hitler did not expect that the French political leaders who attempted to combine boudoir activity with war administration would be very effective. His intelligence service doubtless had informed him that profascist groups in France like the Croix de Feu and the Cagoulards (the hooded men) were aiming (as early as December, 1939) at a separate peace under a ministry of the aged Marshal Pétain.

The terrifying team of the dive bomber and the tank would exploit the break-through effected by the German shock combat squads. Then the French would learn (what General Weygand afterward admitted in agony) that "a modern retreat has no limits; it does not enable one to save matériel or maintain a continuous front." The logistic breakdown confidently predicted by Allied "experts," which was to follow when the German mechanized units outran their supply, was not to occur. The German general staff (which had made plans to prevent its occurrence) knew that it would not. Hitler could well afford to attend the theater the night before the historic blow. It was not done entirely to deceive the enemy.

Surprise in a strategic sense was achieved by a carefully worked out program of diminishing German air activity on the Western front which allayed suspicion of the impending stroke. Military critics had preached as infallible the doctrine that large-scale sustained aerial attacks would precede any assault. How else could one gain mastery of the air? As a result, the Allied air force was caught napping in the early hours of May 10, 1940, and many planes were destroyed on the ground.

Holland, defended by a force of 14 divisions, succumbed in four days to an attack from the sky, the sea, and the land launched by a relatively small force of planes and carried out by six German divisions (including one armored division). Belgium, with a larger force of trained troops (16 divisions) and protected by elaborate fortifications at Liége and along the Albert Canal, and reinforced by a force of 30 Allied divisions, held out for 18 days. The German break-through at Sedan destroyed Corap's Ninth French Army on May 14 and reached the sea on May 21. The heroic resistance of small French and British forces at Calais held up the advance of the German forces northward. The sea was calm. A mist covered the beaches at Dunkirk, and the RAF, thrown belatedly and fully into action at Dunkirk, covered the evacuation of 335,000 British and Allied troops. On June 5 the first stage of Hitler's battle against France was completed.

The same day (June 5) the German army launched its final assault on the hastily formed Weygand line, which ran from the Somme to the Aisne to the Maginot line proper. The fact that the German army was able to overrun three countries (including Luxemburg), capture all their armed forces and equipment, drive the Allied expeditionary force out of Flanders in 26 days, and then be prepared to renew the attack without the delay of a day evidenced the highest kind of military organization and control.

One German break-through of the Weygand line occurred on

the Somme. It isolated small units of Allied troops on the coast and menaced Paris from the west. Another penetration was made on the heights of the Aisne, near the Chemin-des-Dames battleground of World War I. It menaced Paris from the east and enabled the mechanized troops of Kleist and Guderian to roll southward toward the Swiss frontier *behind* the Maginot line. When Weygand in desperation withdrew most of his 27 divisions from the Maginot line, it was broken at Saarbrücken by the army of General Witzleben, which captured Verdun on June 15. Farther south the weakened Maginot line was pierced at Colmar by the army of General Dollmann. As a junction of these forces with the armored columns of Kleist and Guderian neared, and as the slow advance of the Italian forces pointed to junction with the German forces, Marshal Pétain made his appeal for an "honorable peace." In his words "there were no more military possibilities."

When fighting ceased at 1:35 A.M. German time on June 25, the German line of occupation in France ran from Rochefort to Poitiers to Limoges to Clermont-Ferrand to Saint Étienne, to Bellegarde. The occupation of the whole French Atlantic coast continued until the French-Spanish frontier was reached in the Pyrenees.

VII

WHEN men recovered from the stunning effect of the fall of France, the secrets of the German military success slowly became apparent. The Wehrmacht worked like a superbly trained combat team. Allied mechanized and aviation units were thrown piecemeal into the struggle without co-ordination or cumulative effect. They did not attain anything like the close and continuous two-way radio communication between units that characterized the German operations. Allied soldiers with rifles had little chance at close quarters against German shock troops and tanks or at longer range against the fire of German howitzers and mortars. Even more decisive was the lack of adequate anti-aircraft protection against the nerve-shattering attacks of German Stuka squadrons. The German engineer units were trained and equipped to maintain communications with the breath-taking pace of German motorized columns. Their rubber boats and special bridge-building equipment enabled the German forces to cross water barriers at a speed that upset all Allied calculations. Tank trucks kept the mechanized forces of the nazis moving when the Allied tank forces were rendered immobile by fuel shortages. The supreme lesson of the campaign had already been demonstrated in Poland and Norway: air power was essential to success in modern warfare. The tired and beaten Allied troops evacuated from the hell of Dunkirk kept mumbling that they had never had a chance to fight, that given air support on a scale comparable to the Germans there would have been no disaster.

The most amazing aspect of the great battles leading to the collapse of France was the relatively small number of casualties suffered by both the attackers and defenders. The French army, which numbered nearly 2,000,000, was brought to surrender without having more than 200,000 of its troops killed in battle. German casualties were even less. They were officially reported as being 27,074 killed, 18,384 missing, and 111,034 wounded. Nearly 2,000,000 prisoners were in German hands. All the equipment of 30 Dutch and Belgian divisions, all the heavy equipment of the Allied force (30 divisions) in Flanders, all the equipment of 55 French divisions, and the equipment of the Maginot forts fell into German hands. From a material standpoint this was the largest bag of military booty in history. From a military standpoint it was the cheapest and quickest conquest of a great state in modern times.

Hitler's emotional nature and flair for the dramatic were again demonstrated in the last agonies of France. When the news of the armistice request reached him, he danced an awkward jig of joy. Hatred and inexpressible scorn appeared on his face when he saw the Allied armistice monument in the forest of Compiègne. He insisted that the armistice car of 1918 be used, and that the stain and humiliation of 1918 be expunged

(at least orally) by a preliminary statement read by General
Keitel to the sad Frenchmen who had come to witness by their
signature the collapse of French military power. Bells of joy
were rung (by order) throughout the Reich, and Hitler set the
seal of triumph on the French campaign by visiting Paris, where
his "body photographer" caught him against the swastika-topped
Eiffel tower and peering poker-faced at the tomb of Napoleon.

The Wehrmacht was rewarded in true Napoleonic fashion by
the creation of a whole "school" of marshals. Göring, already
a field marshal, was made marshal of the Reich. Keitel, Brauchitsch, Rundstedt, Leeb, Bock, List, Kluge, Witzleben, Reich
enau, Milch, Speerle, and Kesselring were raised to the rank of
field marshal. Halder, the chief of the general staff, was merely
raised one grade, although most critics feel that he worked out
the details of both the Polish and French campaigns.

It required two full months for the Wehrmacht to count its
prisoners, collect its booty, and move its bases forward for an
attack on Britain. The conquest of France and the Low Countries
had rendered the German military position on the Continent
secure. The whole northern coast of Europe, from the Arctic
capes of Norway to the Pyrenees, was now in Germany's hands.
Judged by the standards of World War I, this alone should have
made the British position hopeless. Germany had also acquired
the doubtful aid of Italy. A total Axis force of 200 divisions and
the combined German and Italian air forces made it inevitable
that the small nations of Europe, Hungary, Rumania, and
Bulgaria should fall into the Axis orbit. A triumphant Hitler
could either consolidate his position on the Continent, and
defy Britain to face a long war with no prospect of winning a
military decision, or (as was inherent in the national socialist
philosophy) strike out against Russia for European domination.

VIII

THE CONQUEST of France ended the revolutionary phase of
Hitler's war leadership. For the land campaigns in western

Europe from 1939 to 1941 German military preparations and doctrines fitted the requirements exactly. In the limited space and against the relatively feeble resistance encountered, the German plans and weapons were entirely adequate. The combination of the short-range dive bomber and the tank-infantry team, coupled with the revolutionary technique of undermining enemy resistance by propaganda and intrigue, successively overwhelmed Poland, Norway, Holland, Belgium, and France. These campaigns were conducted so swiftly, so surely, and so economically that they served to dwarf all previous military achievements. Exploited by a malignant and brilliant propaganda machine, they made the German army seem utterly invincible.

The tremendous impact of these victories has affected all our judgments on military events since that time. Even the Germans themselves were not immune to the intoxication of success. Therefore one key to the later strategic embarrassments of the Third Reich may be found in the unexpectedly easy successes of this period. They may have led Hitler and the German high command to believe that the extended phase of the war after the fall of France could be successfully carried on with the weapons and doctrines of the limited phase. Hitler became obsessed with the certainty of future successes; for him the word "impossible" ceased to exist.

The Führer and his high command faced an entirely new set of conditions after France fell. The war, hitherto confined to the relatively narrow limits of western Europe, was now destined to extend beyond the immediate range of the Luftwaffe and Wehrmacht. Perhaps the highly illogical resolution of Britain to continue the war alone against Germany and Italy was an eventuality on which they did not plan. We can now assume that a war between the rival nazi and Soviet revolutions was a fundamental part of the over-all German war program from the first. This being true, the continuation of the war in the west after the fall of France was embarrassing. To German military minds, the stubborn refusal of Britain to accept a peace on approximately the terms that Hess later carried to England was plainly absurd. Under no foreseeable condition, they must have argued, could Britain hope to defeat Germany and Italy alone. Therefore, there was no sense in continuing the war. It was not as if by a sturdy and prolonged resistance Britain could ultimately win better terms; the terms then available were, to the German way of thinking, already "reasonable."

So the first departure from German traditional methods of conducting war was their decision to make a strategic attack on Britain with a tactical air force, the Luftwaffe. In this case, the Germans followed a British irrationality with one of their own. A great measure of the German success in the land campaigns of 1939–40 can be attributed to the fact that the Luftwaffe was then carrying out the ground co-operation role for which it was designed and trained. When operating with virtually no air opposition it provided just the necessary additional power and terror needed to make the Wehrmacht seem irresistible. But when the Luftwaffe was called upon to carry out the mission of a strategic air force, it failed signally as in the Battle of Britain.

The Battle of Britain entailed something more than the failure of the Luftwaffe. It revealed that for the first time in World War II the German high command had undertaken a campaign the end of which was not clearly foreseen and which was only indirectly related to the supreme impending struggle with Russia. The air assault on Britain would only make sense in the German tradition *if* it were successful. At no time in the venture could any German predict the course or outcome of the battle. It violated many of the fundamental tenets of German military thought.

In September, 1940, mass nazi air raids on London began. These were met by the RAF, operating with superior machines from their own bases, enjoying a well-developed scheme of aircraft warning. The RAF beat off the daylight attacks with such heavy losses that the Germans resorted to night bombing. Immense property damage was inflicted, but the spirit of Britain rose superior to the great demands of the occasion. For once Hitler's plans did not succeed. He was dealing with a people who had not been undermined in advance and who drew strength from peril.[4]

The full implications of Germany's errors and defeat in the Battle of Britain were not immediately apparent. In contrast to tactical errors, which are quickly revealed and punished by an alert enemy, mistakes in the realm of higher leadership are sometimes concealed for a long period. By leaving Britain to her own devices in 1941, Hitler allowed one enemy to remain on Germany's flank whose bases of military power were now relatively secure against attack. The makeshift, post-Dunkirk British army could be steadily replaced by a newly armed and strenuously trained force. Very early in the war Britain began to concentrate on the production of heavy bombers capable of carrying out a sustained strategic attack on the Reich. Thus, instead of repeating the mistakes of the Luftwaffe by sending poorly defended, low-capacity bombers designed for short-range tactical support of ground forces on *strategic* bombing missions, Britain was adequately equipped in 1942 to begin a systematic assault on Germany's bases of military power and her war industries.

As a result of the drain on his air resources in the Battle of Britain and his eagerness to engage all possible strength against Russia, Hitler overlooked the tremendous opportunities open to him in the Mediterranean after the fall of France. A full development of this theme would require more space than is available here, but the failure to exploit the opportunities for consolidating the Axis position in the Mediterranean and North Africa, at little cost in 1940–41, is certain to go down in history as one of Hitler's great "lost opportunities." The way was thus prepared for the ultimate Anglo-American conquest of North Africa and the withdrawal of Italy from the Axis.

Intent on the impending death struggle with Russia, Hitler concentrated his main strength against Russia and let Rommel

[4] Mr. C. C. Grey, former editor of the authoritative British aviation magazine *Aeroplane,* has recently been allowed to publish the fact that when the Battle of Britain ended, the RAF's fighter plane reserves were almost untouched. *The Luftwaffe* (London, 1944), p. 186.

carry on in North Africa as best he could with limited forces. His remarkable successes, up to the autumn of 1942, with relatively small forces seem to indicate that far-reaching results might have followed the detail of larger German forces to this theater.

Before Hitler could turn from the failure of his air assault on Britain to the more promising program of attacking Russia, he was forced to rescue his ally and protect his southern flank by a campaign in the Balkans in the spring of 1941.

The Balkan campaign of April, 1941, demonstrated all the veteran competence of the nazi army, but it was in a sense a campaign that should never have been fought. Except for the task of policing the conquered areas, the Wehrmacht was idle. Thirty divisions were concentrated in Hungary, Rumania, and Bulgaria. Theoretically, the Balkans should have fallen into Hitler's hands without a fight. The tough but ill-equipped Jugoslavs, fighting with French methods that had proved fatal to their teachers, were driven to surrender in 11 days. The Anglo-Greek forces maintained a delaying resistance, but nazi air power and armored forces proved too invincible even in the difficult terrain. Field Marshal List handled the campaign with consummate skill, but Hitler with his fine instinct for the dramatic arrived on the front to "take charge of operations" after complete success was assured. His personal chief of staff, General Jodl, signed the armistice with Greece. Hitler's control of Europe now extended from the North Sea to the Aegean.

The German victory in the Balkans was accompanied by the advance of General Rommel in Libya and followed almost immediately by the air invasion of Crete. These triumphs appeared to threaten Britain's position in the Mediterranean. An overland Axis campaign against Suez seemed indicated. Yet that campaign so confidently predicted by the military experts did not materialize. Instead, wild speculations of future German plans followed the flight of Rudolf Hess to England. As the attitude of the United States hardened toward the Axis, Hitler prepared another great surprise. He cynically scrapped the Russian pact of August 23, 1939, and sent his gray-clad veterans marching into the vast Soviet Union. This was on June 22, 1941. It marked the second decisive turn in the course of the war.

IX

THE WAR against Russia brought Hitler to a new period in his military career. During the easy conquests in the west, he was content to let Brauchitsch and the high command conduct the routine phases of the war. But, as if to recognize the formidable and revolutionary character of his Soviet adversary, Hitler's own headquarters now began to issue the official communiqués. In the summer of 1941 Hitler resumed his old post as head of the propaganda wing of the Nazi party and took over the verbal task of "annihilating" the Russians.

It was commonly rumored in Berlin that in deciding upon the strategy of the Russian war, Hitler rejected the plan of General Erich Marcks, which called for a major concentration of strength in the south and a gigantic eastern Cannae following a Russian advance in the north and center deliberately provoked by German weakness in those sectors. Instead, Hitler decided upon a triple penetration which aimed at three lesser Cannaes. Success here depended on whether or not the Russians would attempt to hold the forward areas with heavy troop concentrations. In view of the Russian plan of defense in extreme depth, it would seem that General Marcks' plan held greater promise for decisive results than the one Hitler adopted; but both plans were based upon an unrealistic view of Soviet preparations and doctrines. In any event the Führer's headquarters expected an early collapse of the Soviet regime following the annihilation of the Red armies on the frontier.

Soon after the battles on the frontier, it became painfully clear to the front-line soldiers that the Red army was no ordinary antagonist. For the first time the Wehrmacht encountered real defense of all arms in great depth, a total resistance which included guerrilla warfare and the scorched earth. This knowledge soon reached the people on the home front. On July 6 the readers of the *Frankfurter Zeitung* were told that: "The enemy in the east reacts to the German tactics of wedges and extensions in a wholly different manner than the French. The spiritual paralysis which usually followed the lightning-like German break-through in the west did not occur in the east, or not to the same degree." Foreign correspondents in Berlin testified that it was a matter of some surprise to the German people "to learn that the German high command had actually planned the campaign in Russia on the model of the campaign in France." But a blind belief in the Führer's leadership, fed upon the sweeping claims of the communiqués, persisted until the great battles before Moscow.

Then, as the campaign of annihilation dragged out into the autumn, Hitler took the first great step to undermine the confidence of the German people in his leadership. On October 9, 1941, he had Dr. Otto Dietrich, nazi press chief, assert "on his word of honor" to the representatives of the foreign press that all Russian resistance was broken and that a final decision was impending. Then came the loss of Rostov, the failure of the final nazi offensive on the Moscow front and the bitter winter of 1941–42.

On December 8, 1941, Hitler announced the end of offensive operations on the Moscow front. The dramatic nature of this confession of failure was heightened by the simultaneous announcement that Field Marshal Brauchitsch was relieved of his position as head of the Wehrmacht and that henceforth the Führer would direct operations in person. Hitler now assumed the position of *Feldherr* or sole director of Germany's military destiny.

When Japan struck her treacherous blow at Pearl Harbor, Hitler followed this with a declaration of war on the United States. Here again his innate provincialism manifested itself. Grossly underestimating the industrial and military strength of the United States, confident that the war would be won by the Axis in the year 1942, he was willing to risk war with the most powerful nation in the world whose bases of military strength were immune to attack. His narrow, bigoted clique of advisers told him that the United States was decadent and could not make its weight felt in time, that the U-boats would hold up American shipping. So he boldly repeated the mistake Ludendorff made in 1917 when he sanctioned unrestricted submarine warfare. "The position of the United States," said Hitler in January, 1942, "is of no importance in the war."

The attack on Russia and his decision to challenge the United States betrayed the weaknesses of Hitler's war leadership. His intelligence system could not have left him in doubt about the physical fact of Russia's war preparations; they were described in great detail in German military periodicals. Perhaps he counted upon a political and moral collapse in Russia. He certainly expected a victory before the onset of winter in 1941. When this failed to materialize, he did not admit the basic cause for the German failure—namely, that he had mistakenly applied the methods and techniques of 1939–40 against an enemy fully prepared to meet them. Instead, he merely called for more and greater efforts of the *same kind* which had failed to produce victory in 1941. In the two and a half years of war that followed, Hitler did not introduce a single successful important strategical or tactical novelty in the east. After his first great effort before Moscow, he lost all power to shape events in the grand manner of 1939–40. From that time on he progressively lost control of the course of the war.

Hitler's willingness to engage in war with the United States was based upon a profound ignorance of the vastness, the resources, and the power of our country. Untraveled, unlearned, bigoted, unwilling to listen to unpleasant facts, he accepted the Hollywood version of the American character. Like his political and military counterparts in 1917–18, he condemned the German people to learn of American toughness, military efficiency, and implacable resolution on the battlefield. This time, however, it was not to be on distant fronts in other countries, but amid falling bombs in German cities, and ultimately on battlefields in the Reich itself.

No war leader whose fanaticism blinds him to the realities of the war potential of other countries can escape disaster for long. Hitler's luck ran out the moment his strange madness urged him to proceed beyond the range of knowledge into the realm of personal "intuition."

Writing after World War I General Hans von Seeckt pointed to the graves of "countless thousands of German soldiers far from home which stood as solemn witnesses against those who (in 1914–18) attempted to raise German might beyond human limits and had ended by destroying the very foundations of Germany's strength."

X

WHEN the Red army winter offensive of 1941–42 threatened to overwhelm the hastily constructed defense line in Russia, Hitler made his last successful intervention in military matters against the advice of his generals. He insisted on holding the front despite the suffering of the troops. Thus he brought the German army through its first great trial and reverse. The front was held. In the *Volkischer Beobachter* for May 10, 1942, Colonel Walther Scherff, a nazi military historian, strained the limits of eulogy in describing Hitler's military genius in saving the German army on the Russian winter front. "Henceforth," said Scherff, "the Führer ranks with the greatest military captains of all time." With this and the promise of "new and decisive weapons" to be employed against the enemy, the German people were prepared for the campaign of 1942.

The waning power of the German army was revealed in the campaigns of 1942. Hitherto German strategy was based on the traditional concept of defeating the main armies of the enemy. Throughout the early summer and fall of 1942, however, the whole German war effort was confined to a stroke by Rommel in North Africa which failed to be decisive and a great offensive in southern Russia. The strategy of annihilation so characteristic of German military thought was replaced by a strategy of oil and limited objectives. A long-drawn-out battle for Stalingrad followed. Once again Hitler repeated his psychological blunder of October 9, 1941. This time his own lips spoke the words. He solemnly assured the German people and the world on September 30, 1942, that Stalingrad *would be taken and held*.

Then came the Russian counteroffensive which destroyed the whole German Sixth Army at Stalingrad on February 3, 1943. The "intuitive" leadership of Hitler had led the German army to the greatest defeat in its history. Twenty-two divisions, including some of the finest shock troops Germany had ever put in the field, were destroyed or captured. General Seidlitz, captured along with many other German commanders at Stalingrad, later revealed that Hitler had insisted on holding the position at Stalingrad against the advice of all of his staff except Göring. The latter made the absurd promise that the Luftwaffe would supply the garrison even if it were cut off. General Paulus proposed that the Sixth Army make a break-out attack, but again Hitler rejected this action until it was too late.

The Stalingrad disaster stunned the German nation. There was universal mourning and bitterness over what had happened. According to a Swedish correspondent in Berlin few Germans "looked upon it as an unaccountable natural catastrophe; it was plainly the result of bad leadership,—everybody had a clear idea of who was responsible." Public morale was not raised to learn that Kurt Zeitzler, a virtually unknown officer, had replaced General Halder as chief of the general staff.

Hard on the heels of the disaster of Stalingrad came the Axis debacle in Tunisia. Speaking at the Sportspalast on September 30, 1942, Hitler had dismissed the military leadership of Britain and the United States as a pack of "military idiots." Forty days later the whole Axis position in Africa was threatened by the combined El Alamein operation and an Anglo-American landing in French North Africa. The German war machine, obviously caught off guard, hastily improvised a defense of Tunisia, but the troops that they rushed in were ultimately trapped in the Allied victory of May, 1943. Together with the Stalingrad victory, the loss of North Africa marked the turn of the military balance against Hitler in Europe.

The spring of 1943 passed without large-scale military events on the Eastern front. Finally on July 5 the long-awaited German offensive materialized on the Kursk-Belgorod front. Headed by the famous Tiger (Mark VI) tanks the Germans made a determined bid to break the Russian front as they had done in 1941 and 1942. This time the attack was stopped dead in its tracks by a hurricane of Russian artillery fire, and before the German attacks had ended the Red army seized the initiative. In a sustained offensive throughout the summer, it drove the Germans back across the Dnieper.

The Allied army, which had destroyed the Axis Empire and army in Africa, now surged across the Mediterranean and knocked Italy out of the war on September 8. Germany and her unhappy satellites were isolated in Europe. The disastrous turn of German fortune was reflected in the frustrated ramblings of Hitler's speeches and the unmistakable actions of the remaining European neutrals. The small neutral powers which were forced to obey Germany's will from 1939 to 1942 now felt strong enough to resist openly.

On August 15 Sweden terminated the right to move goods across her borders, which Germany had forced her to grant in 1941, and on August 20 she stopped the transport of German troops. If this could be accepted by the master race as merely a negative act, the decision of Portugal on October 12 to permit the use of the Azores as an Allied base was a different matter. It was a positive act of assistance to the enemies of the Reich and the meekness with which the news of this act was received by the German ambassador in Lisbon was a measure of the Reich's impotence at the moment to intervene or object. Although the immediate military significance of Italy's declaration of war on Germany on October 13 was not great, its political significance was great.

XI

TWO YEARS of Hitler's leadership as *Feldherr* had brought Germany into a position where defeat was inevitable. From the beginning of 1943 onward it was no longer possible for Germany to destroy the main armed forces of her three great enemies, or assail their bases of power, or effectively protect her own. Therefore the intellectual basis for a positive German strategy no longer existed. Germany had lost the war—although the United Nations had not yet won it. There remained only the negative aim of "wearing down the enemy's will to war" or of exploiting a possible division among the United Nations. Colonel Scherff now wrote that the "genius selected by fate to be the *Feldherr* of the Reich should not be censured with criticism. He is censured by fate itself." For once Colonel Scherff was right.

The transition of Germany to the defensive and the adoption of "attrition strategy" in 1943 was accompanied by a great propaganda campaign to popularize this kind of warfare, which went counter to the basic tenets of German military thought. Military writers and commentators in the Reich performed miracles of distortion in order to make this program acceptable to the German mind. Frederick the Great, long hailed as the prototype of nazi *Angriffsgeist,* or spirit of attack, was now offered as support for a war of attrition. But the greatest creation of the nazi mind for giving a semblance of intellectual basis to Germany's deplorable strategic position in 1943 was the concept of the *Festung Europa.*

In the great days of mobile warfare and "destruction strategy," it was customary for Germans to scoff at Maginot lines and formal fortifications. But now, concrete and steel liberally distributed over the peripheries of Europe suddenly became the chief embodiment of German hopes. There is a kind of supreme paradox in the fact that the inherent dynamism of the nazi revolution was the motivating factor in the establishment of the static *Festung Europa.* It arose from the fact that having conquered

the western European nations, Hitler forced these nations into
the "new order," pillaging the resources of the conquered areas
and dragooning their peoples into German war industry. To
do this he had to garrison all conquered Europe. An evacuation
of these areas would have entailed an admission that the dynamism of the nazi movement was exhausted. "Revolutions can't
retreat—and live." Because Europe was a nazi prison, it had to
become a fortress.

German military reverses in 1943 seemed to call for a ruthless
retraction of German strategy to a defense of the homeland
proper. But this could not be done without scuttling the "new
European order." Nor could territory be surrendered in the west
without providing new bases for the growing air fleets of the
Allies.

So the Wehrmacht had to be spread ever thinner around the
perimeter of Europe and the home front bolstered up to with-
stand Allied air attacks by threats and vague promises. Field
Marshals Manstein, Rundstedt, and Rommel now appeared to
bear most of the nazi hopes for survival. The older generals were
shelved one by one. The *Waffen SS* (fully armed SS divisions) and
the Gestapo grew in power. The tactical skill and morale of German troops on all active fronts was still high, but the weaknesses
of the German strategical position could no longer be concealed
from them. With even an elementary knowledge of tactics, the
German troops knew that a cordon defense of Europe was a
military absurdity. Nor could they escape the conviction that
both the Red army and the Anglo-American troops possessed
weapons, tactical skill, and fighting spirit equal if not superior
to their own. No one could tell them that the German armies
which in September, 1942, were fighting on the Volga and before
El Alamein and which one year later were fighting on the
Dnieper and Volturno were waging a victorious war. With their
own eyes, they could see the steady decline of German air power
on all fronts.

The incredible strategic disadvantages of Germany's position
in the fall of 1943 did not appear on the surface, but to any

officer schooled in the old German concepts of war, they must have appeared staggering.

If, before the war, it had been suggested to any well-trained German staff officer that after four and a half years of "victorious" battles the armed forces of the Third Reich would have lost the initiative everywhere, that they would be spread out from northern Finland to the islands of the Aegean, that the bulk of the German ground forces would be battling for its life on a 2,000-mile front in Russia, that Germany would be at war with the only important former member of the European Axis, that she would be "occupying" her Balkan "allies" in order to keep them in the war, that German troops would be fighting in Jugoslavia to hold territory supposedly "conquered" two years before, that enemies whose war industries were immune from counter-attack would be slowly bombing Germany's war industries to destruction, that the manufacture of all civilian clothiers would be discontinued in the fatherland, and that public morale would be maintained with the headsman's ax—he would have dismissed such suggestions as too fantastic for serious consideration.

Realistic Germans knew that the only hope of an effective defense of the Reich lay in the ultimate withdrawal to a defensible area in which interior lines would afford the Germans certain advantages. German military literature suddenly abounded in references to Frederick the Great's achievements in this type of warfare. This program would not waste German manpower and resources in garrisoning outlying areas however important from the political or ideological angle, but would concentrate everything on the strictly military defense of the German citadel. But Hitler seemed to have decided upon a dispersal of German military strength. Only in the east, under the increasing pressure of the Red army, were there large-scale German withdrawals to new lines; but the sustained intensity of fighting on that front precluded the possibility of economizing on troops by the mere retreat to new positions. Perhaps Hitler hoped to achieve the impossible once again (as he did in the winter of 1941–42) and have his troops hold or die on their distant fronts.

In 1918 the Germans waited too long before deciding to abandon Belgium and all their heavy supply depots in the north in order to shorten their line. Their failure to take this drastic action enabled the Allies to win the war in 1918 instead of 1919. By holding to their program of a perimeter defense of Europe in 1943 and 1944, Hitler ran the risk of finding it impossible later to make a "disengaging movement" on the scale required.

XII

THERE is a good deal of speculation as to the manner in which Hitler functions as *Feldherr* or supreme commander of the armed forces of the Third Reich. It would appear that most of the important military decisions of the war are arrived at in conferences at Hitler's field headquarters. In these meetings representatives of the staffs of all three branches of the armed forces as well as members of Hitler's personal staff participate. One matter is clear. Hitler makes the decisions involving important military operations *himself* and thereafter assigns a definite objective to Keitel.[5]

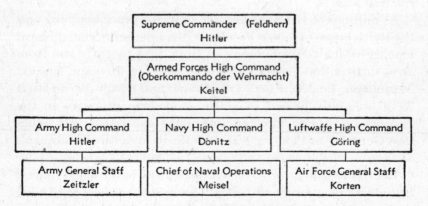

Organization Chart of the German High Command 1944

[5] At least this was true until the spring of 1944. The long silences of the Führer and the absence of press notices about him may indicate that the leaders of the army are again taking control of Germany's military destiny.

After the operation is thoroughly discussed by the commanders in chief of the three branches, Hitler picks a task-force commander who chooses his own staff, draws up detailed plans for the operation, and requests units and matériel to carry it out. The date for the operation is set by the Führer with due regard to the training time required and the political situation.

It was in the field of air warfare and its effects upon the German homeland that Hitler made his most glaring miscalculations. These were errors that could not be concealed from the German citizens whose homes and factories were being slowly bombed to destruction by the Allied air fleets that Göring promised would never be able to reach the Reich. As the increasingly heavy raids of British and American bombers laid one city after another in ruins, it became painfully clear that the fortress of Europe might have walls but that it had no roof. A two-way strain, to which no other nation was similarly subjected, was placed upon the Reich. German soldiers in the field worried about their families at home and the families at home worried about the men at the front. A heavy apathy descended upon the Reich which could not be raised by the most frantic efforts of the nazi leaders.

As millions of Germans became homeless from bombing and the Reich began to show scars of war, the immunity from physical damage which Germany enjoyed from 1914 to 1918, and from 1939 to 1942, was ended. Cologne, Hamburg, Bremen, Rostok, Mannheim, Emden, Essen, Düsseldorf, and finally Berlin itself were progressively laid in ruins. It became necessary in the autumn of 1943 to threaten those who expressed their belief that Germany had lost the war with death under the headsman's ax.

In early 1944 as in 1918, the German army in the field retained its fighting morale and efficiency. Lower commanders continued to show a virtuosity in minor leadership which made the German fighting machine seem capable of prolonged and bitter resistance. But there was no longer any intellectual basis for German strategy, no *raison d'être* for fighting beyond the mere prolongation

of the struggle. The Moscow and Teheran conferences precluded any possibility of "splitting" the United Nations. There
remained only the playing out of the meaningless and tragic
drama of the final hours.

The fall of Il Duce provided Hitler with an unmistakable
personal portent. His frenzied and melodramatic attempts to
"rescue" Mussolini and re-create the fiction of Italian fascism
showed how keenly he felt the blow. It was only natural that in
the final days of the war he would take increased concern for
the superfanatical nazi *Waffen SS* divisions which he created for
just such an emergency. He made their chief, Heinrich Himmler, minister of the interior with wide powers. Thinking back
on the bitter days of 1918, Hitler once observed: "It would be
intolerable, in critical internal situations to send German armed
forces conscripted from the entire population into action against
their fellow-citizens. Such a step would be the beginning of the
end. But what a conscript army cannot be expected to do,
another body (such as the *Waffen SS*) capable on any and every
occasion of representing and asserting the authority of the Reich
—will do." His oft-voiced threat, that in defeat he would "pull
down the pillars of European civilization with him," now meant
that he would probably end his political career as he began it,
by fighting the German people.

CHURCHILL

☆

"He was the co-ordinator of victory."

TWO men were gazing across the English Channel in July, 1940. One stood on the cliffs of Dover, a short, plump, hearty, cherubic man in an outlandishly improvised uniform in which the naval influence predominated. He was wearing a tin hat, carrying a gas mask, puffing a fat cigar, and sweeping the Straits of Dover with a pair of field glasses. Overhead, pursuit planes of the RAF flashed by with snarling motors. Batteries of long-range guns in the emplacements near by threw an occasional shell toward the coast of France. Accompanied by a squad of photographers, Winston Churchill was inspecting the bastions of Britain.

On the beach near Boulogne stood another short, faded-looking man in an *opéra bouffe* adaptation of the nazi field uniform. He appeared flattened by an oversized military cap. Disdaining glasses, he gazed long and menacingly toward the mist-shrouded cliffs of England. Not far away a company of soldiers was dragging a battered Hurricane out of the surf. Accompanied by his personal photographer, "Professor" Hoffmann, Adolf Hitler was making a tour of the newly occupied coast of France.

Not even by torturing the imagination could one conjure up the vision of two less military-looking men. Churchill looked like an elderly naval reserve officer who had been fitted out higgledy-piggledy with spare equipment after his ship had been sunk. Had Hitler's face been hidden, one might have passed him up as a bus-driver's assistant in a badly fitting cap. Yet upon these two strange men the destiny of more than Europe depended at that hour. They personified the military effort of two empires

—two ways of life—linked in a death struggle. From origins entirely different and by roads fantastically dissimilar, they arrived at their cross-Channel observation posts in July, 1940.

Winston Spencer Leonard Churchill was born prematurely at Blenheim palace on November 30, 1874. His father was the famed, eccentric, Conservative chancellor of the exchequer and his mother the beautiful Jennie Jerome of New York. Though in his best moments the boy impressed Lord Randolph as a "good un," his father honestly thought the lad had no prospects in England and sought a place for him in South Africa. Winston summed up his own hopes with the words: "I'll be a soldier, of course, while there's any fighting to be done. After that I shall have a shot at politics." Schooled at Ascot, Harrow, and Sandhurst, he joined the 4th Hussars as a subaltern in 1895. There was a slight impediment in his speech which he overcame by sheer will power and practice. Like Hitler, his great military and oratorical adversary, Churchill gained his matchless powers of persuasion through constant discipline and application.

He escaped from the boredom of Aldershot in 1895 to cover the Cuban revolts for the London *Daily Graphic.* He brought back the Spanish Order of Military Merit, awarded for his impromptu part in repulsing the insurgent attack on Trocham. Capitalizing upon his acquaintance with British military leaders, he "crashed" the Malakhand expedition in 1896 and the Tirah expedition the following year. Two weeks after he reached the Malakhand frontier he was mentioned in the dispatches of Sir Bindon Blood. To save time, he published his account of these operations, *The Malakhand Field Force,* without bothering to have the proofs sent out to India. His reputation as a "young man in a hurry" and a juvenile critic of military operations grew rapidly. Officers in the Indian army ironically referred to this book as "A Subaltern's Hints to Generals."

Despite Lord Kitchener's stern attempts to discourage him, Churchill wangled his way into a minor post in the 21st Lancers when the sirdar's army marched into the Sudan to crush the dervishes in 1898. Professional soldiers in the Egyptian army were determined to "break his heart" by horseplay and criticism. The bumptious Churchill gave them plenty of openings—by immediately capturing a "friendly" dervish who was trying to make his way to the British camp with information. His second exploit was hardly more helpful. After reporting the advance of the dervishes to Lord Kitchener, Churchill estimated that they would give battle within two hours. They waited until the following morning. On September 2, 1898, he fought in the last great cavalry shock action in history—the Battle of Omdurman.

Covering the Boer War as a correspondent for the *Morning Post,* he was captured by Louis Botha after laboring heroically to free an armored train which had been derailed by the Boers. His bravery and resourcefulness saved part of the train and led Sir Howard Vincent to declare that, had Churchill been a regular officer, he probably would have been awarded a Victoria Cross for this action. After escaping from Pretoria, Churchill made his way with the assistance of friendly farmers to the security of Delagoa Bay and Durban. He was overwhelmed with publicity and, after serving briefly in the South African Light Horse, successfully stood for election as a conservative candidate for Parliament for Oldham in 1901.

From that time on, with the exception of a few very unhappy years of temporary political eclipse, Churchill has been almost constantly in the House, generally on or near the front bench. He carried the same restless energy that characterized his journalistic-military exploits into the stuffy atmosphere of Westminster. He switched parties in 1906, obtained a post in the Liberal Ministry in 1908, and was made first lord of the Admiralty in 1911.

II

WITH this appointment began Churchill's direct connection with World War I. He fell to the task of preparing the navy for war with furious zeal. Among the elegant and ponderous members of the liberal cabinet "he moved like a panther among seals." Every stick and spar of the Royal Navy was inspected. Subordinates at the Admiralty were kept on their toes by sudden entrances of the first lord with the query: "What happens if war comes with Germany tonight?" He fell under the dangerous spell of Lord John Fisher, the stormy petrel of the Royal Navy. Fisher was the creator of the dreadnought; he was a burly, forceful, messianic giant who backed kings into the corner, bowled over grand duchesses, and overwhelmed his listeners with great dollops of frantic talk which ranged from watertube boilers to Shakespeare, Nelson, Isaiah, Blake, and "Admiral Buggins"—which was Fisher's term for admirals who had won their posts solely by seniority. From his retirement in Switzerland Fisher poured a steady stream of striking letters into the dispatch box of Winston Churchill. He pointed to the inevitable war with Germany, urged Churchill to plunge for bigger and better naval programs, cried for bigger guns and more speed in ships, begged him to trample on "protected cruisers," hurry up aviation, lay down supersubmarines, superbattle cruisers, to "make Admiral Buggins' wife a widow and his house a dunghill."

Fisher's letters steeled Churchill to plunge for the 15-inch naval gun, which was adopted without waiting for the trials of the pilot model. Churchill also adopted Percy Scott's system of director firing, which had been shelved repeatedly by previous administrations. Unfortunately for Britain, this reform was barely completed in the capital ships of the fleet before Jutland. When the crisis of 1914 grew acute, Churchill kept the fleet mobilized after the review at Spithead, and gave secret orders to send the fleet to its war station at Scapa Flow before the declaration of war on Germany.

During the crisis of 1914 Churchill was passing the time by playing bridge with a number of other political figures. A dispatch arrived telling of the German declaration of war on Russia. Churchill calmly turned over his hand to Beaverbrook—who found that the first lord with typical nonchalance had overbid his hand, leaving his substitute in an extremely vulnerable position—and went to send the "war" telegram to the fleet. In the words of Philip Guedalla:

As the slow darkness deepened across Europe, one actor seemed to get the last ounce out of his part; and when he marched across to Downing Street to report that the war telegram had gone out to all the ships, one somehow feels no surprise that a sharp-eyed lady at the foot of the stairs saw him "with a happy face" striding toward the double doors of the cabinet room.

The first public reaction to Churchill's action was one of relief. As Lord Kitchener said to him in the hour of Churchill's political disaster in 1915, "One thing they can't take from you: the fleet was ready."

III

THE war brought Churchill into the pitiless glare of publicity. For a time it increased his popularity, but it also revealed his tendency to "mistake frothy bubbles for great waves." He was not content simply to exercise the functions of his important office, but his mind ranged the whole field of the war. He suffered torment when convinced that lesser men were muddling affairs. When Kitchener began to expand the army Asquith observed that "Churchill's mouth watered at the sight and thought—of all these glittering commands—to be entrusted to dug-out trash." [1] For hours he would pour out to any important person who would listen torrents of schemes, criticisms, invectives, and appeals. Plans for running the war rolled off his tongue and pen so glibly that the prime minister commented: " 'Tis like a hen laying eggs."

Despite Churchill's zeal, a series of irritating reverses attended the British attempt to control the seas. The two German warships, the *Goeben* and *Breslau*, escaped the British dragnet in the Mediterranean and, by taking refuge in Turkish waters, bolstered up the shaky Ottoman Empire. The commerce-raiding cruisers *Königsberg* and *Emden* made trouble in African and Indian waters. Spee, with the German Far Eastern fleet, was on the prowl and soon massacred Admiral Cradock's small fleet at Coronel. In a single day an old German submarine, the U-9, sank

[1] "Dug-out" is British army slang for a retired officer called back into the service.

three big British armored cruisers which were keeping an absurd cold-meat patrol off the Broad Fourteens near Holland. Churchill was just one day late in canceling this stupid "duck march." With the main German fleet kept in cotton wool, there was no major fleet engagement early in the war.

Churchill, who followed the events in France with great attention, discussed with Sir John French the prospect of joint military and naval action along the coast of Belgium. During the "race to the sea" he saw the importance of prolonging the Belgian resistance at Antwerp. When the Belgian command threatened to surrender that city, Lord Kitchener asked Churchill to make a flying trip to bolster the Belgian resistance. Sensing the strategic importance of the mission, Churchill set off at once in the uniform of an elder brother of the Trinity House with the only forces immediately available, the Royal Naval Division. Asquith, who still regarded the war as a sort of supreme garden party, interesting as a means of seeing how his political associates performed in new situations, wrote: "The intrepid Winston set off at midnight. I do not know how fluent he is in French, but if he is able to do himself justice in a foreign tongue, the Belges will have to listen to a discourse the like of which they have never heard before."

The ill-equipped naval division reached Antwerp in time to stiffen Belgian resistance for a time, but many were driven into Dutch territory and interned. The Antwerp intervention, though it saved valuable days, and probably the channel ports, was widely criticized as "Winston's folly." It was vain for one distinguished British general to class it "as one of the two acts of intuition in the war"; the public thought it was a failure. The atmosphere of hazard and irresponsibility with which Churchill's character became associated in the public mind soon undermined his position. He was regarded as being "half a Pitt and half a Puck."

There were a few fleeting moments of triumph. In October, 1914, Churchill brought the tremendous energies of Lord Fisher to bear upon the problems of the Admiralty. With the advent of Fisher, the atmosphere of the Admiralty became increasingly bizarre. Scriptural phrases for striking down the enemy were heard. Nelsonic poses were struck; annihilation—not victory —became the watchword. With instant action Fisher dispatched Sir Doveton Sturdee and two battle cruisers to the Falkland Islands. There, on December 8, they clawed Spee and his squadron to death. In a single stroke the seas were cleared of remnants of German sea power. Churchill in a rash speech threatened to "dig the German submarines out of the nests like rats," but they went on torpedoing British ships. Fisher's appearance in the Admiralty supported Churchill for a time, but in the end it brought about the downfall of both men.

Fisher was notorious as a one-idea man. To his mind the way to win the war was to land troops on the Pomeranian coast of Germany. This entailed breaking into the Baltic and transporting Russian troops in shallow-draft vessels to the Gulf of Stettin, where, Fisher was never tired of hammering home, Frederick the Great got the biggest scare of his life when the Russians landed during the Seven Years' War. A vast armada of shallow-draft vessels was planned. But while these preparations were under way Churchill's mind was toying with the idea of forcing the Dardanelles with the great fleet of pre-dreadnought battleships which were not fit to fight in the line of battle in the North Sea. The War Office, it should be pointed out, never regarded the Baltic plan as a sound operation.

Although Churchill and Fisher shared the responsibility for inaugurating the ill-fated attempt to force the Dardanelles with battleships alone, Churchill was identified in the public mind with the failure. Once the die was cast, he forced the venture with resolution and, despite their distaste for the business, won over such strong men as Fisher and Kitchener to his point of view. When the naval attack on the Narrows failed on March 18, 1915, Lord Kitchener took over the responsibility for the success of the venture by throwing the makeshift army of Hamilton into the balance.

Disaster followed disaster in a nightmare of muddle and hesitation. German U-boats appeared in the Aegean and sank the *Goliath,* the *Triumph,* and the *Majestic.* Then Fisher decided that the affair had gone too far. He suddenly resigned on May 17, expecting to replace Churchill as first lord. An intense political crisis followed. With Churchill's head on the block, there came a wireless flash saying that the German fleet was putting to sea. Working without his first sea lord, Churchill desperately threw every scrap of British naval strength across the supposed path of the German fleet. But the battle never came off. Looking back over the long hours he had watched with Churchill through the night of May 17, Beaverbrook wrote:

> I cannot help reflecting on the extreme duality of mind which marks Churchill above all other men—the charm, the imaginative sympathy of his hours of defeat, the self-confidence, the arrogance of his hours of power and prosperity. That night he was a lost soul, yet full of flashes of wit and humour.

In the political changes which followed, Churchill lost the Admiralty because the Conservatives would no longer tolerate him. He was relegated to the virtual inactivity of the Duchy of Lancaster but retained a place in the War Cabinet. He would not endure this "well-paid inactivity" and finally resigned his post to fight with the 6th battalion of Royal Scotch Fusiliers.

The Dardanelles affair was a legitimate gamble, yet, barring the fantastic muddling which characterized its conduct, it was by no means a hopeless affair. The official historian of the Gallipoli campaign, in summing up the situation at the eve of the naval attack, said:

> The enterprise was perhaps still capable of accomplishment, if the government were ready to face the inevitable loss of ships. This was the opinion of the German Admiral von Usedom, who knew better than anyone the strength and weakness of the fortress and the capacity of its defenders. But there must be no indecision, no faltering, and no delay. Nothing but iron will and grim determination, both at home and on the spot, could snatch the hazardous victory.

Setting aside the question of the wisdom of the venture, when once the issue was drawn, Churchill's conduct most nearly approximated these demands. On his part there was no indecision, no faltering, no delay. He alone of all the leaders connected with the enterprise showed iron will and grim determination. He was the one man who ruthlessly pushed things into the domain of action.

IV

As A major and later a lieutenant colonel of the 6th battalion of the Scotch Fusiliers, Churchill reached the depths of political and personal eclipse. When his battalion entered the line at Plugstreet, certain officers were not above gloating over a fallen politician accused of overriding his professional advisers. He was brusquely warned by one of his superiors: "We want no politics here." He looked ridiculous in the regimental Glengarry bonnet of the Scotch. When he attempted to repair his political fences on leave, his speeches in Parliament were coldly received. Finally he was able to return to active political life when his battalion was broken up for replacements and he pushed his own officers for the key posts. The military men were frankly relieved at this unselfishness. Castoff politicians were not welcome in France. Churchill took his place on one of the back benches in Parliament and began to fight his way back to power.

Lloyd George, who became prime minister in 1916, preferred to have Churchill as a colleague rather than as a critic, so he made him minister for munitions. By this time Churchill's bold and imaginative step in fostering the tank became known.

Of course Winston Churchill never claimed to be the inventor of the tank. The path to the War Office was virtually paved with the bones of inventors who had offered a rough equivalent to the tank to the high priests of the military status quo, and who had died of neglect. It took an unconventional man, "one profoundly ignorant" of the niceties of professional soldiering, to make the tank a reality. As is frequently the case with a new weapon, the Mark I tank was wildly misused at the Somme in 1916. Some 48 ambitious youngsters were thrown through the mud at the German lines in an attempt to save Haig's dying of-

fense. The initial failure of the tank was so complete that Ludendorff did not pay the British the compliment of imitating it. Yet
the concept of the tank was a brilliant one, and in the end it
served (with American help) to turn the tide of battle against the
Central Powers. The parliamentary commissioners who investigated the origin of tanks at the end of the war gave Churchill a
deservedly large share of the credit for the origin and perfection
of this weapon.

Churchill soon had the munitions ministry organized on such
a systematic basis that his delegation of authority to subordinates
allowed him time for consideration of the larger aspects of the
conduct of the war and for writing. He was asked to draw up the
official communiqué on the Battle of Jutland. The ministry
brought him into close contact with American supply agencies
after the United States entered the war. This experience provided a basis for a frequently expressed desire to see a closer tie
between the two Anglo-Saxon nations.

His experience in the munitions ministry gave Churchill an
insight into the organizational and administrative aspects of
modern warfare. His department was so well organized in
1917–18 that he was able to come to Italy's rescue after Caporetto
with vast supplies, and when disaster overtook the British Fifth
Army in March, 1918, he was able to rush 2,000 guns to France
out of his reserve stocks. With Lloyd George and others he
planned for the campaign of 1919, which was to see movement
and surprise restored to the Western front by masses of tanks
and mechanical troop carriers. To an extent these vague plans
foreshadowed the blitzkrieg methods by which the Germans kept
their offensives in motion once a break-through was made in
Poland and France.

V

CHURCHILL embodied his views on the events of 1914–18 in a
magnificently written four-volume account, *The World Crisis.*
It is a curious combination of personal narrative and history.
Because of the important positions he held and the access he had

to information, and above all because of a fascinating style, *The World Crisis* has become one of the classic works on the war. British soldiers regarded it as a dangerous document, full of errors and inconsistencies, and marked by strong personal bias. Civilian reviewers agreed that as a picture of war it could be compared favorably with those of Tolstoy and Napier. It buttressed Churchill's claim to the possession of the finest prose style of any writer in the English language.

Since these volumes probably reflect Churchill's views of war as he wages the second great struggle against Germany, they are worthy of some attention. One can be certain that they have been studied with great care by the present rulers of Germany. They show Churchill's high qualities and weaknesses in clear relief. He took a broad view of the war and never wavered from his strong optimistic concept of Allied supremacy and ultimate victory. Mr. Churchill is generally right on big things, but likely to be caught up on little things which make big things go wrong in war. Thus his strong belief in 1914 that no German submarine could navigate the intricate and swirling channels of Scapa Flow submerged may have led to the disaster of the *Royal Oak* in 1939. His optimistic declaration in 1915 that the Royal Navy would dig the German submarines out of their nests like rats was paralleled in 1940 by his promise that the Royal Navy would sink every German transport en route to Norway in the Skagerrak. Both bold speeches foundered on the simple realities of the situation. German mines rendered the first promise abortive; German air power rendered the second impossible.

Churchill could not resist the temptation to "personify" the war of 1914–18. He demonstrated strong attractions and equally strong dislikes for various leaders. The failure of the initial French plan of war confirmed his suspicion of Joffre as a "bullheaded, broad-shouldered, slow-thinking, phlegmatic, bucolic personage." His naïve acceptance of the Gallieni legend and his account of the Marne battle have been savagely ridiculed by

General Sir W. S. Bird and Major General Sir Frederick Maurice. He had little sympathy for the "professional formalism" of General Sir William Robertson, who was chief of the imperial general staff from 1915 to 1918. To his way of thinking, Haig was equally lacking in imagination, though he paid tribute to the British commander's insight regarding the possibility of a German collapse in 1918. Jellicoe received scant praise in Churchill's account of the Battle of Jutland, but the many shortcomings of Admiral Beatty were studiously overlooked. Churchill admired Michel, Foch, Mangin, Hoffmann, Hotzendorff, Allenby, and gave the credit for the German victory at Tannenberg to General François, for his courageous acts of insubordination.

To Churchill's mind "the Germans were, of all enemies in the world, the most to be dreaded when pursuing their own plans; the most easily disconcerted when forced to conform to the plans of their antagonist." He lamented the fact that Britain did not use her great amphibian power to the full during the war. He did not want to fight the war the way the Germans wanted it fought. The dreary process of exchanging an Allied life for something less than a German life on the Western front appeared to him to be the very negation of military intelligence. He felt that the failures of 1915 made the war of attrition inevitable, that after the Dardanelles "governments and individuals merely conformed to the rhythm of tragedy in the west." What made his criticism of the conduct of the war worthy of some attention was the fact that it was made *at the time,* and not in the light of afterknowledge. The memoranda published in *The World Crisis* were all circulated to the cabinet or the Committee of Imperial Defence at the time. While Pétain was rigidly defending Verdun at a cost in casualties greater than those suffered by the attackers, Churchill urged that a false front be built up behind the lines and the Germans lured into prepared pockets, where they might be cut to bits. He wanted to use terrain intelligently, was prepared to give up French ground in order to strike the moving, quivering enemy line of battle with counteroffensives on a large scale. Craft and cunning, as well as character, he felt should be among the first requirements of a great commander.

The only cheerful aspect of the dull and costly Somme offensive of 1916 he found in the heroic constancy of the Kitchener armies, which found their graveyard in the muddy fields of the Somme. The Haig-Kiggel-Robertson program of "no surprise" on the Somme produced only the results he anticipated, but the spirit of the Kitchener armies gave him hope for the future.

Churchill supported the idea of a defensive strategy on the Western front, arguing that the Allies did not possess sufficient force to wrest a victory from the enemy in that theater. For that reason he opposed the slaughter test of Passchendaele in 1917 which Robertson admitted he stuck to "more because instinct prompted him rather than any argument which he could muster to support it." After the first Dardanelles failure, and after the Turkish armies had been dispersed to other fronts, Churchill urged another attack at Gallipoli, on the assumption that the Turks would never anticipate it. He made several proposals for landing part of the Salonika army behind the Turkish lines in Palestine. These counsels, the soldiers correctly pointed out, did not take into account the problems of transport and supply. He carried his belief in the power of the defensive war in the west to the point of asserting that Ludendorff destroyed the German army by his offensives of 1918.

Churchill held that the German leaders forfeited all hope of victory when they challenged America in 1917. In his words:

Of all the grand miscalculation of the German high command none is more remarkable than their inability to comprehend the meaning of war with the American Union.—The war effort of 120,000,000 educated people, equipped with science, and possessed of the resource of an unattackable continent, nay of a New World, could not be measured by the number of drilled soldiers, of trained officers, of forged cannon, of ships of war they happened to have at their disposal. It betokens ignorance of the elemental forces resident in such a community to suppose they could be permanently frustrated by a mechanical instrument called the U-boat. How rash to balance the hostile exertions of the largest, if not the leading, civilized nation of the world against the chance that they would not arrive in time upon the field of battle! How hard to condemn the war-torn, wearied, already out-numbered heroic German people to mortal conflict with this fresh, mighty, and, once aroused, implacable antagonist! [2]

There is sufficient similarity between the conditions existing in 1917 and those in 1941 to give this passage more than casual significance. It seems safe to say that when France collapsed in June, 1940, Mr. Churchill placed his sole hope of British survival and victory on the prospect of bringing the aid of this "fresh, mighty, and implacable antagonist" to bear against the rampant German force.

Churchill agreed in general with Hitler's view that the German higher leadership in 1914–18 was not equal to the exploits of its soldiery. That he did not then and probably does not now underestimate their military prowess can be gained from his summary of the German war effort of 1914–18. He wrote:

In the sphere of force, human records contain no manifestation like the eruption of the German volcano. For four years Germany fought and defied the five continents of the world by land and sea and air. The German armies upheld her tottering confederates, intervened in every theatre with success, stood everywhere on conquered territory, and inflicted on their enemies more than twice the bloodshed they suffered themselves. To break their strength and science and curb their fury, it was necessary to bring all the greatest nations of mankind into the field against them. Overwhelming populations, unlimited resources, measureless sacrifice, the Sea Blockade, could not prevail for fifty months. Small states were trampled down in the struggle; a mighty Empire was battered into unrecognisable fragments; and nearly twenty million men perished or shed their blood before the sword was wrested from that terrible hand. Surely, Germans, for history it is enough!

Amidst the present overwhelming chorus of praise for Churchill's leadership and courage, it would be well to remember that at the close of World War I many sober men felt that he was utterly unfitted by temperament and mentality to guide a nation at war. Admiral Sir Reginald Bacon summed up his work at the

[2] This and the quotation in the following paragraph are from Winston S. Churchill's *The World Crisis* (Charles Scribner's Sons, N.Y., 1931) and are reprinted with the permission of the publisher.

Admiralty with the observation: "In an executive command in the field, Mr. Churchill would in all probability have earned undying fame. But temperamentally he was unsuited to fill the post of civilian head of a mighty technical department." Still another professional naval officer, Captain W. D. Puleston, USN, went so far as to assert in 1927 that Britain could in all probability survive another world war, but it could never survive another Churchill.

VI

In the postwar period of disenchantment the great leaders of the British war effort lost their popularity. Churchill was no exception. His career from 1918 to 1939 followed his usual erratic political pattern. He served variously as minister for war, air, colonies, and finally as chancellor of the exchequer, his father's old post. During this period he gave aid to the armies of Kolchak and Denikine in their war against the communists in Russia, but they lost the war and he lost many supporters. He had a hand in settling the Near Eastern problem, and brought the hitherto irreconcilable Irish enemies to a final conference table. But the political sands were shifting; the Liberal party went to pieces, and Churchill ultimately found himself out of Parliament. This gave him time to write a number of books, including *The World Crisis,* and to undertake a monumental six-volume life of Marlborough.

When he re-entered Parliament as a conservative, Churchill found himself suspect by all political parties. As the long shadow of Hitler began to fall across Europe, his conservative leaders were content to live in a fool's paradise of half measures and appeasement. British prestige during the Ethiopian and Spanish wars fell to a new low. The tightly harnessed German industry began to turn out arms for the nazi Wehrmacht. Churchill once more assumed the role of prophet. He made the nazi air force the subject of his constant warnings. In the Commons and throughout the country he spread the tale of impending danger. It was of no avail. Glib explanations were offered on the floor of the

House, but the RAF lagged ever farther behind the growing Luftwaffe. The poeple were indifferent or tired of "Winston's nagging." He had cried "wolf!" too often in the past. They remembered his wild tirades against the Red desperadoes of the Kremlin and scoffed that he was merely manufacturing another "scare" in order to get ahead in politics. The House was filled whenever he talked—but he influenced no votes. He lost additional prestige by his forlorn support of Edward VIII in his marriage difficulties with the Archbishop of Canterbury and the hosts of righteousness in England. For six long years he was tolerantly regarded by the "smart" young men of the party as an interesting relic of the "imperial wild oats" sowed during the Victorian and Edwardian period.

But, as the inevitable crisis with Germany approached, he could no longer be denied. When Mr. Chamberlain firmly bowed his neck to the nazi heel at Godesburg and Munich, Churchill thundered at his leader. He was the most embarrassing and relentless opponent of the prime minister. By midsummer 1939 he had the old man of Birmingham hanging on the ropes, dazed by his merciless beating. The British public, slow to suspect its leaders, pathetically eager to believe the "peace-in-our-time" pledge of Mr. Chamberlain, finally made its voice heard. It became clear that Churchill could not be kept out of responsible office. The Conservative party was torn by dissension in August when Russia and Germany signed a pact behind the back of British and French missions in Moscow. When the tired prime minister announced to the House on September 3 that Britain was once more locked in a death struggle with her ancient adversary, he called Churchill aside, saying: "I would be most grateful if you'll help me now." Churchill took over Lord Stanhope's post at the Admiralty and sent another war telegram to the fleet. This time he did not stride "with a happy face" toward the cabinet room.

The strange calm at the beginning of the war gave cause for false assurance. As in 1914 the Royal Navy again controlled the surface of the sea. Again a British expeditionary force moved unhampered into France. No bombs hissed down on sprawling cities. General Gort's divisions took up their places behind the Maginot line and trained; Gamelin pushed feebly at the outer fringes of the Siegfried line while the army of Poland was struck down in 18 days. No one in high place in France or Britain seemed to read the lesson of this campaign. The static war in the west was good-naturedly accepted in the slim hope that the blockade would hamstring Germany or force the nazi command to throw its conscript armies against the tank traps and slaughter pens of the Maginot line. Air Marshal Newall's small but efficient fleet of British bombers piled up an impressive total of millions of reconnaissance miles flown, but dropped nothing more harmful than leaflets on German soil. Only those who were aware of the kind of military-social-political revolution that had taken place in the Reich, and who knew also the actual state of British preparations, could judge the extremely hazardous position of the British.

The British Empire never began a war under less promising conditions. After having betrayed the bastion of Czechoslovakia, her military position and that of France in relation to Germany became increasingly hopeless. Her army was small and would not benefit by the adoption of conscription for some time to come. Her artillery and tank establishments were incomplete, her antiaircraft protection elementary. The RAF, though of high quality, was kept in cotton wool until after May 10, and then found itself heavily outnumbered. Only on the sea did Britain have temporary reason to feel secure. That was Churchill's domain, but even here plentiful embarrassments awaited and ultimate disaster threatened the empire, which declined to fight at a time inconvenient to the enemy.

Churchill's appointment to the Admiralty gave the British public considerable ground for assurance. He at least could express himself vigorously. But a series of embarrassments similar to those of 1914 arose. The loss of the *Royal Oak* and the aircraft carrier *Courageous* showed that the Royal Navy still retained some of its traditional backwardness in the matter of war methods. In November, 1939, when it appeared that the German submarine menace was under control, the nazi enemy brought out a surprise magnetic mine which piled up British and neutral wrecks along the east coast.[3] German pocket battleships broke into the Atlantic, massacred the auxiliary cruiser *Rawalpindi* and sank merchant shipping. These losses were offset by a brilliant victory over the *Graf Spee* in December and by showy action in February, 1940, in which the destroyer *Cossack* boarded the German prisonship *Altmark* in Norwegian territorial waters and released British seamen captured by the *Graf Spee*. Then came the Norwegian campaign.

The British public began to suspect the futility of its leadership during the Finnish war, but its confidence was utterly shattered in the Norwegian campaign. At the eve of the astonishing German victory in Norway Mr. Chamberlain made the profound mistake of saying that Hitler had "missed the bus." General Sir Edmund Ironside, chief of the imperial general staff, let it be known that he was "ten times as confident" as he was in September, 1939. Then came a campaign which in treachery, thoroughness of preparation, speed and ruthlessness of execution set a new record in the annals of warfare. According to the old concept of war, Hitler had overreached himself. The idea that he could maintain lines of communication 1,000 miles long seemed absurd. Optimism in Britain flared to the sky. Here, obviously, was the chance for the navy. Even Churchill went off the deep end of reality by asserting that every German transport in the Skagerrak would be sunk. There followed a series of heartbreaking failures in which the Royal Navy failed to bring any heavy German naval units to decisive battle, in which a pitiful Allied expeditionary force was driven from its perilous perch on the hills outside Trondheim by murderous attacks of the German Luftwaffe and by the incredibly rapid advance of German armored columns through the mountain valleys from Oslo. When it was all over the German navy had lost only seven destroyers to the

[3] The Admiralty was quick, however, to solve the mystery of the magnetic mine and soon provided naval vessels and merchant ships with the de-gaussing belt.

Royal Navy. The three cruisers lost by the Germans fell to the stanch Norsemen. The lesson of air power had been driven home to the British fleet, whose tasks were multiplied by the German control of Norwegian bases.

Mr. Chamberlain clung to office yet a little while. He was stung to the quick by the refusal of 40 members of his party to vote for him in a test of confidence on May 8. Not a single member of the Conservative party connected with any of the fighting services supported Mr. Chamberlain. British politicians were busy over the Whitsun holiday of May 9 preparing for a shift in the government. On May 10 the German stroke fell in the west. There was nothing Mr. Chamberlain could do but resign. The king asked Churchill to form a cabinet late that day.

VII

IT MUST be regarded as the very refinement of irony that, although Churchill's lifelong ambition was to hold the prime ministry, he was to achieve this goal only at a moment when the military fortunes of the British Empire were at the very bottom of the abyss. He took over the reigns of government from Mr. Chamberlain, but there was nothing he could do to avert the military disaster which the nazi command had prepared for the Allies in Flanders and which was already in motion. Allied armies, it is true, marched, fought, and issued communiqués. But once the trap at Sedan was sprung upon the Allied armies which had rushed to the defense of Holland and Belgium, all forces north of the Somme were destroyed from a military point of view. Only the heroism of the RAF and navy and the traditional fortitude of British troops in adversity made the miracle of evacuation possible at Dunkirk.

There is little evidence to show that Churchill had any effect on the course of the Flanders battle or on the events that led to the French collapse in June. He repeatedly flew to France to encourage continued resistance and in the final hours proposed a merging of the two empires. At least he was thinking in broad

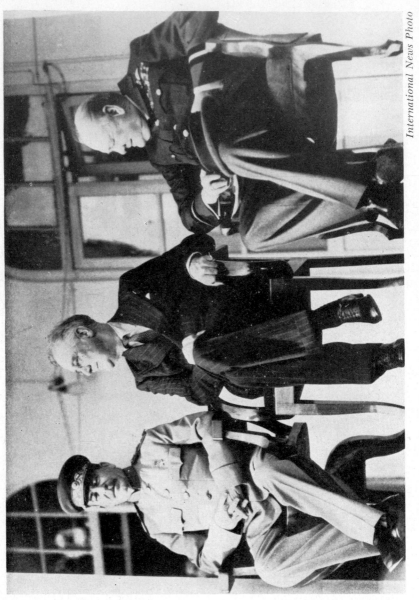

STALIN, ROOSEVELT, and CHURCHILL (at Teheran)

terms under pressure. When Pétain had his way and asked for an "honorable peace," Churchill withdrew the last British division from France and prepared for a defense of the islands and the British Empire. His oratory and leadership rose to new heights of effectiveness. He became the very embodiment of the British will to resist. Tireless and sturdy, he promised the British people only work, suffering, tears, and sorrow. They gave him what free peoples always give strong leaders in an emergency—hearty support and growing affection. In July, August, and early September Britain was turned into a fortress. There was no longer any room for the comforting, enervating idea that others were to do the fighting. While Britain nerved herself to face the inevitable final struggle, the Wehrmacht took two months to count its prisoners, collect its booty on the Continent, and move its bases forward to attack "the last enemy." Air warfare in new fury broke out on Britain in September, 1940.

At this hour, despite the survival of the British fleet and air force, a victory over Germany seemed beyond hope. At war against Germany and Italy without an ally, Churchill called upon the untapped reserves of British courage. His challenge will live along with the priceless treasures of English prose.

> Hitler knows that he will have to break this island or lose the war. If we can stand up to him, all Europe may be free and the life of the world may move forward into broad, sunlit uplands. But if we fail, then the whole world . . . will sink into the abyss of a new Dark Age made more sinister, and perhaps more protracted, by the lights of a perverted science. Let us therefore brace ourselves to our duties, and so bear ourselves that, if the British Empire and its Commonwealth last for a thousand years, men will say "This was their finest hour."

It must be counted among the least of Britain's sorrows that when he came to power the military situation did not permit Churchill to demonstrate the kind of imaginative, farsighted war that he was master of explaining in prose. Before him was the long and uncertain fight for equality and then supremacy in the air. As long as the mighty force of German divisions remained intact in Europe there was no chance of military operations on the Continent. He felt certain that, as the war drew out, America would see the wisdom in preserving British control of the Atlantic rather than face at some future date the combined Atlantic and Pacific threat of a triumphant Axis.

When Britain decided to continue the war alone after the fall of France, Churchill could not foresee the future of the war or the empire, but he saw three possibilities for an ultimate British victory. One was that Britain could somehow wrest control of the Mediterranean from Italy. The second was that Hitler's all-consuming ambitions would ultimately drive Germany into war against Russia. The third was that the United States would some-day range its vast potential power alongside that of Britain.

Since the war could no longer be confined to Europe, Churchill resolved to bring what force he could to bear upon the shaky foundations of Italy's African empire. With the German Wehrmacht poised as if to invade England, Churchill sent naval, military, and air forces to the Mediterranean which enabled General Wavell to destroy the greater part of Marshal Graziani's army in Libya, made it possible for Admiral Cunningham to strike two crippling blows at the Italian fleet, and insured the collapse of Italian East Africa.

When Germany prepared by diplomatic and military means in the winter and spring of 1941 to aid her Italian ally, who had come to military grief in Albania, Churchill boldly took the risks of opening a campaign in the Balkans. He hoped for a strong defensive fight by the Greeks, Jugoslavs, and British Expeditionary Force. There were, as he eloquently pointed out, factors of morale and prestige involved. He had promised to fight for the whole eastern Mediterranean, and, although the British army suffered another minor Dunkirk, in one sense he had forced Hitler to fight an unnecessary battle. Hard on the heels of the Greek disaster came the bitter defeat in Crete. Despite these reverses the British African empire was still intact when the whole course of the war was altered by the German invasion of Russia on June 22, 1941. It then became clear that Churchill's decision to fight, after the collapse of France in June, 1940, had finally forced Hitler to engage in the only kind of war Britain could conceivably win—a world-wide war on distant fronts.

Churchill's flair for strategic prophecy, for knowing what is going on in the enemy mind over the hill, never appeared more clearly than in the weeks preceding the German invasion of Russia. While German and Russian official sources were insisting that the "pact of eternal friendship" of August 23, 1939, would never be broken, he warned of the coming invasion. In a similar manner he had formerly warned the Scandinavian neutrals, the Low Countries, and the Balkan powers. Churchill had been (and remains) a lifelong enemy of communism, but he brushed aside the obvious nazi attempt to divide Britain on ideological grounds by preaching a crusade against communism. He promised all possible aid to Russia and signed an alliance with her. When the campaign in Russia required the main strength of the Luftwaffe in that theater, the RAF, which Churchill looked upon as a strategic weapon of great potentiality, took the offensive over France and western Germany.

It was in the sphere of coalition war that Churchill's talents for inter-Allied co-ordination were fully revealed. Before the United States entered the war, he helped arrange the bases-for-destroyers transfer. He negotiated lend-lease agreements which brought American military equipment to the British armies and food to the homeland. In August, 1941, he made his first dramatic war missions to an Atlantic rendezvous where he signed the Atlantic Charter with the American president. Immediately after Japan struck her treacherous blow in December, 1941, he flew to Washington to lay the groundwork for future Anglo-American military collaboration. He was in Washington again in May and June, 1942, where plans for the defeat of Rommel were framed and the Allied landing in North Africa projected.

His first attempt to reach a close understanding with Russia apparently failed during his visit to Moscow in August, 1942. In January, 1943, he took part in the Casablanca conference where the final plans for the conquest of Tunisia and Sicily were made. He followed this with a visit to Adana for a conference with Turkish leaders. In August of 1943 he dealt with Pacific problems at the Quebec conference. Finally in November and December of 1943, he completed his efforts to get all the important United Nations leaders together at the Cairo and Teheran conferences.

Churchill will probably emerge from the war as the "coordinator of the victory." He alone has attended all the conferences which have made unity of effort possible. The 68,000 miles he has traveled to do so have taken a heavy toll of his health. Among the heads of states he has been the pre-eminent exponent of strategic air warfare.

Not all Britons are satisfied with Churchill's conduct of the war. Though he saved Britain from conquest by Germany, he is charged with the loss of her empire in the Far East. During the long period of defeats in the Middle East there was considerable criticism of Churchill's interventions in military affairs by some officers. These men with their local point of view could not see the over-all picture of the war as clearly as Churchill. Perhaps it was partially toward them that he directed his remarks before the Congress of the United States on May 19, 1942. Describing his role and function in the war he said: "Modern war is total, and it is necessary for its conduct that technical and professional authorities be sustained and if necessary directed by heads of government, who have the knowledge which enables them to comprehend not only the military but the political and economic forces at work and who have the power to focus them all upon the goal." This is the clearest brief description available of the function of a statesman-soldier in modern war.

In summarizing Churchill's contribution to Britain's ultimate victory it is appropriate to use the words of an erstwhile critic. Harold J. Laski does not see eye to eye with Mr. Churchill on all phases of his policy, but concerning his major achievements as a war administrator and as the personification of Britain's will to victory, he speaks without reservation.

No citizen of Great Britain with any love for his country is likely to underestimate the debt it owes to Mr. Churchill. He took over the command of its fortunes when they were at a lower ebb than anytime since Austerlitz. . . . Yet within a few months his energy and his courage had awakened among the people a spirit of resolution which no enemy could break. He brought a unity of heart to the nation, a determination to die rather than surrender, which, as in the weeks of the Battle of Britain, made a Nazi victory unthinkable. To the outside world, the fate of Britain might seem to hang by a thread; to its own citizens, confidence in triumph was born in the hour when, beyond its shores, defeat seemed most inevitable. That is Mr. Churchill's triumph, and it is no other man's.[4]

[4] Harold J. Laski, "Winston Churchill in War and Peace," in the *Nation,* vol. CLVII, December 18, 1943.

TIMOSHENKO

☆

"We shall grind down the enemy and then destroy him."

FOR three terrible years from the autumn of 1939 to the autumn of 1943 the military dynamism of the Axis was in the ascent throughout the world. Before its tremendous surge could be checked, many nations were overwhelmed, countless people enslaved, and incalculable devastation was wrought on the face of three continents. By the end of 1942 the forces opposing the Axis had been able by herculean efforts to establish a hazardous equilibrium. Gradually this balance was turned into an effective United Nations offensive which wrested the initiative from the Axis in every theater of conflict. In this transfer from a United Nations defensive to a state in which there was no longer any reasonable chance of an Axis victory in Europe, the Red army played a leading role.

From June, 1941, onward it engaged the main military forces of the Axis in Europe. In bloody struggles which tried the Russian nation as it had never been tried before, the Red army checked the frightful momentum of the nazi war machine and finally turned it back in general retreat. Led by new officers steeled in two years of bitter war, the Red army then began to reap the rewards of its magnificent defensive achievements.

Few soldiers who begin at or near the top of the military hierarchy can expect to finish a long war in that position. Hindenburg and Haig were the exceptions in World War I. Keitel, who has been retained as a kind of concession to the regular elements in the Wehrmacht, has thus far been the outstanding exception in World War II. Of the three leading Red army generals, Budenny, Voroshilov, and Timoshenko, only the latter survived the first winter of the war. Already in 1942 Timoshenko's pre-

eminence in the Red army was overshadowed by such men as
Zhukov and Vassilevsky, but because of the supremely important defense role he played in the first stages of the war, Timoshenko will be accorded a place among the leading soldiers of
his time.

Semion Konstantinovitch Timoshenko, the "blitzgrinder"
and "teacher" of the Red army, was born on February 18, 1895,
the son of a landless peasant in Furmanka, Bessarabia. He had
practically no education and was working as a farm laborer when
the tzarist draft board placed him in the army in 1915. Service as
a machine gunner in the 1st Oranienbaum Regiment and in the
4th Cavalry Division did not set him apart from his fellows,
though an act of insubordination in October, 1917, nearly
placed him before a firing squad. Court-martialed for having
struck an officer, Timoshenko was "freed" by the November
Revolution of 1917. He fought against General Kaledin's forces
in the Don region and rapidly rose to command of the 6th Red
Cavalry Division.

His most spectacular exploit during the civil war was a cavalry
break through of the White army's siege lines around Tsaritsin
(Stalingrad) in November, 1918. This success brought him to
the attention of Stalin, Budenny, and Voroshilov. He took part
in the ill-fated invasion of Poland and was severely wounded
fighting against the armies of Baron Wrangel at Perekop in
September, 1920. Before he recovered from his wounds, the
main battles of the civil war were over; the Red-army had finally
freed Russian soil from its many invaders and defended the
revolution against internal enemies.

Timoshenko now came in contact with the central government of Russia. He met Lenin for the first time in 1920 at the
Bolshoi Theater in Moscow. When Lenin commended him on
the fine showing of his division in the civil war, Timoshenko
volunteered that in many cases he had been successful because
he relied on suggestions and advice from the men in the ranks.
This pleased Lenin who said: "Good! Good! Always be able to
count on the support of your men. The main thing is to be at

one with the masses!" Timoshenko seems to have acted upon this advice throughout his subsequent career, for according to all reports, he never allowed himself, even at the height of his power, to lose touch with the men in the ranks.

In the post-civil-war period Timoshenko came under the influence of Frunze (Trotsky's successor as war minister) whose name was given to the Red Army Military Academy; of Shapozhnikov, one of the outstanding professors on the staff; and of Tukhachevski, the brilliant field commander. These men showed the illiterate Timoshenko that he still had a great deal to learn about war and reawakened early desires for an education which the poverty of his parents had denied him. Along with other self-made leaders of the civil war, he became a student at the military academy where he found study much harder than fighting.

In 1925 Timoshenko was made joint commander and commissar of the III Cavalry Corps, a position he held until 1930. He attended the Political Academy for Higher Commanders and visited various European maneuvers in 1933. From 1933 to 1936 he was assistant commandant of the Kiev Military District under General Yakir. He held brief commands of both the Caucasus and the Kharkov military districts in 1937. Returning to Kiev as commandant in 1938, he was serving in this post when Germany attacked Poland in September, 1939.

Timoshenko's membership in the Communist party dates back to 1919. His loyalty to the Stalin regime was unquestioned, for though heads fell all around Timoshenko during the purge, no suspicion of disloyalty fell on him. He had belonged to Tukhachevski's suite and Yakir's staff; he had succeeded Koshirin in command of the Caucasus Military District and Dubovoy at Kharkov. All these men disappeared in the purge, but Timoshenko remained in the favor of the government. He did not purchase favor by slavish adoption of all the party military policy; even after the purge, he continued to support Tukhachevski's program for ridding the Red army of the impractical dual command inherent in the system of political commissars.

TIMOSHENKO

II

AT THE outbreak of World War II the Red army was 21 years old. It had undergone tremendous changes in that brief period. The product of a revolutionary movement, the Red army had passed through various stages of evolution from a volunteer force to a permanent conscript army. Separate military units organized on a territorial basis gave way to a single national army. Back of the army and the array of organized reserves was a population schooled in total preparedness for war through the Osoaviakhim and the Soviet education system. Russian industry was designed and located primarily with defense considerations in mind. The army and the nation were spiritually prepared to defend their homeland against a total attack. "The nation and the army," said Stalin in 1928, "compose one entity, one family."

The doctrines and war methods of Soviet Russia are the products of many minds. Timoshenko was but one of the officers who helped to prepare the Red army for the great trials that lay ahead of it. Early in the history of the Soviet Union, Lenin insisted on the total dedication of all state resources to war as an absolute requirement in the event of a foreign attack. "Once we have to fight," he said, "everything—the entire internal life of the country—must be subordinated to the war. On this point we can permit no deviation." Mikhail Frunze, the war minister, saw that until Russia's industrial production reached a parity with the most advanced European states, she would have to employ such defense methods as guerrilla warfare and the scorched earth. In the vast spaces of Russia he saw a resource of inestimable value wearing down the enemy. Military experts at the Red Army Military Academy such as Svechin and Verkhovsky stressed the potentialities of a war of attrition as against the prevalent German concept of a war of annihilation. Verkhovsky went so far as to suggest that in a war against a continental European enemy, "it might be far better for the Red army to surrender Minsk and Kiev than take Bialystok and Brest-Litovsk." Stalin himself repeatedly stressed the difficulties of carrying out an uninterrupted offensive against a formidable opponent. He saw that regrouping of reserves, halts for security reasons, and transport problems would slow down a modern army despite mechanization. Space and time were important factors in Russian military calculations. Because of its vast size, Russia could, if necessary, purchase time with space.

Thus the main lines of Russian military policy were laid out in advance. Against a well-prepared adversary like nazi Germany, the Red army would face great initial disadvantages. These would have to be overcome by a program of defense in extreme depth, a total resistance of the whole population, a war of attrition which aimed at the destruction of the enemy's strategic reserves, to be followed by an eventual Red army offensive. As Max Werner described them, the principles of Soviet war are: (1) Husbanding of forces and accumulation of reserves, so as to be stronger than the enemy in the second half of the war. (2) Systematic weakening of the enemy by defensive and offensive operations. (3) A final offensive aimed at the destruction of the enemy's fighting forces.

Like all other aspects of Russian life, the Red army shared the trend toward mechanization which followed the consolidation of the revolution. If the tractor became the symbol of Russian agriculture, the tank became the symbol of the army. Many officers were carried away by the appeal of mechanization to the point where they felt that machines could solve most of Russia's military problems. Timoshenko did not share their full enthusiasm but insisted that human factors, the discipline, training, and spirit of the soldiers, were equally important. Mechanization enthusiasts talked glibly about the almost unlimited possibilities of the offensive, but Timoshenko knew that the offensive was merely one face of a coin. The other was the defensive. Some zealous political leaders thought that the political indoctrination of the Red army was in itself an all-sufficient preparation for war, but Timoshenko insisted that this had to be augmented by military skill and adequate armament.

Not long after he was convicted of having struck an officer in

the tzarist army, Timoshenko found that he could not handle
his guerrilla cavalrymen without real discipline. On taking over
command of the 6th Cavalry Division in 1918 he said: "Lack
of discipline and inefficiency are crimes. I shall not tolerate
slackness or lack of discipline in my division." Certain Red army
leaders placed their faith in "revolutionary" or "conscientious"
discipline, but Timoshenko doubted whether this kind of discipline by its mere presence could make an army out of a mass
of men. At the base of the Red army's discipline and command
problem was the long-debated and much-condemned "party"
institution, the political commissar. Timoshenko's attack on
this institution was not made on political but on purely military
grounds. If it was not efficient in war, it should be abandoned.
He had seen the evil effects of this system operate in the Red
army defeat before Warsaw in August, 1920.

The modern Red army had its baptism of fire on the Man-
churian frontier in 1938 and 1939. Here Russian infantry,
mechanized forces and planes successfully resisted the encroach-
ments of Japan. Changkufeng and Nomanhan were the first "defeats" suffered by the Japanese army in modern times. Though
the outside world paid little attention to these "frontier" episodes, the Japanese, who were on the receiving end, got a sufficiently clear picture of the military prowess of the Red army to
influence their future plans for war against the United Nations.
In the same month that Hitler invaded Russia, Lieutenant General Kommochi Okura, former manager of the South Manchu-
rian Railway Company, wrote a long article in the Japanese
magazine *Taiheiyo* realistically appraising Russian industrial
and military strength.

There were still many elements of weakness in the Russian
military establishment and these showed up clearly in the Finnish War. The winter campaign against Finland, which began
November 30, 1939, provided a number of unpleasant surprises
for the Red army. The small, highly mobile, and skillful Finnish
forces trapped and decimated Red army divisions strung out
along the forest roads of central and northern Finland. The

mere possession of mechanized equipment did not save the hapless Red army troops. Serious shortages in Russian winter equipment and marked deficiencies in training were revealed. If the Kremlin expected to crush Finland in a quick politico-military campaign with the use of second-line troops, this hope soon faded. Finally, in late December, after initial Russian attacks had been repulsed with heavy losses, Stalin entrusted the command on the Karelian front to Timoshenko with orders to break through the Mannerheim line.

This was Timoshenko's first important fighting command and his introduction to war on a modern scale. The defenses of the Mannerheim line were formidable by any standard. The garrison that defended these positions was of high quality with excellent equipment and morale. Early victories over much larger Russian units gave the Finnish soldiers and their commanders confidence that the Mannerheim front could never be broken.

The whole month of January, 1940, was spent preparing for the assault on the Mannerheim line. Russian communications were improved; new divisions were brought in; artillery was moved forward into position; massive ammunition depots were built up. Timoshenko had models of the Mannerheim redoubts constructed behind the Russian lines and gave the troops practice in assaulting them. On February 1, 1940, he was ready to strike.

The second phase of the Finnish War was ushered in by an unprecedented artillery bombardment of the Mannerheim line. Subsequent operations revealed the Red army at its true value. No longer were Russian divisions allowed to work their clumsy way into Finnish traps. Slowly the tremendous power of Russian resources and the training of the troops began to manifest themselves. Under this massive attack the Finnish troops were forced into a desperate step-by-step defense. By day and night thousands of shells fell on their positions. There was no chance to sleep or bring up reinforcements. Working in close co-operation with Soviet artillery, engineers and infantry removed minefields

and blasted away tank obstacles. Infantry in armored sledges
were towed into battle by Russian tanks. One by one the Finnish
forts and pillboxes were undermined by the rain of Russian
shells. Acquainted with the technical details of the Mannerheim
forts, the Red army artillerymen deliberately fired high-
explosive shells into the ground in front of the pillboxes. Since
the forts had no concrete frontal aprons, many of them sagged
forward into the shell holes. This threw their guns out of align-
ment and rendered them useless.

The Red army functioned like a machine in this period; the
high courage of the Finnish garrison availed them little. Their
scanty reserves were pinned down by Russian diversions north
of Lake Ladoga, and they could not reinforce threatened points.
On February 25, the Red army captured Koivista, the eastern
anchor of the Mannerheim line. Then Timoshenko directed
the attack toward Viipuri. A bold advance across the ice at
Kronstadt Bay outflanked the Finnish position on this front.
On March 3, 1940, the Red army reached the outskirts of Viipuri. The Finnish position was now hopeless. Unable to face
Russian mechanized forces behind the Mannerheim line, the
Finns were forced to accept Russian terms on March 12.

The performance of the Red army from February 1 to March
12 was highly impressive, although in the public mind it failed
to offset the Russian blunders in the early phases of the campaign. Timoshenko was rewarded for his part in the victory with
the rank of marshal, the Order of Lenin, and the title "Hero of
the Soviet Union." On May 7 he appeared with Stalin in his box
at the Bolshoi Theater in Moscow. The day following this public recognition, he was named People's Commissar for Defense
and member of the Supreme War Council. Timoshenko had
"arrived."

III

At the age of 45 Timoshenko was at the summit of his physical
and mental powers. He carried his 6-foot, 200-pound frame with
the tireless grace of a well-developed athlete. His booming bass

voice carried to the remote corners of a lecture room or to the outer edges of a group in the field. He now had power enough to effect the reforms necessary in the Red army. The first institution to be "reformed" was that of the political commissar. Though the political commissar was revived in the war against Germany, it was primarily to maintain morale and control and expedite guerrilla warfare, not to supervise operations in the Red army proper. Finally, on October 9, 1942, the whole system of political commissars was abolished. The officers thus released were trained as combat officers and absorbed by active divisions. Their years of front-line activity made them a particularly valuable source of new officer material.

Feeling that the Red army's prewar training had placed too much emphasis on technique and too little on field training, Timoshenko worked out a rigorous training program which extended from the battle practice of small units to maneuvers embracing several armies. Everywhere he strove to achieve realism in training and maneuvers. His "Disciplinary Code of October 12, 1940" restored military titles and ranks for commissioned officers, re-established the salute, and greatly increased the severity of military penalties. Soviet officers were now given the authority to inflict the death penalty on insubordinate troops, but at the same time Timoshenko tried to improve the officer-soldier relationship by putting it on a personal basis.

The large-scale maneuvers of the autumn of 1940 gave Timoshenko a chance to bring home the lessons of the Finnish War. His penetrating critiques were directed solely at improving the battle efficiency of the troops. He found serious fault with the reconnaissance practices of the Red army. He preached the doctrine of building up the efficiency of the army on the foundation of the infantry squad. From the nazi campaigns in the west, he foresaw that all kinds of units, big and small, would be forced to fight on their own in the fluid conditions of modern war. The smallest unit in the Red army was taught not to surrender merely because it was "cut off" by enemy mechanized units. It was to fight on, to effect a counterencirclement of enemy units if possible. He strove to develop a high sense of personal initiative in officers and men. "Numerical superiority alone," he used to say, "is valueless without personal initiative." He combined his appeals for discipline and initiative saying: "In war you must obey but you must also think for yourself. Battles are often won by men who think for themselves and fight it out in the last ditch. Obey—but think for yourself!" His concern for the individual soldier was reflected in a rollicking Red army song which, overlooking Timoshenko's status as a bachelor, had a refrain running: "He treats his soldiers like his sons."

In his emphasis on the training and spirit of the soldier, Timoshenko did not overlook the importance of doctrine and equipment in war. Three months before the outbreak of the war with Germany he made General J. F. C. Fuller's *Field Service Regulations III*, the long-neglected treatment of mechanized warfare by the brilliant but embittered British tank expert, a "table book" for all Red army reading rooms. He is said to have ranked Fuller's books along with Clausewitz's *On War* and Douhet's *Command of the Air* as one of the outstanding military works of recent times. As a corollary to his emphasis on the operations of well-disciplined small units, Timoshenko stressed the need for even greater quantities of automatic weapons to increase the fire power of the infantry and urged closer co-ordination between infantry and artillery.

On two occasions in 1941 Timoshenko warned his countrymen against a surprise attack. When, on June 22, 1941, Hitler set his vast armies in motion on the Russian frontier, Timoshenko was in command of the central army group barring the German route to Moscow. Despite the immensity and thoroughness of Red army preparations and the alertness of the Soviet government, the German attack on June 22 did achieve a measure of surprise. Before Russian mobilization could match that of the enemy, months of retreat and bitter defense battle had to intervene. Even then, as Stalin pointed out in his message to the Red army on February 23, 1943, it took two full years to bring the army to the peak of its battlecraft and strength.

Although action was joined all along the immense front, the first German effort to encircle and destroy a major portion of the Red army, took place on Timoshenko's front. This was the battle of Bialystok-Minsk (June 22–July 18). For a considerable time the world was deceived by the blatant claims of the German communiqués into believing that the Red army had stupidly crowded large numbers of troops into the frontier zone and that these forces (two whole armies) were encircled, captured, or destroyed by Field Marshal Bock's armies. For this misconception the hitherto reliable character of the German official communiqués was responsible. However, on the Russian front Hitler issued the communiqués himself, and they proved to be utterly untrustworthy. The average reader in the outside world could only judge the course of events in the Russo-German War by the admitted losses of both sides. Other claims had to be accepted with extreme caution. Two revolutionary systems were locked in a death struggle and both frankly employed their communiqués for fullest propaganda effect.

Thus the German claims to have captured 323,000 prisoners in the battle of Bialystok-Minsk must be compared to the frank admission of German military critics that the Russian troops fought with "insensate tenacity," that they scorned capture, and resisted to the death. Since the Russian *armée de couverture* in the Bialystok-Minsk zone in all probability did not exceed 300,000 men, it was physically impossible for the Germans to have killed them all as Colonel Soldan, the military expert of the *Völkischer Beobachter,* contended or to have captured them all, as the communiqués claimed.

From the Russian point of view, Timoshenko's great accomplishment at Bialystok-Minsk was to delay for 26 days the first German all-out drive against Moscow. He fought a modern defensive battle of all arms on a limited scale and slowed up the Wehrmacht. Instead of opening the door to Moscow before the Germans, the battle of Bialystok-Minsk merely opened the road to Smolensk, where the Wehrmacht met the real strength of the Red army for the first time.

For two and a half months at Smolensk, Timoshenko conducted a defensive operation of all arms in great depth on a scale and at an intensity hitherto unmatched in history. The breaking of the so-called Stalin line by the Germans in the first phase of the Smolensk battle only led to more intense fighting. This illustrates more clearly than anything else, the difference between the Russo-German War and the German campaigns of 1939–40. The methods employed by Timoshenko and his chief of staff, Lieutenant General Vassily Sokolovsky, consisted of a systematic concentration of men and weapons on a scale surpassing that of the invader. To "grind down" the enemy, Timoshenko employed the Red army resources, including tanks, planes, mechanized artillery, land mines, and motorized infantry on a prodigal scale. It was an "active" defensive characterized by the use of massed artillery and counterattacks of great strength. Enemy tank spearheads were allowed to penetrate forward Russian lines and then Red army counteroffensives were launched at the supporting German infantry units. German panzer units cut off from infantry support were assaulted with antitank guns and attacked by individual infantrymen armed with antitank rifles, Molotov cocktails and grenades. As General Sokolovsky described it, "the process resembled Verdun but in terms of 10 or 100 times its destruction."

The Russian methods of fighting in extreme depth gave the German troops a new experience in warfare. Colonel Soldan tried to explain it to Germans back home by saying: "A [German] division seeks to push on, though it knows that in its rear the hole that has just been torn open will immediately close, cutting it off from adjoining units and supplies. It is certain to face a new enemy soon—an enemy as mobile as itself who may appear on the left or right, in front or in the rear—or perhaps everywhere at once." By August 15, 1941, Timoshenko had forced the Germans to abandon their major offensive efforts at Smolensk and, while German troops were withdrawn in the second phase of the Smolensk battle in order to strengthen the nazi offensive in the Ukraine, the Red army actually held in the initiative on the Smolensk front from August 15 to October 1.

The character of Russian resistance at Smolensk is indicated by the fact that even in the late summer of 1941 the Germans did not have strength enough to make decisive attacks in several sectors simultaneously. When troops were withdrawn from the unproductive Smolensk area to be sent southward, German military critics now described positions east of Smolensk as "having to be left to their own" or being "held by a few machine guns and the carbines of gun crews." Thus, early in September Timoshenko's sudden offensive at Yelnya caught eight German divisions off guard and crushed them. Conducting a party of British and American newspapermen over the Yelnya battlefield shortly after the engagement General Sokolovsky observed that the Germans were already on the defensive and digging in. "What lies ahead of them," he said, "is trench warfare, mud, Russian roads, and winter."

General Sokolovsky's predictions did not materialize until early in December. The reinforced Wehrmacht made its supreme effort to take the Russian capital and knock out the Red army in a series of mighty offensives on the Central front from October 1 to December 5. These gigantic operations fall into several distinct phases. The first, from October 1 to October 20, fell in the period of Timoshenko's control of operations on this front. It was preceded by a statement from Hitler that the Russian army was crushed and would never rise again. So confident was the Führer that he allowed Press Chief Otto Dietrich, on October 9, 1941, to pledge his word to the representatives of the German and neutral press that: "With the crushing of Timoshenko's army group the campaign in the east has been decided. The military decision is final. . . . These blows have finished the Soviet Union in a military sense. The Red army no longer has at its disposal units with any considerable freedom of action. The divisions which were hurled against the Germans (at Yelnya) were in fact the last ones."

The German offensives against Moscow launched over a wide front in October were the mightiest efforts in the history of war.

In terms of tanks, guns, planes, and men employed these operations dwarfed the most intense phases of the Smolensk battle.
Timoshenko's armies were forced to give ground before this
overpowering onslaught. City after city fell into the hands of
Marshal Bock's troops. On October 15 the Red army communiqué hinted at the loss of Možhaisk and frankly admitted the
gravity of the situation. On October 18 the German communiqué announced the "annihilation" of Timoshenko's eight
armies and the capture of 640,000 prisoners. General Westhofen
exalted in the pages of *Der Neue Tag:* "The incredible has happened! The enemy has been beaten even before the coming of
winter!"

These rejoicings were wildly premature since the German
communiqués on which they were based were completely inaccurate. The eight armies referred to (those of Golikov, Boldin,
Below, Rokossovsky, Vlasov, Govorov, Kuznetsov, and Leluishenko) were still very much "in being." In fact, they were to
be the spearhead of Zhukov's successful counteroffensive on December 7.

Timoshenko did not share in the Red army's repulse of the
final German offensives against Moscow in late October and November. In one of those abrupt transfers of command that illus-
trate Stalin's gifts as a military administrator and a judge of men,
Timoshenko had replaced Budenny on the Southern front on
October 24, and General Zhukov, who was soon to prove his
skill in conducting a major counteroffensive, had been placed
in command of the Central front.

The great battles before Moscow were the first rewards of
the Soviet plan for exhausting the enemy's strategic reserves.
The German Wehrmacht reached the limit of its powers on December 5. It captured Klin some 35 miles northwest of Moscow.
One German tank column actually reached the outskirts of
Khimki only 15 miles from Moscow, but this was the last spasm
of the dying offensive.[1] The bitterest winter in recent years and

---

[1] Walter Kerr, *The Red Army, Its Men, Its Leaders, and Its Battles* (New York,
1944), p. 37.

the Red army counteroffensive followed. On December 8 the German high command announcd the suspension of offensive operations on the Central front. "Warfare in the east," it said, "will henceforth be conditioned by the arrival of the Russian winter." This unmistakable admission of failure was emphasized by Brauchitsch's removal as commander of the Wehrmacht.

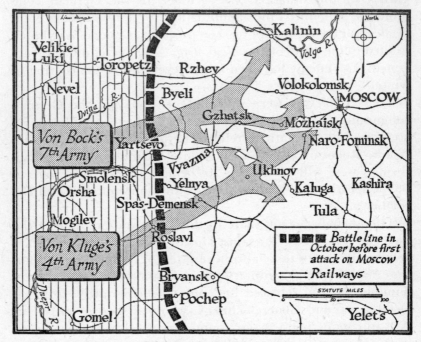

The Battle for Moscow

Meanwhile Timoshenko had raised the curtain on the first Red army counteroffensive by slashing at Kleist's extended lines north of Rostov. On November 29, 1940, the outside world was electrified by the news that the Red army had recaptured Rostov. This was the first important city to be recaptured from the Wehrmacht since 1939; its recapture made Timoshenko a world figure.

The spectacular German advances in the south up to that

time made Timoshenko's exploit at Rostov appear all the more impressive. Kharkov had fallen on October 28, the same day the Germans broke through the Russian position at Perekop and overran the Crimea. By November 16, the Germans had reached the outskirts of Sevastopol and captured Kerch. On November 22 the army of Marshal Kleist took Rostov, the gateway to the Caucasus. It appeared for a time as if the heroic achievements of the Red army before Moscow would be canceled by the disasters in the south.

The situation that Timoshenko took over from Budenny was desperate indeed. Yet within three weeks of assuming command he had put into operation plans for the assumption of a counter-offensive. On November 7 the army of General Schwoeder made a diversionary attack in the Donets area. As this movement drew German reserves northward, the Ninth Red Army under General Remisov crossed the Don late in November and attacked Rostov from the south. At the same time the Fifty-sixth Army under General Kharitonov cut at Marshal Kleist's extended lines from the north. Under the impact of these twin blows, the German army in the south suddenly recoiled toward Mariupol, leaving Rostov in Timoshenko's hands on November 29. A surprising Red army attack across the Kerch straits wrested this bridgehead from German hands on December 30. Thus the year 1941 closed with two spectacular triumphs for Timoshenko's armies after nearly six months of uninterrupted misfortune on the Southern front.

The successful Russian defense of Leningrad and Moscow, the repulse of the Germans in the south, and the Russian winter offensives represent a kind of superbattle of the Marne. The German objective of knocking Russia out of the war before the onset of winter was frustrated. Time had been gained in which to marshal Russian resources for the long struggle of attrition. Though the Russian winter counteroffensives of 1941–42 did not liberate any important strategic point or solve the problem of the German "hedgehog" defense of key cities, the winter was one of ever threatening danger and great suffering for the German armies on the Eastern front. The German army survived the harsh winter of 1941–42, but it never was able to strike with the measure of superiority it had achieved at the outset of the campaign in June, 1941. The frank tone of relief with which the German leaders welcomed the return of spring testified to the critical character of the period.

IV

AFTER their failure to destroy the Red army in 1941 the Germans had only one more year in which to exploit their military advantages. After that the scales would be weighted progressively against them. The entrance of the United States in the war meant that ultimately the tremendous resources of America would be added to those of Britain and Russia. If Russia could be knocked out of the war or enough of her territory and resources captured *before* the Anglo-American forces could open a second front in Europe, then the German military position was not unfavorable. If Russia survived the year 1942 with armies and spirit intact, then Germany's military doom was sealed.

Accordingly, the year 1942 was one of utmost hazard and importance for all the belligerents concerned. It was the critical year in the European theater of operations. All signs pointed to the early resumption of the Axis offensive against Russia. The Red army had checked the first powerful thrusts of the Wehrmacht. Now it had to continue its policy of systematically weakening the enemy for the final offensive in concert with the developing plans of the United Nations.

The balance of forces in the east was revealed early in 1942 when it became apparent that the Wehrmacht was not powerful enough to assume the offensive on more than one front. Abandoning their traditional program of destroying the enemy's armed forces, German strategy now seemed directed at limited objectives—territory and oil. Anticipating that the Southern front would be the main theater of 1942, Timoshenko attempted to delay their attack and divert nazi forces from the Crimea by launching an offensive in May on a 100-mile front from Volchansk to Krasnograd which aimed at the recapture of Kharkov. The Russian attack, which was pressed home vigorously from May 12 to 30, met some success but failed to take Kharkov or prevent the Germans from carrying out their preparatory operations on the Crimea. On May 23 the Germans captured Kerch. From June 7 to July 1, General Manstein subjected Sevastopol to an attack of unprecedented intensity. The city finally fell after a heroic defense which showed the population and army fighting to the last. Timoshenko's gains south of Kharkov were lost to a nazi attack which began in that area in June 10 and reached the eastern bank of the Oskol River by June 28, but his May offensive aided in the prolongation of Sevastopol's defense. This set the nazi timetable back and contributed to the successful stand at Stalingrad.

When the big attack came, it was a twin advance aimed at the Caucasus and at cutting Russian communications on the Volga at Stalingrad. Tremendous gains were made, but repeated German attempts to take Voronezh failed on July 20. Held here, the nazi wave surged southward, and, although the failure to take Voronezh was overlooked at the time in view of the far-reaching nazi success in the south, this was a decisive episode in the campaign of 1942. The failure to capture Voronezh laid the German armies in the south open to the Russian counteroffensive which followed the victory at Stalingrad. Thus Timoshenko's defense of Voronezh and the great defense battle on the Don bend prepared for the nazi debacle in the fall and winter of 1942–43. These operations, next to the defense of Moscow, are ranked by certain American observers as among the most important steps in the preparation for the Wehrmacht's final defeat in Russia.

Farther south, the armies of Marshal Manstein raced forward. Rostov and Novocherkassk were captured on July 28. Then the German attack branched off in two directions. One advance aimed at the Caucasus, the other at Stalingrad; both made spectacular progress. Krasnodar fell on August 20, Mozdok on August 26, Novorossiisk on September 12.

The apparent collapse of Russian resistance in this area led some to speculate that the failure to defend Rostov and Novocherkassk to the death caused Timoshenko's abrupt transfer to the Central front in August.[2] But the Russians do not defend every city to the death; they only do so if the military importance of the area justifies it. Timoshenko was, in fact, transferred from the Southern front in August, but to assert that his "failure" to defend Rostov and Novocherkassk seriously upset Russian plans is refuted by Mr. Churchill's speech in the Commons on September 21, 1943. He revealed that on his visit to Moscow (August 12–16) Stalin then assured him that Stalingrad would be the main line of defense, that it would be held and that plans were underway for an offensive to destroy the German Sixth Army. Walter Kerr, who interviewed many of the commanders who participated in the operations, says that one of the important factors in the Stalingrad victory was "the brilliant manner in which Timoshenko retreated in the early weeks of the German offensive, conserving his men and material for future battles." [3] Though less melodramatic than Mr. Stowe's rumors, this would seem to be a more reasonable explanation of the Rostov and Novocherkassk affair.[4]

The battle for Stalingrad began late in August and raged through September and October. The crack German Sixth Army under Lieutenant General Paulus, supported by Rumanian and Hungarian forces, was entrusted with the capture of the key to the Volga. Fighting of extreme intensity raged over a wide front. The terrain at Stalingrad offered the defenders few

[2] See Leland Stowe, "The Evolution of the Red Army," in *Foreign Affairs*, XXII, 94–105, October, 1943.

[3] Walter Kerr, *op. cit.*, p. 226.

[4] This incident was connected with the Axis separate-peace efforts of August, 1943. Colonel von Wedel, chief of the German high command press department, released copies of the alleged captured Red Army Order of the Day for July 28 which condemned army leaders who surrendered cities without fighting to the death. Foreign correspondents in Berlin regarded it as a German trick to undermine the confidence of the Russian people in their leaders.

of the advantages they enjoyed before Moscow in 1941. Rail communications had been severed by the German advance and Russian supplies had to be ferried across the Volga under German fire. Aside from the fortified position built up around the city, the defense rested on the courage and fortitude of the Red army and the population. A step-by-step defense delayed the German advance to the outskirts of the city until September 12. German units reached the Volga north and south of the city on that day.

Street fighting went on ceaselessly in the rubble of battered Stalingrad. Progress was exasperatingly slow. Russian artillery made every German gain costly; each house had to be reduced separately. Debris which clogged every street prevented the full use of nazi armor, and a note of irritation crept into the German communiqués. Finally, on September 30, Hitler solemnly assured the German people that Stalingrad *would* be captured and *held* against all attacks.

Like the ill-starred promise of Otto Deitrich on October 9, 1941, this speech was to boomerang back at the Führer's head. As Russian counterattacks at Stalingrad developed, the German communiqués began to alter their confident tone. On October 8, 1942, the nazi high command reported that the "essential objectives at Stalingrad" had been attained. Stalingrad was *not* taken—and a Russian counteroffensive followed which trapped and destroyed the whole German Sixth Army.

As at Moscow in 1942, Timoshenko did not share the final defense or victorious counterattack at Stalingrad. The actual house-to-house defense was conducted by Lieutenant General Vassily Chuikov, who acted on the assumption that any city was a fortress if every house was defended room by room. The victorious Russian counterattack north and south of Stalingrad which cut off and destroyed Field Marshal Paulus' army was led by Generals Zhukov, Vassilevsky, Voronov, and Rokossovsky. Stalin had once again intervened in the critical stages of the campaign to change commanders, and transferred Timoshenko to the Orel-Leningrad front.

Meantime, the Russian offensive south of Voronezh, which began on January 16, drove the nazi armies back to the line held in the spring of 1942. The steady Russian advances in the south were followed by the assumption of the offensive by Timoshenko's army group near Lake Elmen on March 1, 1943. This seems to indicate that his transfer from the Southern front was part of Stalin's program for using his leaders where he felt they could serve Russia best. The Russian communiqué announcing the March offensive gave the lie to German propaganda reports that Timoshenko was "out of favor with Stalin" and that he had been "sent on a mission to Washington." The action on the Central and Northern fronts widened as Rzhev fell on March 3 and the advance of Timoshenko's forces menaced Staraya Russa.

V

THE COMPLETE reversal of position on the Russian front in the summer of 1943 was revealed when the Red army launched its summer offensive at Orel in mid-July after an abortive German attack on the Belgorod-Kursk front. What part Timoshenko played in the operations of the summer and autumn of 1943 was not made clear until October 9, when he was awarded the Order of Suvorov for expelling the Germans from their Caucasus bridgehead on the Taman Peninsula. This made it clear that Timoshenko was no longer playing a leading role in the supreme direction of the war.

The present and future stages of the war are bringing new men, methods, and matériel to the fore in the Red army. A whole new corps of young battle-tried officers bursting with offensive spirit and know-how, a perfected method of tank-artillery-infantry penetrations and encirclements, a vast array of streamlined small infantry divisions, powerfully equipped with artillery and automatic weapons, give promise that future Russian offensives will find the Wehrmacht outmatched in fighting capacity as well as numbers. That Stalin has chosen other leaders to conduct this phase of the war is not a reflection on the

men who successfully conducted the defensive phase of the war
as much as it is a clear indication that the Red army has now
embarked upon a carefully considered policy of all-weather offensive warfare. The relative ease with which it stopped the only
offensive effort the Wehrmacht could make in July, 1943, at
Kursk and turned that abortive attempt into a sustained Russian
offensive that brought the Red army to the Dnieper in late September is convincing proof of this development.

The new leaders of the Red army's offensive are a group of
young colonel and lieutenant generals who average 45 years of
age and who were almost unknown in Russia three years ago.
They include Leluishenko, Boldin, Dovator, Konev, Govorov,
Kuznetsov, Malinowski, Bagramian, Tolbukhim, Yeremenko,
Rodimtzev, Chuikov, Rokossovsky, Golikov, and Tulenev. We
may assume that the average age of divisional commanders is
even lower. Under Marshal Stalin the supreme direction of the
war is entrusted to a group of young marshals: Vassilevsky (chief
of staff), Zhukov (vice-commissar of defense), Novikov (air
forces), and Voronov (artillery). These men are convinced exponents of the war of matériel and showed their ability to conduct a sustained offensive over a 700-mile front in the summer
and fall of 1943.

Other indications that the Red army has reached a new stage
in its development are revealed in Stalin's address of February
23, 1943, on the anniversary of the founding of the Red army.
It had taken two long years of war, he said, to school, reform, and
temper the Red army. Now it is equal or superior to the Wehrmacht in all phases of war. Outwardly the changes in the Red
army appear in the regulations regarding the uniform and insignia of service as well as in the formation of elite units. To all
intents and purposes it now follows the pattern of traditional
armies. The establishment of the Suvorov School for military
cadets is another step in this direction.

The chief feature of the Soviet conduct of war has been their
refusal to depart from the long-term strategic plans and doctrines built up for a war with Germany. Now that the defensive

phase of the war has been successfully passed, it is inevitable that men like Timoshenko will find less scope for their talents. Yet there is every indication that the Kremlin and the people appreciate the role played by him and other leaders in the early days of the war. Eve Curie, visiting Russia in 1942, found that next to that of Stalin, the face of Timoshenko appeared most commonly on Russian posters. Trying to supply a parallel that a group of American correspondents would understand, Stalin said late in 1942: "Timoshenko is my George Washington."

In dealing with an adversary as formidable as the Third Reich, attrition is a necessary step to victory.

MacARTHUR

☆

"He survived almost fatal gifts of personal charm and language to be ranked among the great soldiers of his day."

TO THE American military leader who first met the concentrated military might of the Japanese Empire after the paralyzing stroke at Pearl Harbor, it was an unmistakable act of fate that placed him there. No soldier ever had more confidence in his "mission" or "destiny" than General MacArthur. The news of the Japanese attack on Oahu brought from him only the response: "My message is one of serenity and confidence."

Yet, as he viewed the military situation on December 7, 1941, General MacArthur must have known that American interests in the Far East were in extreme jeopardy. The great Philippine commonwealth which he had been sent out to protect was about to be invaded by an overwhelming Japanese force. American naval power, always regarded as the shield of our outlying possessions, had been dealt the most disastrous blow in its history. A peace-at-almost-any-price philosophy had led us to forego even such an elementary precaution as fortifying Guam for fear of "antagonizing Japan." A national indifference to matters of defense, resulting in financial restrictions that prevented the acquisition and adequate dispersion of modern aircraft, placed him in a situation where he could not safeguard even the small forces at his disposal. Large-scale reinforcements in both men and supplies were en route to the Philippines when war came, but their delivery was impossible.

So on December 7, 1941, Douglas MacArthur was forced to fall back upon his small force of American troops and a partly trained and inadequately equipped Philippine army. The fate of his army was sealed on December 7. It was doomed to defeat and capture. Nothing that the greatest industrial and the greatest potential military power in the world could do *then*, nothing that General MacArthur could do, would change the tragic pattern of events from December 7, 1941, to the fall of Corregidor. Admiral King's report on naval operations through March 1, 1944, shows that even if the United States fleet had not been attacked at Pearl Harbor, it could not have proceeded to the Philippines to relieve MacArthur's forces.

For a time the fate hanging over MacArthur's army was concealed by the fog of war and the general public ignorance of military factors in the Pacific. Until these were dissolved by a relentless Japanese advance, the common man in America took some comfort from the bold, confident manner of the American commander, from his rich and colorful language, from his instinct for publicity, from his personal magnetism which once brought to the lips of a grizzled soldier in France the outburst: "My God! What a man!" Then followed the grim and heartbreaking drama of Bataan and Corregidor.

II

Douglas MacArthur was born at Fort Little Rock, Arkansas, on January 26, 1880, the son of Captain Arthur MacArthur of the 13th Infantry and Mary Hardy. Reared in the military atmosphere of an army post on the fringes of the frontier, he followed his father's profession, attended the West Texas Military Academy, and entered West Point on June 13, 1899, where he graduated first in the class of 1903. His all-round record at West Point surpassed all others for a quarter of a century.

He served with company I, 3rd battalion of the engineers in the Philippines after his graduation, accompanied his father to Japan in 1904 as a military observer, and witnessed the bravery and discipline of Japanese troops at the battle of Mukden. For two years he was an aide to President Theodore Roosevelt. A term at the Engineer School of Application was followed by appointments as instructor in the Mounted Service School and the Army

Service School at Fort Leavenworth. He was with Funston at Vera Cruz, Mexico, in 1914, and held the rank of major when the war broke out in 1917.

Transferred in September, 1917, from his post as chief censor in the general staff to that of chief of staff to the 42nd Division, MacArthur rapidly rose to the rank of brigadier general. His flair for colorful language gave the name "Rainbow" to the 42nd Division. When Secretary Baker suggested a division made up of National Guard units from all the 48 states in the Union, MacArthur burst out with the comment: "It will spread over the country like a rainbow." The name stuck and was immortalized by the achievements of that division in France.

MacArthur was a young man no one could ignore, but his youthful ardor was not always appreciated in high places. When he protested vigorously against GHQ plans for using the 42nd as a replacement division, Pershing slapped him down with the observation: "Young man, I do not like your attitude!" In the end the division was not broken up. MacArthur was cited for gallantry at Rechicourt on March 9, 1918, took part in the defensive operations in Champagne (July 4–17), and the Aisne-Marne offensive operation (July 25–August 3). He commanded the 84th brigade at St. Mihiel (September 12–16) and in the Meuse-Argonne operation (October 1–31). From November 1–11 he commanded the 42nd Division. The best commentary on his fighting record in France occurs in the citation at the time he received the Distinguished Service Cross and Oak Leaf Cluster: "On a field where courage was the rule, his courage was the dominant feature."

He came home from France with many decorations, bearing a reputation for lush language and irrepressible buoyancy. His penchant for novel military garb was revealed when he appeared on the deck of his transport bound for New York wearing a huge raccoon-skin overcoat fastened at the neck with a long wool scarf. To a brigadier general who could maintain his dignity in such a costume, the design of a special cap, permitted by his rank as field marshal in the Philippine army, presented no mental hazards in later years. These eccentricities, which afforded a good deal of mild amusement to conventional brother officers, stood MacArthur in good stead later. Perhaps like Rommel and Montgomery, he realized that one of the few devices by which a commander can quickly make an impression on troops is by striking deviation from the norm either in manners, speech, or attire. Modern armies are too big and complex to permit the kind of personal domination achieved by commanders in the past. Besides elasticity of mind, technical competence, and personal drive, a field commander can use a touch of Barnum or Billy Rose.

On June 12, 1919, MacArthur was appointed superintendent of the United States Military Academy. He entered upon his new duties with a zeal that startled the old academy. As he saw it, the end of World War I closed an epoch in the history of the academy. Its new mission was not simply to prepare officers for the army but to prepare them for the next war. The new conditions required that future officers have "an intimate understanding of the mechanics of human feelings, a comprehensive grasp of world and national affairs." While retaining the academy's time-tested concepts of "duty-honor-country," he attempted to bring its curriculum up to date by establishing new courses in the cultural, social, historical, and scientific fields. His consistent interest in athletics led him to stress their importance at the academy and accept the presidency of the United States Olympic Team in 1928.

His term at the Point was followed successively by command of the Military District of Manila, the 23rd infantry brigade, the Philippine Division, the IV and III Corps areas, the Philippine department, and the IX Corps Area. He was made chief of staff of the United States army on November 21, 1930. At the age of 44 MacArthur had reached the summit of the peacetime army hierarchy. His term as chief of staff was extended beyond the statutory limit, a fact that enabled him to submit five annual reports.

The years from 1930 to 1935 were not only the years of the

great depression; they were also the years in which the fascist states were preparing their rearmament programs and launching their first attacks on the postwar status quo. His annual reports to the secretary of war therefore constitute MacArthur's professional opinion on the state of American defenses and the nature of a future war. Taken as a unit they provide an insight into American military thinking of the period.

MacArthur's years as chief of staff were spent primarily in an attempt to reform army organization. When he took over, the small forces of regular infantry in the United States was distributed among 24 regiments located at 45 different posts with a battalion or less at 34 posts. Seven artillery regiments and an equal number of battalions were distributed over 16 posts. Under these circumstances training of larger units was virtually impossible. Beyond the corps areas there was no higher organization and these existed largely as "skeleton" units.

In 1932 MacArthur put through the four-army organization that divided the United States into four army zones of nine corps areas to provide defense zones as well as a mobilization and command basis for future emergencies. Until this reorganization was effected there was no complete chain of tactical control paralleling the administrative system of the corps area commands. Therefore on mobilization the army would have consisted merely of "skeleton" divisions reporting directly to the War Department. The four-army plan with a general headquarters headed by the chief of staff was intended to provide a tactical chain of command controlling the whole organization. The general headquarters also was charged with the planning for future eventualities. For any single-theater war, this arrangement would have sufficed; but for the kind of a multitheater conflict in which we found ourselves involved in December, 1941, the control and planning arrangement of GHQ proved to be inadequate.

MacArthur's second great reform was the establishment of the GHQ air force in 1934. Like the GHQ arrangement, it did not meet the needs of a multitheater conflict, and was supplanted in 1942 by the reorganization of the army. He established a tank school at Fort Knox, Kentucky, which became the foundation on which the armored force was ultimately built. But beyond these considerable reforms, the claims of his ardent supporters that he prepared the army for the immense and unforeseen tasks that lay before it in 1941 seem excessive.

No chief of staff in 1930–35 could, on the basis of the existing foreign and domestic policies, envisage or prepare for the participation of the United States in a war of the character that faced it on December 7, 1941. Claims that MacArthur foresaw its nature clearly are refuted on page after page of his reports. His concepts of what war might be like was set down at some length in his final report (1935). He compared the idealized conduct of modern war to that of Genghis Khan and wrote:

> The successes of that amazing leader, beside which the triumphs of most other commanders in history pale into insignificance, are proof sufficient of his unerring instinct for the fundamental qualifications of an army.
>
> He devised an organization appropriate to conditions then existing; he raised the discipline and morale of his troops to a level never known in any other army, unless possibly that of Cromwell; he spent every available period of peace to develop subordinate leaders and to produce perfection of training throughout the army, and finally, he insisted upon speed in action, a speed which by comparison with all other forces of this day was almost unbelievable. Though he armed his men with the best equipment of offense and defense that the skill of Asia could produce, he refused to encumber them with loads that would immobilize his army. Over great distances his legions moved so rapidly and secretly as to astound his enemies and practically paralyze their powers of resistance. He crossed great rivers and mountain ranges, he reduced walled cities in his path and swept onward to destroy nations and pulverize whole civilizations. On the battlefield his troops maneuvered so swiftly and skillfully and struck with such devastation and speed that times without number they defeated armies overwhelmingly superior to themselves in number.

This is one of the few "purple" passages in the reports where one feels that the language employed is "the real MacArthur." In all probability this is the way he would like to have waged war.

It was MacArthur's misfortune that the major "publicity"

attending his tenure as chief of staff was connected with his role in evicting the "bonus army" from its makeshift encampment in Washington. No European chief of staff would be burdened with such a "politically hot" function. Yet, when all the screaming was done, MacArthur accomplished the thankless job without the loss of a single life.

When the equally publicized "trial" of General Mitchell took place, MacArthur was on the panel of judges. Others turned the courtroom into an auditorium for various kinds of oratory and invective, but he sat through the long session without uttering a single word. Mitchell's biographer says that MacArthur voted against the conviction of Mitchell, but the evidence offered is merely hearsay.

III

In 1936 MacArthur was made director of the organization of the national defense of the Philippine commonwealth with the rank of field marshal. He retired from the United States army on December 31, 1937, at his own request. With its splendid capacity for taking the short view of things, the liberal press sharply criticized his mission to the Philippines as "an attempt to militarize the Filipino people."

Six months after reporting for duty in Manila, MacArthur surveyed the problem of Philippine defense and outlined a program that envisaged a period of peaceful independence after 1946. Despite the immense difficulties involved in protecting the 7,000 islands making up the Philippine group, MacArthur expressed confidence that given 10 years, the conquest of the Philippines could be made so costly that under normal circumstances few powers would care to undertake it. Naturally his defense scheme was based on the assumption that British and American naval power would continue to be important factors in the Pacific. He contemplated a Philippine army made up of a regular element of approximately 1,000 officers and 10,000 men, plus a civilian reserve. Chosen on a basis of universal service, an annual class of 40,000 reservists would receive five and a half months training. The army would be supplied with American arms and equipment. When the system was fully developed, MacArthur believed that a successful invasion of the Philippines would require an initial force of 300,000 troops, plus 75,000 service troops, and a monthly replacement of 40,000 men.

The only nation that could conceivably bring such a force to bear on the Philippines was Japan. Yet in the fall of 1939 MacArthur gave an interview which implied that in his opinion Japan had no immediate designs on these islands.[1] In less than two years, however, the threat of impending hostilities in the Pacific became so clear that dependents of American army personnel were evacuated from the Philippines. MacArthur was placed on active duty on July 21, 1941, and designated as commander of United States army forces in the Far East. In the following month President Roosevelt ordered the mobilization of the Philippine army. War loomed as inevitable.

How accurately did General MacArthur estimate the situation in the Pacific and the nature of the coming war? There is, of course, no way of determining this at present; but in the middle of May, 1941, John Hersey, known for his consistent admiration of MacArthur, had an interview with him on this subject. His report, often overlooked because it is in the back of his book, reads as follows:

General MacArthur pops up behind his desk and walks halfway to meet you. He is brisk and quick in spite of the oppressive heat. . . . The General is in a mood to talk. He begins to discuss Philippine defense. He speaks in involved sentences punctuated with historical references, philosophical asides, technical strategic points, and pure MacArthurisms.

Conversation turns to the subject of war clouds over the Pacific. The General is emphatic, analytic, precise, and seems very sure of what he says.

He says he thinks that the Germans have told Japan not to stir up any more trouble in the Pacific. That is because Japan is helping Germany more by not fighting than she would by actually going to battle. By remaining a threat Japan does several pro-German things. First, she ties down most of the United States Fleet at Pearl Harbor. Second, she has

[1] This interview is quoted in F. C. Waldrop, *MacArthur on War* (New York, 1942), p. 310.

caused Great Britain to put a great number of troops, perhaps as many as 125,000 or 150,000 of her best fighters, in Malaya. Third, she has made the Dutch spend $300,000,000 in arming the Indies that might otherwise have gone toward the war effort in Europe. And finally, she has made Australia hold most of her war effort in the Far East.

If Japan entered the war, he says, the Americans, the British and the Dutch could handle her with about half the forces they now have deployed in the Far East. The Japanese Navy would be either destroyed or bottled up tight. In other words, strategy would be a much more concentrated affair than the widespread checkmate strategy in force now.

Not that General MacArthur underestimates the Japanese Navy. He emphatically does not. But he points out that it is a rule of modern warfare that the highly complex nations of today can't fight much more than four years of war. In two months Japan's war in China will be four years old.

Degeneration, he thinks, has already eaten into the foundations of the highly complex economic and military structure of Japan. It is not a question of degeneration at any single weak point; it is a general matter. Resources have been burnt out; Japan has overspent herself.

In the purely military field, MacArthur thinks that about half the Japanese Army has been reduced in effectiveness from first-class to third-class standing. The rest, which has not yet seen action, is still first-class in his opinion. Japan, he says, apparently has very little in the way of military reserves. . . .

You ask: what about Japan in Indo-China and Thailand?

That, says the General, is the only kind of effort the Japanese are capable of now—a *coup de main*. . . . The South Pacific is beginning to present a bristling united front. . . . The Philippine situation looks sound; twelve Filipino divisions are already trained.

Then, as unexpectedly as he started talking, the General stops, comes over, shakes your hand briskly and says good-bye.[2]

"Thus," said Hersey later, "even the best men are not right all the time."

When the blow fell MacArthur faced it with a total force of about 130,000 men. There were 19,000 United States troops including 8,000 air-force personnel, 12,000 Philippine Scouts, and 100,000 troops of the Philippine army. A considerable part of the Philippine army had never functioned as regiments.

[2] Quoted from John Hersey, *Men on Bataan* (Alfred A. Knopf, New York, 1942), with the permission of the publisher.

There were about 250 military aircraft in the Philippines, of which 107 were P-40 fighter planes.

IV

WAR came to the Philippines eight hours after Pearl Harbor in the form of Japanese air attacks on Clark, Iba, and Nichols fields which destroyed the greater part of the American air force. Controversy has raged over MacArthur's alleged failure to disperse planes adequately, but General Marshall's report brushes this controversy aside saying that "the destruction of a large number of our planes [was] due to the limited dispersal fields and lack of sufficient radar warning equipment, antiaircraft guns and other matériel." The air force and the batteries at Corregidor were on a round-the-clock alert for several days prior to December 7.

How effectively General MacArthur prepared for the defense of the Philippines within the limits of his resources will not be known until the records are available. By the time the impending blow became apparent, it was no longer possible to take adequate defense measures. The transition to a full war status while we were still "at peace" was impossible. Even after the unofficial news of Pearl Harbor was received, the high command in the Philippines did not dare to launch the small striking force of Flying Fortresses against Formosa "before war was declared." Having lost our opportunity to destroy Japanese bombers on the ground, our own air force was virtually helpless. The single radar warning system in working order at Iba picked up the Japanese air force operating from carriers at sea as early as December 3. A Japanese reconnaissance plane passed over Clark Field at great altitude at dawn on that day.

Everyone who had any experience in modern war knew that nearly all our air-force eggs were tightly packed in a few baskets, but, as General Brereton found out, you cannot disperse planes adequately simply by ordering it done. Frantic improvisation was not particularly helpful. At some of our airfields, which

were not hard surfaced, fighter planes had to wait their turn to
take off while the dust from the propeller of the previous plane
settled enough to permit them to see. This was while the Japanese air force was in action against nearby targets. Even if most
of our planes had escaped destruction in the early raids, they
would have been overwhelmed ultimately by the sheer power,
numbers, and efficiency of the Japanese air force. Even when we
were ready and waiting for them, Japanese bombers flew their
steady course well beyond the range of our antiaircraft fire and
at a speed and altitude that made effective interception by our
P-40's impossible.[3]

There may have been, as Lieutenant Colonel Ind says, "flacid-
ity, a torpidity, and an all-pervading lack of movement and resolution at the headquarters of the Philippine department of the
United States army" when he arrived there in May, 1941; but by
the time war came every man and officer was working to the
point of breakdown. It was not a man or men who were responsible for the loss of the Philippines; it was a national way of life.

From December 10 to 22 Japanese landings were made in
northern Luzon. For a time the hero stories of "Buzz" Wagner,
Colin Kelly, and others concealed the undeniable fact that everywhere the Japanese invaders were reaching their main
objectives. Newspaper reporters, eagerly besieging the headquarters of USAFFE for copy, sent back reports that described
the first Japanese troops that landed on the Philippines as "poor
soldiers." Colonel Pierce told Clark Lee: "My professional opinion [of the Jap army] is that they are no damn good on the
ground. These fellows they sent against us were nothing but un-
trained kids. They are shooting popguns and are dressed like a
ragged mob. To call their doughboys fourth-rate is being chari-
table. They can't shoot a rifle—get confused easily. On the other
hand their tanks and planes were too much for us." [4] The last
sentence, of course, was lost in the "news appeal" of the rest of

[3] For the story of the United States air force in the Philippines see Lieutenant
Colonel Allison Ind's, *Bataan, the Judgment Seat* (New York, 1944), pp. 204–218
et. seq.

[4] Clark Lee, *They Call it Pacific* (New York, 1943), p. 141.

this report. This kind of reporting aroused hopes in the American public that were to have unfortunate repercussions later. General MacArthur ultimately set the reporters right by admitting that the Japanese army was first-rate and could only be defeated with well-trained and well-equipped troops.

Since there was no prospect of putting up more than a delaying action against the Japanese in the Philippines, General MacArthur fell back on the plan for defending the only area that could be temporarily held, Bataan and Corregidor. The evacuation of Manila was accompanied by the flight of thousands of civilians to Bataan. Their presence upset the army's plans for a prolonged defense because they consumed supplies intended for the troops. On January 11, 1942, the entire command on Bataan was reduced to half rations. By the end of March a further reduction was necessary.

Savage fighting raged on Bataan from January to April, 1942, with MacArthur carrying out an active defense as long as the state of his troops and supplies permitted. The loss of all the airfields in Luzon forced him to send the remaining Flying Fortresses to other bases in Allied hands. A few battered P-40's, kept in flying condition by skillful cannibalization, operated for a time off fields on Bataan, but they could only annoy the enemy whose planes appeared at will over the American position.

After the evacuation of Manila, General MacArthur conducted the defense of Bataan from a headquarters set up in the tunnel of Corregidor. Strong Japanese assaults on January 10, 17, 29, and February 1 were repulsed with heavy losses. Then the enemy settled down to the grim business of exhausting the American garrison. Since there was little that MacArthur could do to prolong the defense of Bataan and there was need for his services elsewhere, President Roosevelt in February ordered him to leave Corregidor by any means possible and go to Australia. Reluctantly he turned over the command to General Jonathan Wainwright and undertook the hazardous trip by PT boat and plane.

His departure was followed by a Japanese attack of great

MacARTHUR

strength on March 28 which penetrated the American lines at one point but which was driven back by an unexpectedly strong counterattack. But the doom so long hanging over the gallant defenders of Bataan could not be averted. From April 4 to 9 a relentless Japanese attack finally broke down the defense. General George cut communications with Corregidor and surrendered.

Corregidor held out under combined artillery, bombing attack, and landing assaults until May 6.

This closed the saddest campaign in American history. The loss of Bataan and Corregidor involved the death and capture of thousands of American and Philippine troops. Ironically enough, the surrender of Corregidor took place just one year after General MacArthur had given his optimistic interview on the military situation in the Pacific to John Hersey.

Because the heroic defense of the Philippines presented an encouraging contrast to the quick capitulation of Singapore and other strategic areas, the emotional impact on the American public of the disaster in the Philippines was profound. In the larger picture of the global war, however, the loss of the Philippines and its garrison appeared in another perspective. Hard as it was for the American public to follow the heroic day-by-day defense of Bataan without being able to reinforce or relieve the defenders, the strategic situation called for other measures. General Marshall outlined them as follows: "In view of the enemy's capabilities throughout the Pacific and our untenable position in the Philippines, the major efforts of the United States were directed toward a rapid concentration of defense forces along our route to Australia, the creation of an effective striking force on that continent, and the dispatch of material aid to the forces of our Allies in the East Indies."

February and the first two weeks in March, 1942, saw the darkest period of the war for the United Nations in the Pacific. Singapore with all the hopes that rested upon it fell on February 15. A terrific Japanese bombing attack blasted Port Darwin on February 17. Australia grimly prepared to defend the "Brisbane line." An Anglo-Dutch-American fleet was annihilated off Java. A tiny Australian force of 3,000 combat troops at Port Moresby, New Guinea, with a half-dozen reconnaissance planes and five antiaircraft guns, made ready to meet a Japanese attack, which the weakness of that port and its strategic position invited. They expected to be able to hold out for 36 hours before "retiring" into the jungle.

New Guinea and Australia were virtually defenseless. But then the Japanese made one of the critical mistakes of the war. Instead of striking at Port Moresby, the Japanese landed on the northern shore of New Guinea. That caution may have cost Japan one of her last chances of ultimate victory. Before the Japanese invaders of New Guinea moved forward from Lae and Salamaua to Buna and Gona, an event occurred that changed the course of the war in the Pacific. General MacArthur arrived in Australia.

The news of this event broke over the Australian radio on March 17, 1942, when an excited announcer shouted over the static: "General Douglas MacArthur, American commander of the heroic defense force in the Philippines has arrived in Australia! He has been smuggled out of Corregidor by PT boats of the United States navy and by special aircraft in one of the most dramatic episodes of the war. It is expected that General Mac-Arthur will confer immediately with the prime minister, Mr. Curtin, after which he will take supreme command of all forces in the Australian theater. . . . I repeat. . . ."

In the words of one Australian reporter "the whole country went mad." To newsmen and radio listeners MacArthur used the same language with which he had closed his annual report as chief of staff for 1934—"I shall keep the soldier's faith." Coming as it did in the midst of unrelieved United Nations disasters all over the Pacific, MacArthur's "escape" from the Philippines had the moral value of a military victory. One Australian correspondent wrote that it did more to "lift morale on the mainland than anything that had happened in the war."

The combined chiefs of staff in Washington directed him to

establish a Southwest Pacific command and gave him the mission
of "holding Australia, checking the enemy's advance along the
Melanesian Barrier, protecting land, sea, and air communications with the Southwest Pacific and maintaining our position in
the Philippines." The last objective was more of a statement of
desire than a practical military assignment. For although Mac-
Arthur repeatedly stressed his promise to go back to the Philippines, this was impossible under existing circumstances. All he
could do after he took charge of operations in Australia was to
organize a small bombing raid against Japanese installations in
the Philippines.

No doubt the fate of Bataan and Corregidor made a lasting
impression on MacArthur's mind and affected his subsequent
thinking. It is reflected in little things such as the words used by
telephone operators at his headquarters. As soon as the Japanese
struck at Pearl Harbor anyone calling the headquarters of the
USAFFE at Manila was greeted with the word "war" instead of
the customary "United States Army Forces, Far East." At Melbourne, callers were astonished to hear the headquarters operators say "Bataan speaking." One of MacArthur's earliest pronouncements after arriving in Australia was: "The president of
the United States ordered me to break through the Japanese
lines and proceed from Corregidor to Australia, for the purpose,
as I understand it, of organizing the American offensive against
Japan. A primary purpose of this is the relief of the Philippines.
I came through and I shall return."

But the heartbreaking difficulties and delays to be encountered in "organizing the American offensive against Japan" soon
became apparent. His trip from Corregidor introduced him to
one exasperating factor in the military picture: communications. His voyage by PT boat made him personally aware of what
Japanese control of the sea meant. His plane landed at Port
Darwin in the midst of an air-raid alarm. That was just an additional lesson in what air inferiority meant. Proceeding southward by the tortuous narrow-gauge railway for some 200 miles,
his party then drove by automobile across 500 miles of the bleak-

est desert in the world to Alice Springs. There they took another narrow-gauge train for some distance before transferring to a broad-gauge. Any "American offensive against Japan" based on Australia faced logistic problems tough enough to break a transport officer's heart. Yet it was on such ramshackle foundations that General MacArthur had to base his plans.

To speak of going back to the Philippines while the Japanese were still driving southward toward the outer bastions of Australia seemed a little unrealistic—even if it represented a desire that every American shared. The United Nations were not even able to establish a hazardous equilibrium in the Southwest Pacific until May 4–8, 1942, when a naval task force achieved a timely victory in the Coral Sea battle. This was followed by the stunning defeat inflicted on the Japanese navy at the Battle of Midway, June 3–6. These two engagements marked a turning point in the Pacific war. Their effects soon began to be felt on the perimeters of Japanese expansion.

The last Japanese offensive movement in the Southwest Pacific began on July 21 when troops led by Lieutenant General Tomatore Horii pushed inland rapidly from Gona Mission on New Guinea, crossed the Owen Stanley mountain range, and threatened Port Moresby. By August 3 they had reached Kokoda where they were halted as much by the difficulties of supply as by the small force of Australian defenders. Four days later, on August 7, an event took place many hundred miles to the east in the Solomon Islands which had a profound effect on all subsequent military and naval operations in the Pacific. The marines landed on Guadalcanal. From that moment on the Japanese lost the initiative in the Solomons and never regained it. The effects were soon apparent in New Guinea as well.

Though a Japanese landing was successfully made in Milne Bay, New Guinea, on August 26 to reinforce the threat of the main column crossing the Owen Stanley Mountains, Allied troops were able to force an evacuation of these troops three days later. This was the first Japanese "evacuation" since the outbreak of war. The main Japanese column, however, pushed on from Kokoda and reached Efogi some 40 miles from Port Moresby on September 9. A week later they had advanced an additional 12 miles, but this was the limit of their offensive capacity. On September 26 Australian troops under General Sir Thomas Blamey's command seized the initiative and began to drive the enemy back over the mountain jungle trails toward Buna and Gona.

One of General MacArthur's first major decisions after setting up his headquarters in Melbourne was to defend Australia in New Guinea. He had not been in Melbourne two weeks before he had scrapped the "Brisbane line." When one reporter asked him what was the formula for defensive war, MacArthur snapped "defeat." The complete defeat which his army had suffered in Luzon convinced him that the first requisite of success in modern war was air superiority. As one officer on his staff put it, "the navy can't save Australia if we lose the air." Thus the first round of the battle for New Guinea was directed at gaining control of the air over Papua. This meant throwing P-40's and in some cases even Australian Wirraway trainers and green pilots against crack Jap pilots in Zeros. Later, first-line planes arrived in numbers, but until they did, the air fight for New Guinea was carried on by sheer courage against fearful odds and difficulties.

Gradually the Fifth United States Army Air Force, under the driving leadership of General George C. Kenney, established air supremacy over Papua and and made Port Moresby secure as an advance base. Once Allied air supremacy was attained, Australian troops under General Blamey were able to recapture Kokoda with its air strip after six weeks of fighting. This gave some indication of the slow velocity of military movement in the jungles of New Guinea.

General Horii's first threat against Moresby was turned back, and his army suffered from failure of supply and resultant illness. General MacArthur wanted to use elements of the 32nd American Division to cut off his retreat. Yet the Allied forces in New Guinea simply could not move men and supplies fast enough over the roadless mountain jungle terrain to cut off or destroy his army. It was therefore decided to move the American forces to northern New Guinea by air. This was done but not in time to cut off the Japanese retreat. After a halt at Ovi, the Japanese retreated on November 11, 1942, to a final defense position at Soputa-Sanananda-Gona-Buna. Although General Horii lost his life when the raft on which he was crossing the Kumusi River overturned and his troops were constantly strafed by Allied planes, the survivors took up defensive positions in a jungle Verdun, a veritable maze of log, concrete, and earthen bunkers. They were supported by a force of 1,800 Japanese troops which had been landed at Buna from Japanese transports.

Before General Horii died, General MacArthur talked of the Buna campaign as if it were a trial of strength between the two men. "He had no idea of the plan I was putting into effect—he never believed I could do it." When General Horii's death was reported, one observer noted "an expression of regret" on General MacArthur's face. "An ignominious death," he said, in a manner that made the listener feel as if MacArthur would liked to have killed General Horii with his own hands.[5]

Well-hidden from Allied air reconnaissance by the leafy canopy of the jungle, the Japanese position at Buna and Gona was to be a bitter surprise to General MacArthur's troops. When they reached it after slogging through the muddy jungle, the troops recoiled sharply after heavy losses like one whose hand brushes against a concealed buzz saw. Two months of heart-breaking, morale-cracking, jungle trench warfare were to follow before the remnants of General Horii's army were pried out of these defenses and exterminated.

This kind of fighting, in which the Australians took a leading role, was a far cry from the idealized type described in the famous Genghis Khan passage of MacArthur's *1935 Report* as chief of staff. There was no paralyzing speed or deception here. It was a soldier's battle which had all the disagreeable features of 1915 trench warfare plus torrid heat, heavy rainfall, and jun-

[5] George H. Johnston, *Pacific Partner* (New York, 1944), p. 103.

gle undergrowth. George H. Johnston, who observed the fighting in that area, wrote:

In no other campaigns of this war, possibly in none in any war, has there
been fighting so full of fury, cold-blooded hatred and primitive savagery
as in those bloody clashes in the jungles of the South Pacific battlefronts.
. . . No quarter was asked, none given. Men died in the darkness when
a knife was drawn across their throats by an unseen foe. Men were strangled
to death. Men died as they charged with fixed bayonets against hidden
machine-gun posts. Men slept for weeks in foot-deep mud, drenched to the
skin by the cold, sweeping rains of the tropical mountain passes; slept
while the giant jungle rats nibbled clumps out of their hair. Men lived
for months on starvation rations and in incredible filth, and they died of
terrible tropical diseases.[6]

When units of two United States National Guard divisions,
the 32nd and the 41st, "fresh from the cities of Australia," were
first thrown into this kind of warfare there were disappointments and delays. One American officer lamented this to an Australian officer whose battalion (a veteran unit that fought in
North Africa) had been cut down in battle from 680 officers and
men to 2 officers and 21 men. The latter said: "Good God, man,
you must be reasonable! Those kids are good, make no mistake
about it—your division will be as good as any in the world when
it gets over its growing pains." Johnston saw part of one United
States regiment going into action for the first time against a
strong Japanese position after an earlier attack had been repulsed with heavy losses. "Most of the kids," he wrote, "looked
terrified. Many held their heads in their hands. A few were
weeping—probably from nervous strain. I saw the same unit
making an assault a week later. You would never have believed
that you were looking at the same men. Their faces were iron,
their wrists steel. The only expression in every face was a mix-
ture of hatred and determination. They were tough. . . . They
attacked bravely and they killed coldly."

The Papuan campaign schooled our troops in the harsh tasks
of jungle fighting and showed General MacArthur what air

6 *Ibid.*, p. 202.

power could do in the matter of transporting troops and supplies over the trackless jungles and across water barriers.

When the full logistic difficulties of moving troops and supplies over the Kokoda trail to support an attack on Buna were revealed, General Kenney boldly asserted that he could move a whole division and its supplies by air if suitable landing strips were built on the northern coast of New Guinea. When doubters raised difficulties, Kenney explosively said that he could move the whole army if he were given enough planes. He was as good as his word. When the Kokoda air strip was enlarged and terminal strips built at Wanigela Mission, the Fifth Air Force began flying troop units from Port Darwin, Moresby, and Kokoda. The equivalent of a full combat division (minus artillery) was moved by air together with its supplies and equipment. A few British 25-pounders and one American 105 mm. howitzer were also flown in with a supply of ammunition. A daily average of 115 tons of supplies were landed at advanced bases by transport plane or were dropped by parachute. This tremendous transport feat was carried out under extremely difficult flying conditions. It made possible the victorious termination of the Buna campaign. General Blamey described the United States Fifth Air Force as "one of the greatest and most courageous air fighting forces in the world."

That General MacArthur was quick to see the strategic and tactical implications of Kenney's feat appeared in his communiqué of January 24, 1943, issued the day after Jap resistance ended at Sanananda. To newsmen who crowded into his headquarters MacArthur said:

The outstanding military lesson of this campaign was the continuous, calculated application of air power inherent in the potentialities of every component of the air forces employed in the most intimate tactical and logistical union with ground troops.

The effect of this modern instrumentality was sharply accentuated by the geographical limitations of this theater. For months on end, air transport with constant fighter coverage moved complete infantry regiments and artillery battalions across the almost impenetrable mountains and jungles of Papua and the reaches of the sea, transported field hospitals and other base installations to the front, supplied the troops and evacuated casualties.

For hundreds of miles bombers provided all-around reconnaissance, protected the coast from hostile naval intervention and blasted the way for the infantry as it drove forward.

A new form of campaign was tested which points the way to the ultimate defeat of the enemy in the Pacific.

The offensive and defensive power of the air and the adaptability, range and capacity of its transport in an effective combination with ground forces represent tactical and strategical elements of a broadened conception of warfare that will permit the application of offensive power in swift, massive strokes rather than the dilatory and costly island-to-island advance that some have assumed to be necessary in a theater where the enemy's far-flung strongholds are dispersed throughout a vast expanse of archipelagos. . . .

The correspondents who listened to this erudite announcement took it to mean that General MacArthur was 100 per cent for air power and that there would be no more slogging infantry battles of the Buna type.

V

THE conquest of Papua and the construction of air bases on the northern coast of New Guinea gave General MacArthur the advantages of a central position in operating against the Japanese in Northeast New Guinea and New Britain Island. From this position he could throw his concentrated air power in either direction. A notable illustration of the flexibility of air power took place at the Battle of the Bismarck Sea (March 2–4, 1943) when Allied planes caught a 22-ship Japanese convoy in the Huon Gulf bound from Rabaul to Lae. Under the repeated attacks of Allied bombers and fighters, every Japanese ship was sunk. Units of the 51st and 20th Japanese divisions estimated at 51,000 men were drowned at a cost of one Allied bomber and three fighters.

In two days air power put out of action as many Japanese troops as were killed in five months of hard fighting in Papua. If General MacArthur's communiqué describing this as "a major disaster to the enemy" overstated the importance of the victory (the average weekly intake of new recruits in the Japanese army more than replaced these losses), it was nevertheless a convincing demonstration of the power and range of the air arm.

The character of island jungle warfare must have presented a number of surprises to General MacArthur despite his long study of military history. It had few superficial resemblances to linear or area warfare of the European type. Waged in the midst of vast distances, and on sparsely inhabited, almost completely undeveloped terrain, it discounted our potential superiority in mechanized equipment. Everything used by the army had to be brought in over lines of communications that stretched for thousands of miles. Japanese initiative in the early stages of the war enabled them to determine where they intended to fight their defensive battle. The United Nations were committed to an offensive in areas where all the natural features seemed to favor the fanatical pillbox fighting of the Japanese infantry. Even if we could transport our motorized and armored equipment to these theaters and supply their requirements, we faced difficulties in operating this type of equipment in the jungle. The only element that offered us immediate advantage was the air.

In the Pacific islands communication routes tend to channelize along jungle trails; operating bases are airfields and ports; dispersal areas and supply dumps are necessarily restricted in size. Thus most of the conditions for effective strategic bombing existed.

In certain areas where it was impossible to employ artillery on anything approaching the European scale to blast Japanese pillboxes and bunkers, the bomber offered a substitute.

Accordingly General MacArthur's second campaign, the advance northward toward Salamaua, Lae, and Finschaven, was shaped by these considerations. The weight of Allied air attacks on Japanese bases in New Guinea steadily increased in the summer of 1943. A 123-ton raid on Salamaua on July 23 was followed by a 177-ton raid on August 14. Then all Allied air power was suddenly thrown against Japanese plane concentrations at

Wewak (August 14–19). Some 250 Japanese planes were caught on the ground and destroyed by Allied bombers. Having won local air supremacy over the Salamaua front, MacArthur was ready to begin his advance early in September.

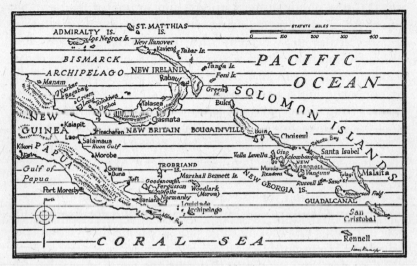

Southwest Pacific Area

General MacArthur now had naval as well as land and air forces under his command. The success with which he carried off his first aero-amphibian campaign shows that he adapted himself rapidly to the particular requirements of island warfare. Allied staff work was of a high order; General Blamey's operations book for the Salamaua-Lae thrust was said to be "fatter than *Gone with the Wind*." Air supremacy enabled MacArthur to surprise and deceive the Japanese command. Part of this deception arose from MacArthur's conventional approach to Salamaua, north and south of the Francisco River as if an orthodox attack was intended. Then, before the advance on Salamaua was driven home, heavy air raids softened both Salamaua and Lae, and Australian infantry and American engineers were landed at Singaua Plantation, 12 miles east of Lae. The beachhead which they established cut off Lae and Salamaua from Japanese reinforcements moving overland. Almost simultaneously a great fleet of American transport planes dropped a paratroop force behind the Japanese lines west of Lae. General MacArthur witnessed the landing from his own Flying Fortress *Bataan,* where Signal Corps photographers caught him in one of his best "action shots" of the war, pointing out of the waist-gun window at the spectacular mass descent into the Markham Valley. The triple envelopment of Salamaua and Lae doomed the garrisons trapped inside them, and after bitter fighting Salamaua fell on September 11 and Lae five days later. Both areas were said to be covered with "masses of wreckage and bomb craters." More than 6,000 Japanese troops were killed in these operations.

Without giving the Japanese commander time to strengthen his forces on the Huon Peninsula, General MacArthur moved against Finschaven. American engineers rushed the Lae airfield into condition for use and another mass landing of paratroops near Kaiapit cut off Finschaven from the northwest. This base fell after 11 days of fighting and gave the Allies virtual control of the Huon Gulf.

These neat and economical operations were impressive for their precision and swiftness. One Australian correspondent described them as "beautiful as a ballet." Brigadier General Charles A. Willoughby, chief of intelligence at Allied headquarters in Australia and author of the well-known book *Maneuver in War,* assured the correspondents on November 15, 1943, that in his opinion "the masterly co-ordination of ground, sea, and air had not had a more brilliant exhibition in modern times." In MacArthur's shifting of his air, sea, and ground balance from one area to another, he found an apt comparison to Lee's celebrated Chancellorsville maneuver. He closed his press conference by describing MacArthur as "a fellow craftsman in a distinguished historical company of great commanders—Napoleon as well as Lee." No complaint about the inarticulateness of the military could appropriately be leveled at this headquarters!

VI

WHILE General MacArthur was completing these operations against the Japanese in New Guinea, the United States navy was gradually building up its strength in the Pacific. After hard fighting, marine and United States army units won complete control of Guadalcanal. Since General MacArthur's zone of authority extended to 160° east latitude and this line ran directly through Guadalcanal, a new division of authority was obviously necessary. When the tide of the American invasion moved westward and north from Guadalcanal, General MacArthur assumed general control of operations in the Solomons.

He was now able to direct a constantly expanding series of blows at Rabaul, the main Japanese base on New Britain Island. Forces under his command occupied Trobriand and Woodlark Islands on June 30, and air bases were rapidly established. Following the invasion of the Gilberts by the United States navy in November, General MacArthur made ready to invade New Britain. Marine and army forces of the United States Sixth Army (Lieutenant General Walter C. Krueger) under the tactical command of Brigadier General Julian W. Cunningham landed on Arawe Peninsula on December 15. Heavy naval and air bombardment preceded the landing which was made at relatively low cost in casualties. By December 19, the enemy air strip at Arawe was captured and General MacArthur then switched his air power to an assault on Cape Gloucester. Four hundred tons of bombs were dropped on Japanese installations in this area on December 19. This was followed by a 300-ton raid on December 23. Four days later the United States Marines under command of Major General W. H. Rupertus landed on the eastern and western sides of Cape Gloucester. In three days of bitter fighting, they captured the enemy air strip and moved forward toward Borgen Bay.

From his central position General MacArthur now lashed out at the enemy from two directions. On January 2, 1944, units of the Sixth United States Army landed at Saidor, New Guinea, 55 miles southeast of Madang. Australian units moving over land joined the American forces 14 miles east of Saidor on February 11, completing Allied control of the Huon Peninsula. At the close of this operation, General MacArthur's headquarters reported that in 18 weeks of fighting on New Guinea, Allied armies had defeated or destroyed a force of 14,000 Japanese troops.

Gradually the Allied net closed in about the Japanese forces in the Solomons. On January 31, 1944, United States forces invaded the Marshalls and captured Kwajalein. Incessant Allied air attacks now rendered the enemy use of Rabaul increasingly difficult and costly. Air reconnaissance on February 10 revealed that the enemy was withdrawing naval vessels and transports from this port. The gradual Allied advance against Rabaul was continued on February 16 when the Green (Nissen) Islands were occupied by American forces. This advance cut off an estimated force of 22,000 Japanese troops on Choiseul, Shortland, Bougainville, and Buka. In the words of General MacArthur: "For all strategic military purposes this step completed the campaign for the Solomon Islands."

The pattern of the reconquest of the Pacific islands now began to be apparent. The Allied high command no longer sought to capture each individual island in series. A massive carrier force enabled them to throw overpowering air forces at first one island group and then another, isolating Japanese garrisons on intervening islands. These troops were condemned to military impotence through gradual exhaustion of supplies and lack of air support. Heavy Japanese losses in merchant shipping made it impossible for them to supply outlying garrisons, and the enemy attempted to make up for his deficiency in transports by the use of wooden barges. More and more the matter of supply became a paramount factor in the Pacific war; and supply was inextricably bound up with control of the air.

Allied superiority in the air was soon felt in all Pacific theaters. A Japanese convoy attempting to escape from Rabaul was intercepted by Allied bombers on February 15–16 with a loss of

MacARTHUR Watching the Landing of Allied Paratroops near
Lae

15 vessels. As if to emphasize Japanese air and naval inferiority, an American carrier force boldly raided Truk on February 20, and on the same day American surface craft shelled Rabaul and Kavieng. These shocking events caused the immediate dismissal of the Japanese army and navy chiefs of staff.

Taking advantage of Japanese weakness in that area, General MacArthur ordered an invasion of the Admiralty Islands north of New Britain on February 29. Under the cover of air and naval transport, the 1st United States Cavalry Division under the command of Major General I. Palmer Swift landed on Los Negros Island and completed most of its occupation in nine days.

So swiftly had the tide of battle turned that Admiral Chester W. Nimitz told newsmen on March 7, 1944, that the main obstacle to progress in the Pacific was not enemy material or resistance—but space.

VII

GENERAL MACARTHUR has been away from the United States for several years. He has fought most of his World War II battles in close co-operation with the Australians. It is worthwhile, therefore, to give the views of one of their distinguished journalists on the character and achievements of the American leader.[7] The Australians admit that General MacArthur is still something of a mystery to them—"yet his popularity in Australia has never wavered." Prime Minister Curtin "would cut off his right arm if MacArthur asked for it." The Australians are "proud of the Americans and grateful for what they have done." The Australian-Yank fighter-air transport-engineer team is making history and developing new techniques in the Southwest Pacific. If American reporters have sometimes been less than just to the predominant fighting role played by the Australians in New Guinea (five out of six troops in that theater were Australian)

[7] The material in this paragraph is based on George H. Johnston's *Pacific Partner* (New York, 1944), pp. 105–118 *et. seq.*

MacArthur has gone out of his way repeatedly to correct this. The American commander is a stanch friend of General ("Typhoid Tom") Blamey. If the Australian troops have at times been disappointed at what one Australian correspondent called General MacArthur's "remoteness," they now have become accustomed to his practice of supervising military operations by working through their officers. When General MacArthur arrived in Australia in 1942, they regarded him as the greatest soldier in the world; after two years of fighting under his command their conviction on this point has increased rather than diminished.

At this stage of the war no one can foretell what General MacArthur's full role in its triumphant conclusion will be. His views about a desirable strategy for the war against Japan have not yet been fully employed because of commitments elsewhere. Nothing would satisfy him more than to lead a liberating force back to the Philippines where his army fought and lost its first great battle. Such an event would be the crowning experience to an unusually rich military life. Few soldiers are permitted by fate to win back a great province that was lost under their care.

On his record to date General MacArthur has shown a marked readiness to learn from experience and a capacity to utilize the full potentialities of air warfare. He became a theater commander after having filled the highest peacetime positions in the United States army. Among American soldiers in high command today, he is the only man to have commanded as large a unit as a division in the last war. For many months General MacArthur patiently learned from defeats inflicted by an enemy superior in all phases of modern war. When once equipped and prepared for aero-amphibious war, his conduct of operations has been imaginative, skillful, and highly economical.

General MacArthur has survived personal gifts of intellect, charm, and language which would have proved fatal to all but the strongest of men. He is certain to rank among the great soldiers of his day.

CHIANG KAI-SHEK

CHIANG KAI-SHEK

☆

"In the beginning make it impossible for the enemy to win and then await the time for the enemy to be defeated."—SUN TZU

NO leader of World War II presents more perplexing problems, more baffling psychological obstacles to a western biographer than Generalissimo Chiang Kai-shek. Rendered inaccessible to all but his most intimate western acquaintances by barriers of language and culture, complemented and in a sense "impresarioed" by a wife of exquisite charm, matchless eloquence, and a sure knowledge of American mores, aided by a corps of subtle aides whose methods and effectiveness are sources of bewilderment and admiration to foreign observers, Chiang has already become a legendary figure.

Most Americans know China only through books. We feel a sense of guilt for the hardships which our previous policy has inflicted on the people of China. We have admired their long and unequal struggle against a barbaric invader. Thus we have built up an idealized picture of fighting China and its leaders which—American visitors to wartime Chungking tell us—is shattered at the first direct contact with reality. The visitor who experiences it for the first time is unprepared for the sight and smell of China's poverty, suffering, and filth. He compares the willingness of the lowly worker or peasant to fight, work, and starve for China's future with the venality of a small circle of political leaders and businessmen who seek to profit by China's misery and danger. The first reaction of a visitor is to blame the generalissimo. But the longer he stays, the more clearly he sees the immense and insoluble character of some of China's problems—and the greatness of Chiang's achievements.

One experienced American student of Chinese affairs has

flatly asserted that no westerner can possibly "understand" Chiang. Disciple and heir of Dr. Sun Yat-sen, political and military reformer, champion of nationalism, enemy and coworker of the provincial war lords and communists, Chiang has been hailed by many as the "maker of modern China" and condemned by others as a reactionary opponent of the advancement of the masses. To some he appears as the personification of Christian leadership, to others as a politician whose opportunism verges upon cynicism. On one point there can be no dispute: through the confusion of China's emergence as a national state, amid the trials and sufferings of revolutions and war, the generalissimo towers above all his countrymen.

First modern practitioner of the military strategy of the scorched earth and the defense in very great depth, convinced believer in the capacity of China's depressed millions to wage effective resistance and to endure the suffering entailed, willing to trade space on a gigantic scale for time, Chiang has achieved one of the greatest military feats in history. For seven terrible years, in which he repeatedly warned the democracies against the real purposes and menace of the Axis, he kept the flame of Chinese resistance burning. He has engaged Japanese military resources, which if expended elsewhere would have placed the other United Nations under far greater strategic handicaps than they now face. He has not only defended the inner ramparts of his country but united his people as they have never been united before. By his tenacity and willingness to endure early slights and injuries by Britain and America, he finally won the assurance that all China's losses since 1895 will be restored after Japan's defeat, and that humiliating restrictions on her sovereignty dating back to the days of western imperialism will be ended. In the fulfillment of Chiang's career and of the promises he has received from the United Nations at the Cairo Conference lies China's chief hope of recovering from her incalculable losses and establishing the future greatness and welfare of her tortured people on an enduring basis.

All these things he has accomplished under conditions difficult enough to break all but the strongest or dismay all but the most tenacious of men. It is against these very great achievements and against the confused background of China's still continuing "emergence from medievalism under a thin crust of modernity" that one must weigh the charges of Chiang's manifold critics.

One student of the China war has dealt with the "might-have-beens" as follows:

China should have started guerrilla activity immediately and should never have made a stand at Shanghai; she should have resolved differently her Kuomintang-Communist differences; she should have adopted earlier the scorched earth policy; she should have moved more of her Shanghai industry to the interior. . . . Yet wars are never as they should be but as they are. China's strength, like Japan's weakness, is a compound of mistake and of genius. . . .[1]

Those who find fault with the generalissimo for failing to institute sound agrarian reforms, for delaying the establishment of a long-range economic program, for tolerating incompetence and venality in Kuomintang circles, could conceivably complain with equal justification at the Creator's failure, amid His other labors to fashion man more convincingly in His own image. One makes revolution and war as one must, not as one would like to.

II

THE generalissimo was born in Chikow, Chekiang Province, on October 31, 1888, the eldest son in a family of five children. After his father's death, the modest resources of his family were devoted to educating Chiang. Like many other great men, Chiang was deeply influenced by his mother who "inculcated a sharp morality, an unrelenting frugality, and a persistent industriousness in her children." His own success in surmounting handicaps of poverty and hardship may have given Chiang an instinctive impatience with the poor and uneducated, and inclined him to regard poverty in the abstract as a personal prob-

[1] Herrymon Maurier, *The End Is Not Yet* (New York, 1941), pp. 82–83.

lem. Thus "leftist commentators, dubbing Chiang a product of landlordism and compradore class interests—explain him through a mystagogic economic determinism" arising from his youthful struggles and success. His deeply spiritual nature was also developed through the example and teachings of his mother. Chiang grew up with a sense of the infinite looming over him. Indoctrinated with the discipline and austerity of Buddhism, he was spiritually prepared to embrace Christianity when it came to him with noteworthy zeal and effect.

As a result of his preliminary education, Chiang "went modern" in 1907 and cut off his queue. In the following year he entered the Paotingfu Imperial Military Academy near Peking. From Paotingfu he went to the Shinbo Gokyo preparatory military academy in Japan. During three years of study in Japan he served with a Japanese artillery regiment (the 13th or Takada Regiment), and joined the Tungmenhei, a secret Chinese patriotic society which prepared the way for the Kuomintang. When the Chinese revolution broke out in 1911, Chiang returned to Shanghai where he began his political and military career as a supporter of Sun Yat-sen.

For Chiang the 10-year period from 1911 to 1921 was filled with diffuse and apparently meaningless activity. He was still just another partially trained young military leader lost in the confusion and failures of the early revolutionary movement. At this stage he hoped to solve China's problems by random bursts of platitudes and well-directed bursts of small-arms fire. Disheartened by Sun Yat-sen's inept military projects, Chiang "retired" for several years to become a Shanghai broker and protégé of Chang Ching-chiang, a wealthy supporter of Dr. Sun. During this period Chiang amassed a considerable personal fortune, a fact which has caused the envious to charge that he was a member of the notorious Shanghai "Green Gang," an organization combining "the features of a protective racket and a benevolent society." These charges, though widely repeated, have never been substantiated. How he earned his money is of less interest than the fact that it in no way dulled his sense of moral and spiritual values or weakened his desire to serve his country. One event of far-reaching consequences for his future career took place in 1921 when his unhappy marriage to a Miss Mao of Fenghua was terminated by divorce. Six years later he was to marry Mei-ling Soong.

The interruption of his military career by the Shanghai interlude ended in 1923; Dr. Sun Yat-sen detailed him as military observer and liaison officer to Moscow under the terms of the new agreement with the Soviet Union. Here a new world opened before Chiang's eyes. Familiar with both Japanese and Chinese military and political institutions, he was now to see the merging of military and political doctrines into a unified revolutionary effort. He came back convinced of the need for military reforms as a basis for further developments of the Chinese Revolution. With him came General Vassili Blücher (Galens) who was to become Soviet military adviser and coworker with Chiang at Canton.

He was apparently able to instill some of his new zeal for military reform into Dr. Sun Yat-sen, for in the year before he died Sun established the Whampoa Military Academy in Canton and gave Chiang the task of training cadets for the new Nationalist army. During a two-year course at the academy the prospective officers of the new army were given basic training in military science, indoctrinated with nationalism, and taught to safeguard the mental and moral as well as the physical welfare of their men. If they came out of their training with a well-developed sense of loyalty to the nation, it was only natural that most of these officers should also extend their personal loyalty to Chiang, who was appointed commander in chief of the Nationalist army in 1926, charged with carrying out a great campaign of unification in the north.

Dr. Sun Yat-sen died in 1925, and Chiang rose to a position of dominance in Chinese affairs in the two-year "northern campaign" from 1926 to 1928. Leading the Nationalist army of 21 divisions, he moved against the provincial armies of Wu-Pei-fu, Chang Tso-lin, Chang Tsung-chang, and Sun Chuanfang. For the first time, since the campaigns of Tso Tsung-tang (1868–78), Chinese armies moved through the countryside without robbing the people. By maneuvers, battles, and "silver bullets," the armies of the provincial war lords were eliminated or absorbed. Chiang kept communist elements and practices, such as the system of political commissars with the troops and communist "advisers," in the Nationalist army until 1927. Then he abruptly purged the Kuomintang and the army. When he captured Peking in July, 1928, Chiang had all the four major political divisions of the Kuomintang party united under his leadership. He was now the chief figure in Chinese life.

The rapid "conquest" of China from 1926 to 1928 convinced Chiang of the value of outside military advisers. Having got rid of his Soviet advisers in 1927, Chiang now imported German military experts to assist him in building up the Chinese army.

The first to arrive was Colonel Max Bauer, who formed the Central Military Academy at Nanking, instituted refresher courses for Whampoa graduates, and set up a model division for training the officers of new divisions. Specialist schools were later established for artillery, antiaircraft, tanks, communications, and staff work. Colonel Bauer was widely credited with the swift crushing of General Li Tsung-jen's revolt in 1929. The influence of his training also appeared in the surprisingly effective resistance of the Chinese 19th Route Army to the Japanese at Shanghai in 1932. Chiang's next advisers were Colonel Kriebel, Major General Wetzell, and General Hans von Seeckt. Creator of the German Reichswehr, Seeckt was a brilliant soldier whose education, manners, culture, and professional skill made a deep impression on Chiang. Seeckt stressed the necessity of accompanying military reforms with the establishment of basic war industries in China. Only in this way could China become militarily self-sufficient. He and his successor, General Alexander von Falkenhausen, worked hard to raise the quality of military instruction offered at Nanking and to improve the staff work of the army. Before much progress could be made, however, the long-smoldering war with Japan broke out in 1937.

In June, 1938, the nazi government, with its eye on the Japanese end of the Axis, recalled General von Falkenhausen and his staff. By that time Chiang was deep in his war with Japan and, though hostilities revealed some officers of extraordinary skill and competence, he never had anything like enough trained combat officers to direct China's vast but ill-equipped armies. Colonel Claire Chennault was brought in to supervise the Chinese air force in 1937, but until American planes and pilots were available in 1942, he could do little to limit the effects of Japan's overwhelming air superiority.

The agelong desire of Chinese patriots for a unified China under a strong and just government was not accomplished merely with Chiang's conquest of the provincial war lords in 1926–28. He soon found himself at loggerheads with the communists and determined to crush their attempts at political and military autonomy.

From 1932 onward Chiang faced two fateful problems: what to do about the Japanese piecemeal conquest of northern China and what to do about the Reds. To the great annoyance and disappointment of many of his former supporters, Chiang merely seemed to dabble with preparations for the inevitable clash with Japan and spent most of his time and energy trying to crush the Reds in Kiangsi. His long-range program of road building from 1931 to 1937 was, in fact, a preparation for war —but was not recognized as such at the time. He launched four campaigns against the communists from 1933 to 1934 and finally drove the Kiangsi Soviet, led by Chu Teh and Mao-Tse-tung, to undertake the greatest military mass migration in history. For 6,000 miles they marched through Kiangsi, Kwangsi, Kweichow, Yünnan, Szechwan, Sikang, Tsinghai, and Kansu, into far northern Shensi. But even this remarkable demonstration of leadership, discipline, and will to survive did not change Chiang's attitude toward the Reds. If anything it may have increased his determination to destroy so potentially dangerous a faction before the rest of China was "infected."

After 1932 the northern Chinese armies showed little interest in helping Chiang battle against the Reds. They had been driven out of their homes by the Japanese and preferred a national war against the invader. When other methods failed to convince Chiang that he should end his battle against the Reds and embark on war against Japan, the "young marshal" Chang Hsueh-liang "kidnaped" him at Sian on December 12, 1936.

The Sian coup (December 12–24, 1936) marked a turning point in Chiang's career and in China's history. This fantastic affair could only have taken place in China in late 1936. In it, spiritual, national, economic, and political forces unique to China were suddenly brought into melodramatic crisis. When the young marshal demanded that Chiang stop his war against the Reds and unite China against the Japanese, the generalissimo refused to negotiate with him though his life was at stake.

Finally, after protracted and infinitely delicate negotiations, Madame Chiang, T. V. Soong, and W. H. Donald (Chiang's Australian adviser), who joined the deadlocked conference, saved face all around. They got Chiang into a plane bound for Nanking with his erstwhile captor riding as a penitent stowaway in the pilot's compartment. Resignations, recriminations, self-condemnations followed from nearly all the participants of the Sian affair. But when all was said and done, Chiang dropped his battle against the Reds and made ready to resist Japan. When the famous Liukouchiao incident of July 7, 1937, precipitated the Sino-Japanese War, Chiang was supported by all the important armies and leaders of China.

III

THE Japanese conquest of China began in 1931 with the occupation of Manchuria, was followed by the absorption of Jehol (1933), Chahar and Suiyuan (1936). Some Chinese leaders assert that Chiang was aware of the necessity for resisting Japan as early as 1934 but felt that China was not then ready to risk all on the outcome of military operations alone. They imply that his conception of the coming struggle involved the use of all weapons: political, psychological, spiritual, and diplomatic. By resorting to war, even an undeclared war, China would be deprived of some of her slender stock of weapons. Chiang's addresses to his officers in 1934 are said to substantiate these claims. Finally, in July, 1937, Chiang felt that Japan's aggressions could no longer be borne. He called upon the Chinese people to sacrifice everything if necessary to resist Japan.

What resources could Chiang count upon in his war against Japan? According to Major Evans F. Carlson of the United States Marine Corps, one of the shrewdest foreign observers then in China, there were about 200 Chinese divisions of 1,260 rifles each in 1937. These were organized into approximately 100 corps and 50 armies. Chiang's own German-trained Kuomintang army numbered about 300,000 men; they were the most efficient force at Chiang's disposal for positional warfare on the European model. Other troops varied in value depending on their leaders, or as in the case of the Kwangsi-Kwantung troops, on their willingness to submerge the class struggle in the national war. The communist armies were of little use in positional operations but proved to be amazingly resourceful and effective in guerrilla warfare and in organizing the inhabitants of conquered areas for resistance.

The equipment and supply of the Chinese army was one of its greatest weaknesses. Lacking industries, China had to rely on foreign purchase for most of its military equipment. Since the years in which she purchased the bulk of her war matériel were years in which the Axis nations were preparing for their own wars of aggression, China never did get first-line weapons. She bought arms where they could be obtained and complicated her already grave supply and maintenance problem with a profusion of calibers and types of weapons. Her tanks and planes were not only of foreign manufacture and limited in number, but her crews and pilots had little or no experience in operating with other forces. Limited training and ammunition supply reduced the value of such artillery as the Chinese army possessed. So, in the last analysis, it was a vast army of infantry on which

Chiang relied to defeat the well-equipped modern armies of Japan.

It is futile to argue that Chiang should have built up a better army in the years from 1928 to 1937. The traditional Chinese concept of the soldier as occupying the lowest rank in society made it impossible to create the psychological and spiritual foundations for a formidable military force in a matter of a few years. Yet there may be some basis to the charge that Chiang's attitude toward the Reds, his distaste for their ideas, his fear of arming the rural masses, the opposition of certain Kuomintang circles, prevented anything like a total mobilization of China's strength in 1937. Edgar Snow points out that despite its immensely greater population China could actually mobilize fewer men at the outbreak of war than Japan.

The potential greatness of the Chinese peasant-soldier has been attested by numerous western observers. He may lack education or mechanical aptitude, but he shows a pathetic eagerness to die for any cause he can understand or leader he can trust. His endurance is phenomenal. The idea that the average Chinese does not respond to training is refuted by Major Carlson, who wrote:

The average Chinese (civilian or soldier) is unusually intelligent and readily absorbs instruction. He is resourceful and possesses initiative. He is traditionally loyal to his family, and is faithful to the point of death to a leader who treats him with consideration. He responds readily to kindness and justice. Basically he is honest and truthful. He appears to lack nerves. He is inured to privation and physical hardship, and he meets death with the same philosophical realism with which he has faced life.[2]

In addition to the vast manpower of China, Chiang could count the immense distances and broken character of the country as important factors in his defense plans.[3] If China lacked modern industries, she had years of experience in the decen-

[2] *The Chinese Army* (New York, 1940), p. 40.
[3] The Japanese failure to appreciate the military importance of vast space in China's defense plans was pointed out by the German correspondent Wolf Schenke in an article entitled "Vast Space as an Instrument of War," *Zeitschrift für Geopolitik*, September, 1938.

tralized system of domestic manufacture. If she lacked modern communications routes and equipment, the fact hampered the enemy more than the Chinese. Behind China's poverty and apparent helplessness was a massive inertness, a resistance to conquest by mere bulk, and an antlike co-operative spirit by which mere numbers slowly—almost imperceptibly—accomplished miracles.

China's war for survival began uncertainly and without a formal declaration of hostilities on the night of July 6–7, 1937, when Japanese and Chinese troops clashed at Liukouchiao (site of the Marco Polo bridge) near Peiping. For a time, while local Chinese commanders tried to "settle" the incident by negotiations, the Liukouchiao affair had all the appearances of just another brawl between border guards. But the speed with which the Japanese moved infantry divisions into the area from Manchuria showed that they were carrying out a carefully prepared plan. Brushing Chinese troops aside they entered Peiping almost without firing a shot. Before the month was over they had also occupied Tientsin—but only after bitter street fighting.

General Count Juichi Terauchi, former Japanese war minister, at the head of four armies, had as his objective the conquest of northern Shansi, Hopeh, Suiyuan, and western Shantung. Operations in the north clearly illustrated the terrible disadvantages under which the Chinese armies fought in 1937. Under a hail of Japanese bombs or artillery projectiles, many a Chinese soldier died without ever seeing an enemy. Machines and high explosives conquered positions, and infantry merely occupied them. There could be no thought of "holding" the Japanese in this area; Terauchi's armies averaged an advance of 12 kilometers a day for five months.[4]

When the fighting spread to the south, Chiang did not intend to surrender territory without fighting. What prompted him to make a stand at Shanghai was not known, but his German advisers reportedly opposed it. Perhaps he counted on embroiling Japan in a conflict with the foreign powers by staging an all-

[4] Edgar Snow, *The Battle for Asia* (New York, 1941), p. 26.

out battle on the very doorsteps of the foreign concessions.[5] If this was his hope, the heroic defense of Shanghai failed, and Chiang used up a considerable number of his best troops. Yet it is possible that the Japanese excesses in Shanghai—and later in Nanking—were decisive factors in uniting China against the invader.

Admiral Harry E. Yarnell, who had a ringside seat at the fighting on the Yangtze, has expressed the opinion that Japan's real motives in 1937 were to secure the northern provinces of China. If this is true, and the course of the war seems to confirm it, then Chiang's decision to fight at Shanghai diverted Japan from her original objective. Had the Japanese limited their activity to North China in 1937–38, the dismemberment of this area could not have been prevented. By hazarding the destruction of his German-trained troops at Shanghai, Chiang forced Japan to attempt the military defeat of all China. As a consequence, all Japanese strategy since that time may have been conditioned by this step, and even her assault on "Greater East Asia" may have been forced upon Japan because of her failure to win a military decision in China.

As long as the Chinese army at Shanghai fought in fixed positions, its performance was spectacular. No other army thus far put up a more prolonged defense of a given area against a modern Japanese army. It equaled the resistance of the American and Philippine troops at Bataan, but the staff work of the army was not equal to the valor of its troops. Acting on intelligence reports of the relief of Chinese troops on the Hangchow coast early in November, the Japanese struck this area in great strength before the relieving troops had occupied their position. The break-through that followed threatened the whole Chinese position and forced a general retreat.

Chinese plans for holding the so-called "Winter line" (Fushan-Soochow-Kashing) some 50 miles west of Shanghai crumbled

<hr />

[5] In his addresses to Chinese officers at Kuling in July, 1934, Chiang is reported to have said: "Japan cannot conquer China with America in her rear, Soviet Russia on her right, and England on her left. . . ." Quoted in W. H. Mallory, "The Strategy of Chiang Kai-shek," *Foreign Affairs*, XVII, 700 (July, 1939).

when a handful of Japanese scouts trailed the retreating Chinese forces into the walled city of Soochow on the night of November 20. Failure to remove the boats from the eastern shore of Lake Tai enabled the Japanese to cross this water barrier and force a further Chinese withdrawal to the west. Capture of Wuhu by a Japanese flying column cut off Nanking from the west, and on December 13 the Japanese army entered the capital.

The fall of Nanking was followed by a monstrous outbreak of violence and rapine on the part of the Japanese troops. European observers described it as a kind of mass schizophrenia and military mutiny. For weeks whole Japanese divisions gave themselves over to pillage, rapine, and sadistic outrages. An estimated 40,000 Chinese civilians lost their lives in this outbreak. Not only were the Japanese troops out of control but their officers were also. Several divisions had to be quarantined before order could be restored, and General Iwane Matsui, the commander, was replaced by General Shunroku Hata.

The importance of the rape of Nanking was overlooked by an "atrocity-satiated" western world. It gave the badly shaken Chinese forces time to retire to new positions. It steeled every Chinese heart to resist the invader and made the thought of a negotiated peace hateful to all but traitors like Wang Ching-wei. It might have prepared the staffs of western armies for the unexpected suicide frenzy of Japanese troops in 1943 when they were about to lose face in defeat at the hands of white troops at Buna, Attu, and Tarawa. The early impression that the Japanese army at Nanking was deliberately allowed to "blow off steam" by the high command is not shared by all informed observers of the China war. Owen Lattimore is convinced that the army in Nanking was definitely out of control.

Japanese confidence in an early collapse of the government of Chiang Kai-shek was indicated by their premature establishment of pro-Japanese puppet governments in Peking and Nanking. They clearly misjudged the nature of Chiang's strategy which called for a long war, for a retirement into the western provinces, for the scorched earth, guerrilla tactics, a struggle of attrition, and an eventual period of Chinese counteroffensive. He envisaged the war in three general stages:

(*a*) A limited period of positional warfare conducted mainly by the German-trained Koumintang armies.

(*b*) An unlimited period of attrition in which the invaders would be drawn deeply into the interior and enmeshed in a yielding net of Chinese forces.

(*c*) A period of vigorous counteroffensives to follow Japanese exhaustion and the beginning of their retirement toward the coast.

It is in wartime addresses to the Chinese people and the world that Chiang's statesmanship and grasp of military realities are revealed. Speaking to the Chinese people on October 9, 1937, in the midst of the Shanghai battle, Chiang warned that the war would not be finished in six months or a year but would go on until Japan was exhausted. The day after Nanking fell he told his people to prepare for two kinds of Japanese strategy: that of "swallowing like a whale" (a phase of the war in which many important Chinese cities would be captured) and that of "nibbling like a silk worm" (a succeeding phase of the war in which Japan would try to convince the Chinese of the futility of resistance by limited harassing operations and intrigue). He then issued his first futile warning to the western powers. "Japan's present aggression in China," he said, "is really the initial phase of her plan for world conquest." He hoped that the western powers would recognize that the maintenance of China's international rights was a matter of enlightened self-interest. He repeated this warning in various forms throughout the war, but without much effect. The foreign powers were forced to accept repeated humiliations at the hands of the Japanese such as the *Panay* incident (December 12, 1937), the machine-gunning of the British ambassador (August 26, 1937), and the stripping of British civilians in Tientsin (1939). Yet they refused to believe Chiang's insistence that "peace is indivisible, and isolation is impossible."

Chiang followed two patterns of resistance. North of the Yellow River he allowed the Japanese to move without resorting to positional defense. Here the strategy employed by the Chinese was one of guerrilla warfare and the "limitless rear." South of the Yellow River, Chiang concentrated the bulk of his Kuomintang-trained troops and resisted every Japanese advance. The Chinese employed what they called "magnetic" strategy. They lured parts of Japanese columns off in pursuit (as steel filings will follow a moving magnet). When the main column was sufficiently weakened or communications overextended, the Chinese would attack their flanks and rear. This has been their major strategy in several victories. Taierhchwang, Changsha (three battles), Ichang, and others. Because it was the first defeat suffered by the Japanese, the battle of Taierhchwang was of great importance.

Early in February, 1938, the Japanese made a determined effort to crush Chinese resistance at the junction of the Tientsin-Pukow and Lunghai railways but were halted in this attempt by General Li Tsung-jen near Suchow. When this venture failed, three Japanese columns were to converge on Taierhchwang, at the junction of the Lunghai railway and the Grand Canal in March. Two of the columns were held up and the third, a mechanized force estimated at 60,000 men, was trapped at Taierhchwang and barely escaped complete destruction after a savage 18-day battle in which the Chinese troops showed an unexpected capacity for offensive action. Taierhchwang was the first great Chinese victory of the war. It raised the morale and hopes of Chinese people everywhere.

But victories like Taierhchwang and Kaifeng, where the Japanese troops had the dikes of the Yellow River cut behind them in June, 1938, could not prevent the loss of the main Chinese communication centers. One by one the railway nets of China fell into Japanese control, although in the north the guerrillas rendered this control exceedingly tenuous. Finally, after a long bitter campaign up the Yangtze River in which the navy played an extremely important role, the Japanese entered Hankow on October 25.

This blow had been preceded by the sudden capture of Canton on October 21, where Chinese forces, feeling secure against the Japanese attack by the nearness to British Hong Kong, did not take adequate defense measures. The loss of Canton cut the last remaining railway line to any Chinese port; it made China dependent upon imports through French Indo-China and Russia. The fall of Hankow was a severe blow to Chiang, but he resolutely moved his capital westward to Chungking in the almost inaccessible province of Szechwan.

After the evacuation of Hankow, Chiang explained his strategy:

> From the beginning our plan has been to establish the bases of our resistance not along the coast or rivers, or at centers of communication but in the vast interior. . . . Our western provinces are the real bases of our resistance. No momentary vicissitudes can shake our resolution. . . . Our war of resistance differs entirely from wars fought for political supremacy. Ours is a war for the very existence of our nation—for the completion of our national revolution. Being such, it is beyond considerations of time or space. It cannot be blocked by factors of finance, economics, or communications. . . .

IV

THE LOSS of Canton and Hankow ended the "eastern" phase of the war and led to the Chungking or "western" phase of resistance. In its clifflike retreat on the junction of the Yangtze and Kialing rivers the Chinese government was virtually cut off from contact with the outside world. At first sight it seemed impossible for a landlocked agrarian state like China to continue resistance against an industrial maritime power whose ships moved freely on every ocean. But the extreme peril of China's position and the misfortunes that forced her to rely on her own resources compensated in part for the loss of supplies from foreign countries. The movement of the government to Chungking was followed by a mass migration of millions of civilians from the zones of Japanese control into the interior. Whole industries were dismantled and moved 1,000 miles into Szechwan. Small factories were built in the western provinces and co-operatives established on a large scale. China became virtually self-sufficient, although no European people (except perhaps the Russians) could have endured the hardships this involved.

The strength of China's resolution to continue the war overcame the disappointments of the year 1939. The Japanese army controlled hundreds of thousands of square miles of Chinese territory, but that control shrank every night to within sight of the nearest Japanese sentry. Chinese guerrilla armies, particularly the Eighth Route and the New Fourth armies, operated effectively in the north and brought the war to the very doorsteps of Peiping and Shanghai. They made sporadic raids on railways and communication lines, ambushed small Japanese units, and organized the peasants for passive resistance. According to the *China Handbook, 1937–1943* at one time there were 800,000 guerrillas operating behind the Japanese lines. The amount of damage they inflicted and the extent to which they hindered the enemy cannot be estimated—but it must have been considerable.

Unfortunately the New Fourth Army proved to be unreliable. Its leader General Yeh Ting disobeyed orders from the generalissimo and made a surprise attack on the Chinese 40th Division on January 1, 1941. As a result this army was disbanded on January 12 and its commander placed under arrest.

On more than one occasion Chiang has resorted to severe measures in order to stamp out treachery, incompetence, and venality among higher commanders. General Li Fu-ying evacuated Tatung in Shansi province in the early days of the war. He was condemned to death by court-martial in September, 1937, and executed. General Han Fu-Chu, governor of Shantung, failed to defend his province and was executed on January 24, 1938. General Shih Yu-san, governor of Chahar, disobeyed orders from the central government and imposed illegal levies on the people. He was shot by a firing squad on December 8, 1940.

After the disaffection and disbanding of the New Fourth

Army, the main guerrilla force operating against Japan was the famous communist Eighth Route Army (now called the 18th Army Group) under General Chu Teh. At the end of the year 1943 it was estimated that some 356,000 guerrillas were still in the field, but the extent to which these armies are dependent upon or are controlled by Chungking is not clear. The discipline and orderliness of these forces, the character, skill, and unselfishness of their leaders, the effective functioning of their cooperative way of life, the loyalty they inspired in the inhabitants of their districts—these will be among the legacies carried into the postwar life of China.

With the end of 1939 the Japanese strategy in China underwent a marked change. From this time on they acted as if the military phase of the China war was ended and the political phase had begun. With the principal Chinese railways, cities, and ports in their hands, with China practically isolated from the outside world, with a great European war about to break out, they felt able to force China to accept defeat by economic and political pressure, accompanied by occasional set-piece military operations.

The Japanese set up a new puppet government under Wang Ching-wei at Nanking on March 30, 1940, but this traitorous former coworker with Chiang had no more success in breaking down Chinese will to resist than his luckless and less distinguished forerunners. The common Chinese expression about Wang's government is: "It equals nothing."

The fall of France enabled the Japanese to extend their control of the approaches to China by occupying French islands and Indo-China. Thus the war in China became synchronized with the Axis war in Europe, although the fact was not clearly recognized by the western powers. Japan used the period from 1940 to December, 1941, to prepare for her long-planned conquest of British, Dutch, and American possessions in the Far East. China provided an ideal training ground for her armies. The skill in landing operations, the mastery of jungle fighting, the march discipline and endurance shown in the conquest of

Malaya, the Philippines, and the Dutch East Indies were not developed in training camps; they were the by-products of the war in China.

The view was once widely held that the Japanese deliberately "held back" in China, that they used only their second-line troops and planes, that they faked an incompetence in the air (for example, their failure to bomb Chungking into surrender) in order to lull the western powers into making a false estimate of their strength, equipment, and methods. This concept, like that of Russia's alleged "purposeful blundering" in Finland to misguide the German general staff, does not stand up under examination. To an alert American news correspondent like Hallet Abend, it was a mystery why the rest of the world continued to believe that the Japanese were poor fliers, inaccurate bombers, and inefficient artillerymen. In order to warn our people against underestimating the Japanese in the air, he wrote an article for the *Saturday Evening Post* (April 19, 1941) entitled "Yes, the Japanese Can Fly." He described the new Japanese Zero fighter, its astonishing speed and maneuverability in some detail. But, he adds, this portion of the manuscript was deleted by the publishers on advice of the "authorities" who apparently did not believe it.[6]

The idea that Japanese artillery practice and military equipment was below European or American standards was also a part of this myth. Yet it must be pointed out that even trained professional observers gave currency to some of these beliefs. For example, Major Carlson, who was later to achieve fame as leader of the Marine Corps Raider Battalion on Makin and Guadalcanal, wrote:

> After observing the Japanese operations at Shanghai for three months, I characterized the army as third rate, as compared with the armies of the Western Powers. My observations during the succeeding year confirmed this appraisal. It is based on inferiority of striking power, poor coordination of transport, poor coordination of the air force with ground troops, inferior-

[6] Hallet Abend, *My Life in China, 1926–1941* (New York, 1943), pp. 265–266.

ity of weapons, poor direction of artillery fire, and lack of imagination and initiative on the part of leaders.[7]

One must conclude that *if* the Japanese army was that bad in 1937–38, then the training it received in China from 1938–41 made it one of the most formidable military forces in the world. Perhaps it was the easy, comfortable thing to do to ignore the realities of the China war and to assume that because they could not end the war on their own terms, the Japanese were inept and inefficient fighters.

Certain aspects of Japanese strategy in China, like some of their naval operations in the Pacific, are difficult to explain according to western concepts of warfare. If the complete military defeat of China was intended, then three strategic keys to the heart of China had to be captured and held. These were the province of Shansi, the crossing of the Yellow River at T'ungkuan, and the Han River valley. According to Owen Lattimore, these three "keys" to China have the following strategic importance:

> The northern mountains of Shansi offer the only good defense in depth against an invasion of North China from Inner Mongolia, and by far the best base for a counterattack against Inner Mongolia. The eastern mountains of Shansi dominate the North China plain. . . . The southern Shansi mountains flank the approaches to T'ungkuan, the second key of strategy. All of these mountains are held by Chinese forces, which are able to keep the Japanese garrison in the central basin of Shansi under perpetual siege.

> T'ungkuan . . . offers the only good passage between the major plain of North China and the inner basin of Shensi. Command of the T'ungkuan passage is absolutely necessary for the movement either of large bodies of troops or of economic transport on a large scale, if the deep hinterland of China is to be controlled. Only from Shensi can Szechwan . . . be invaded.

> The Han River valley, from the southern mountains of Shensi to the Yangtze at Hankow, is the only way of turning the T'ungkuan position, as T'ungkuan is the only way of turning the Shansi position.[8]

Yet the Japanese high command was unwilling to throw in enough men and material to capture and hold these keys.

[7] *Twin Stars Over China* (New York, 1940), p. 301.
[8] "Stalemate in China," *Foreign Affairs*, XIX, 622 (April, 1941).

Japanese strategy in China makes sense only if the role of the navy in the China war is adequately understood. Too little attention has been paid to this side of the war. We forget that the occupation of the coastal cities, the conquests of the river cities, were the results of amphibious operations. Perhaps Japan was testing out in China the expanded aero-amphibious strategy which characterized her attack on Britain, Holland, and the United States.

If this is true, then Japan's refusal to expend enough men and equipment to take and hold the strategic keys of China becomes understandable. Japan might well have felt that time was on her side, and that China would collapse when Japan completed the conquest of "Greater East Asia," and when the trickle of supplies which reached China over the Burma Road was cut off.

V

ONE OF the hopes that sustained Chiang throughout the long years from 1937 to 1941 was that the great western democracies, Britain and the United States, would see the folly of their efforts to appease Japan, would cease to supply her with the materials of war, and would ultimately join China in the war. Because he held such a high opinion of the military and naval power of these countries, Chiang's disappointment at the series of defeats that Britain and the United States suffered from December 7, 1941, to May, 1942, was profound. It is quite possible that he and his military advisers assumed that Japan had put forth her full military effort in China and had failed. They regarded the Japanese attack on the western powers as a kind of military and naval hara-kiri, not as a carefully worked out plan which had a fair chance of succeeding. Chiang expressed this opinion in an address on May 10, 1941, when he declared that "the inconsiderable caliber of Japan would make nonsense of an attempt on her part to grapple with the United States." [9]

[9] *Resistance and Reconstruction: Messages during China's Six Years of War, 1937–1943* (New York, 1943), p. 245.

As a result of the United Nations decision to regard nazi Germany as the first and main adversary, China's position deteriorated with each Japanese victory in the Pacific. At the close

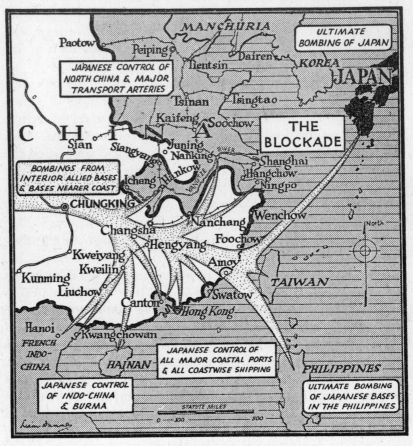

The China War Zone

of the Burma campaign she was entirely cut off from contact with her allies except by air. Spiritual depression and financial inflation followed. During this period Chiang could only repeat his assurance that Japan could never win if China's resistance was maintained. If he could not gain impressive military victories, he at least won notable diplomatic triumphs. On January 11, 1943, Britain and the United States signed treaties with China abolishing extraterritorial rights and special privileges. At the end of the year came the Cairo Conference with guarantees that all of China's territorial losses at the hands of Japan since 1895 would be restored.

A small American air force operated in China during the year 1943, and Chinese troops trained for the eventual liberation of their country. In the spring of 1944 Chinese and United States troops began joint operations in northern Burma. What part Chiang and his troops will play in the final defeat of Japan is not clear, but an increasing body of military and naval opinion holds that the destruction of the Japanese army must take place on the mainland of China. There, after gigantic logistic problems are solved, the full advantages of the mechanized power of the United Nations can be realized.

There we would deal, not with elite troops or Imperial Marines who will fight on remote islands to solitary annihilation or suicide, but with the great mass of the Japanese army whose conduct to date has given no indication that it is capable of similar action. We may be surprised to find that Japanese troops defeated en masse will do what small groups of elite troops will not do—surrender in masses.

But Chiang's work will not end with the inevitable victory over Japan. Before him will stand the equally formidable task of translating the victory into a more abundant and secure life for his gallant, long-suffering people.

EISENHOWER

☆

"The degree of co-operation attained in his command was the greatest single Allied achievement of the war."

A GROUND, sea, or air officer can study his craft in peacetime and perfect his skill in maneuvers, but there is no school for theater commanders of democratic allies in a coalition war—except war itself. Once the governments concerned have jointly chosen a commander for such tasks, they can only wait for events to show whether or not the officer selected has the qualities required. Normal standards and methods of selection are of limited usefulness for such appointments.

What qualifications must a theater commander possess in order to conduct the joint operations of democratic allies with success in modern coalition war? He must be an expert in the theory and practice of modern war. He must know within extremely close limits the capacities of both men and machines. He must be an organizer and administrator of the highest order. He must be a driving executive but at the same time a tactful co-ordinator and diplomat. Where others merely command he must also convince. Articulateness is almost as necessary as professional competence. He must have elasticity of mind far beyond that required of commanders in past wars. Energy, untiring patience, searching vigilance, a sure sense of long-term values, a keen appreciation of the national interests of all groups concerned, must mark his every action. He must win and maintain public support of all the national elements in his command. And when the fateful issues are finally put to the supreme test of battle, an iron will and unshakable confidence in all his subordinates must sustain him in the loneliness of high command.

Had anyone ventured to tell a lieutenant colonel in the United

EISENHOWER

States army, named Dwight D. Eisenhower, who was commanding an infantry regiment in 1940, that he possessed all these qualities to a marked degree, the friendly, open-faced young officer would have broken into laughter or been keenly annoyed, depending on how well he knew the offender. Yet within two years this virtually unknown officer had successfully carried out the complicated "triphibian" operation of the North African landing so effectively that he set a standard for future commanders.

Whatever the shortcomings of our army program of officer training and selection may be, it should be of some comfort for Americans to know that General Marshall could see in a young and relatively obscure officer like Eisenhower, who had never commanded troops in combat, the qualities required for command in a kind of war for which our national policy made little or no preparation possible. It speaks equally well for Churchill's judgment that he could accept such an appointment without reservation and support Eisenhower when this placed him over British officers of wide combat experience.

Few officers in the American army have advanced in rank more rapidly than General Eisenhower has in the last few years. None has had his zone of activity and responsibility increased as widely or rapidly. His capacity to meet these unprecedented tests has revealed him to be one of the great soldier-administrators of our time.

II

DWIGHT DAVID EISENHOWER was born on October 14, 1890, at Denison, Texas, the son of David J. Eisenhower, a construction engineer, and Ida Stover.[1] Graduating from West Point in the top third of the class of 1915, he was commissioned in the 19th Infantry. Though he did not serve in France during World War I, he picked the tank corps as one of the coming organizations in the army and became commander of the tank training

[1] There is the usual dispute about the birthplace of Eisenhower with Tyler, Texas, in close second.

center at Colt, Pennsylvania, where he won the reputation of being a first-rate organizer. The Distinguished Service Medal, awarded for the excellence of his command, was accompanied with a citation commending his zeal, foresight, and marked ability in organization.

In the postwar period he served a two-year term as executive officer and commander of the tank troops at Fort Meade, Maryland, and a similar period as executive officer at Camp Gaillard, Panama Canal Zone. After passing through the Command and General Staff School and the Army War College, he spent three years in the office of the assistant secretary of war where, in addition to his other duties, he attended the Army Industrial College. General MacArthur took him on in the office of the chief of staff from 1933 to 1935. The next four and a half years he spent as an assistant military adviser to the Philippines where he organized the system of flying fields on the islands. Coming back to the states in February, 1940, he commanded the 15th Infantry at Fort Lewis, Washington, for a few months before becoming chief of staff to the 3rd Division. From February to June, 1941, he was chief of staff to the IX Corps with the temporary rank of colonel and became chief of staff to the Third Army on June 24.

It was in the autumn maneuvers of 1941 in Louisiana that Eisenhower began his meteoric rise. Here, as chief of staff to General Walter Krueger, he directed the operations of 200,000 men in the Third Army with such skill, intelligence, and good humor that he won the admiration of all observers. At the end of the maneuvers Eisenhower was raised to the rank of brigadier general. Shortly after the outbreak of war he was made head of the War Plans Division.

Few Americans realize what a tremendous revolution in outlook and planning necessarily preceded and accompanied the entrance of our army into World War II. Within less than two years, the army was forced to abandon its traditional role as a small defense force with the limited responsibilities prescribed by our national policy and transform itself into an organization capable of conducting multitheater operations in a global coalition war.

For six months after his appointment to the War Plans Division, Eisenhower worked night and day on plans for utilizing our expanding army to the best advantage. The period Eisenhower spent in the War Plans Division was one of heartbreaking defeats for the United Nations. At that time the military dynamism of the Axis seemed irresistible. Before the immense potential power of the United States could make itself felt on the battlefields and oceans of the world, the tremendous offensive surges of Germany and Japan had to be slowed down and checked. Certain essential bastions and bases had to be held at all costs. The first task of the War Plans Division was to ascertain what defensive areas had to be held and allocate just enough strength to safeguard each. To the uninformed outsider this looked like a wasteful dispersal of American military strength in small garrisons all over the globe. Certain military critics and commentators asked how we could expect to counter enemy concentration of strength by such methods and spoke disparagingly of our "amateur" leadership as compared to the "professional" skill of the enemy.

Yet our underrated American and British military leadership contrived to bring about under these disadvantageous conditions the great strategic surprise of November 8, 1942 which, combined with the El Alamein operation, caught the Axis off guard in North Africa. Together with the mighty efforts of the Red army at Stalingrad, this stroke wrested the initiative in Europe from the Axis.

Since Britain was the only bastion of the United Nations in western Europe, our plans for operations against Germany necessarily began there. After a chain of the defensive outposts had been secured in the Atlantic, a headquarters for the European theater of operations was set up in London. To head this command General Marshall chose Eisenhower.

When Eisenhower arrived in London on June 24, 1942, to assume command of the ETO (European theater of operations),

Tobruk had just fallen with a loss of 30,000 British troops. Rommel was advancing in Egypt and before his momentum could be checked at El Alamein further grievous losses in men and equipment were suffered. The nazi drive in southern Russia was still making great gains and few men dared hope for the magnificent victory which the Red army later achieved at Stalingrad. Defeatist sentiments were widespread. Eisenhower set the standard for "atmosphere" in the ETO at his first staff conference. "Defeatism and pessimism," he said, "will not be tolerated at this headquarters. Any soldier or officer who cannot rise above the recognized obstacles and bitter prospects that lie in store for us has no recourse but to ask for a release—those who don't will go home anyway!"

As thousands of American troops poured into England, Eisenhower faced the dual task of training them for combat and at the same time welding the American and British forces into a fighting partnership for coming battles. There were immense problems to be solved in the field of mass human relationships. The American soldier landed in bomb-battered Britain bringing his relatively large army pay and his traditional self-assertive Americanisms with him. We were in the difficult position of being guests of necessity in the British homeland. An "allied army of occupation" has many of the same objectionable traits as an enemy army of occupation. Our troops found British games, shows, taxis, and language amusing. They griped at the weather, the food, the general dumpiness of British clothes, the grim, unrelieved seriousness of the people. Coming from a country and a people untouched directly by war, it was hard for our troops to appreciate what the British people had endured. So Eisenhower set up a program of sight-seeing visits to the bombed areas and trips to historic spots for the troops. Army newspapers and recreation officers concentrated on Anglo-American co-operation. Thus the lull before the battle was used to weld British and American forces into a team that had absolute confidence in the other fellow. Part of Eisenhower's great success in North Africa and Italy stemmed from this preliminary achievement in Britain.

Since the plans of the joint chiefs of staff called for an invasion of North Africa before Europe, the choice of a theater commander came up. Churchill, who lunched with Eisenhower twice a week during the period of preparation in England, got a firsthand impression of Eisenhower's tact, common sense, vision, and grasp of military realities. The smoothness and precision with which the ETO headquarters worked gave him a measure of Eisenhower's efficiency as an administrator. Thus he felt justified in entrusting the command of British military and naval forces to a man who had never directed combat operations.

Perhaps it was the thoroughness with which Eisenhower and his colleagues in the War Plans Division had studied the subject of co-ordinate command that singled him out as the man to command the North African venture. The American government and General Pershing had been among the strongest supporters of a unified command in France in 1918. Then Foch was essentially a co ordinator of ground operations in a single theater with limited authority. Each national army in France kept its own staff intact. The effectiveness of this arrangement depended solely on the willingness of individual army commanders to co-operate with Foch. Negotiations between staffs were conducted on the diplomatic lines of the late nineteenth century. Personalities such as those of Weygand, Bliss, and Henry Wilson were essential to its success. These arrangements would not suffice in World War II. The attempt to revive the old system under Gamelin broke down as soon as the Germans struck in the west.

According to Demaree Bess, as soon as the North African invasion was determined upon, Eisenhower called British and American officers together in Norfolk House and pointed out where and why the command arrangements of 1918 were inadequate for projected operations in the Mediterranean theater.

Logistics alone required something more. All shipping had to be pooled; common bases had to be used; equipment, information, supplies, even personnel had to be combined or used on an interchangeable basis. For land, sea, and air operations of such magnitude, mutual trust and confidence must exist from the bottom of both armies to the top. A joint staff with Americans and Britons in alternating layers would have to be fused together like a plywood board. Eisenhower chose an American, Major General Walter Bedell Smith, for his chief of staff but took British Major General J. F. M. Whitely as his deputy chief of staff. The G-1 section (personnel) was headed by Brigadier General Benjamin W. Sawbridge, United States army, with Brigadier Victor Westropp of the British army as deputy chief. Forty-three-year-old Brigadier K. W. D. Strong of the British army headed the G-2 (intelligence) section, with an American, Colonel Thomas E. Roderick, as deputy chief. At the head of G-3 (operations) he placed Brigadier General Lowell Rooks, United States army, with Brigadier C. S. Sugden of the British army as deputy. The complicated and all-important post of G-4 (supply) was headed by Brigadier General Clarence Adcock, United States army, with Brigadier R. R. Lewis of the British army as deputy. These men were welded together as a solid unit in an exhaustive series of preliminary conferences until they understood each other's methods, language, and eccentricities.

Never before in history have two allied powers merged their military identities more completely in a single effort. Not that Eisenhower became "British" or that the British became "American." The American commander was too solidly "Midwestern" to take up British mannerisms or fall into their linguistic usages. Any ETO officer who ripped off "cheerio" or "I say there" was fined a half a dollar. His own personal staff, headed by Major Ernest Lee and Lieutenant Commander Harry Butcher, was a stanchly American affair. Time and again Eisenhower nipped incipient Anglo-American disagreements in the bud by getting both sets of offending officers together in the same room and forcing them to thrash out their differences. Those who persisted in criticizing the other side "were sent home on a slow boat."

Eisenhower's methods were direct. He made himself accessible to anyone who had business with the commander in chief. To nervous juniors who tiptoed about his office door waiting for a chance to see him he said: "Dammit, you don't have to tiptoe around here. This office isn't a boudoir! If you have anything to show me, bring it in!" He insisted that reports be simple and direct. Ponderous memoranda bounced back to the officers who wrote them marked: "This is too complicated for a dumb bunny like me! What's it all about?"

Newsmen were captivated by Eisenhower's assumed "country boy" naïveté and his apparent eagerness to take them into his confidence. He flattered them by asserting that newsmen were quite as important in total war as soldiers. He was willing, he said, to treat them like staff officers and give them the information that they needed to understand the broad picture of operations—only they could not publish it. As long as the correspondents co-operated and played the game within those limits, he promised to tell them the "score" frankly. But changing, as he often does, from good-natured urbanity to bleak seriousness, he warned, "God help anyone who lets me down!" To correspondents accustomed to Auchinleck's chilly conferences, to the petty handouts from Ritchie's public relations officers, or to Montgomery's showmanlike but irrelevant interviews, Eisenhower appeared to be a man of "broad vision" and remarkable articulateness. One British reporter described his manner of speech as "like that of an intelligent Oxford don combined with the facility of a Rotarian speaker." Blasts of pure American, such as "I told that so-and-so to peddle his papers elsewhere," interspersed long, lucid analyses of a military or political situation. His talent for clarification tended to make his hearers feel "intelligent and well informed." Eisenhower kept the respect of every correspondent in Tunisia except one, who, during the agonizing period of Axis victories, came to the conclusion that

Ike was "merely a clever charlatan." In the end, even this hard-bitten critic confessed his complete error in sizing up the American commander.

III

THE decision to invade French North Africa involved General Eisenhower in the most complicated amphibious operation in military history. While the Japanese operations in the Southwest Pacific in 1941–42 may have equaled it in size, they did not face nearly as many imponderables or complex problems. The Japanese had exact knowledge of the military resistance to be encountered. The Anglo-American invasion of North Africa was made without knowing definitely whether the French would offer resistance or not. Plans had to be made on both assumptions. If the landing was opposed, then everything depended on the merciful swiftness of the operation. One of the main Allied objectives in driving the Axis out of North Africa was to provide a basis for the military and political recovery of France. A prolonged and bitter struggle might make it psychologically impossible to bring all non-Vichy French elements back into the war against the Axis. Eisenhower was intensely anxious to avoid the shedding of French blood, but it was impossible for security reasons to prepare the political groundwork long in advance of the landing. The date of the landing was not even given to the French officials with whom we were negotiating until four days before it took place.

Despite the immensity of the project, the North African landing achieved a degree of strategic surprise seldom equaled in war. Certain American military writers have described it as "the worst-kept military secret of the war," but the fact remains that with over 100,000 men involved and with planning that dated back to January, 1942, the landings unquestionably caught the Axis off guard.

Eisenhower had to shoulder immense responsibilities from the outset. The initial landing of 107,000 Allied troops had to be carried out from British and American bases over thousands of miles of submarine-infested waters. Air support had to be provided by carriers or based on distant fields in Malta and Gibraltar. Transports, bombers, and long-range fighters all had to be cleared through the bottleneck of Gibraltar. Had this air base been subjected to heavy Axis bombing at the eve or during the first hours of the operation, the whole project might have been endangered. Eisenhower had to accept the possibility of Axis counteraction through Spain and that the enemy might bomb the single railway connecting Casablanca and Oran. An additional risk lay in the fact that the American troops were meeting their first trial in battle. A great deal more than the mere conquest of North Africa depended on how they performed in combat.

In this connection future military historians will doubtless point out what many critics and commentators have thus far failed to observe; namely, that the North African landing was a supremely important training operation for our new army. In modern war troops cannot be completely trained in camps. Part of their transition from civilian trainees to front-line fighters must come from combat itself. The landings in North Africa gave our troops the advantage of carrying out their first operation against "semisoft" resistance. The training value of this experience and the losses which it minimized when we met the battle-hardened German forces in Tunisia cannot be overestimated.

Though landings at Bône, Philippeville, and Tunis were seriously considered, shortage of shipping and air ruled out these possibilities. Three major landings were planned. Two were prepared in Britain, the third in the United States. An American task force under Major General Lloyd Fredendall was to capture Oran; a mixed British and American force under Lieutenant General K. A. N. Anderson was to seize Algiers; and an American task force, organized in the United States under Major General George S. Patton, was to capture Casablanca. A mass descent of American paratroops was to insure the early use of the airfields at Oran for Allied fighter plans shuttled in from Gibraltar. The daring feature of this operation was that the troop-carrying transports were to make a 1,500-mile flight from England. General Eisenhower established his command post at Gibraltar three days before the landing.

If the French army in North Africa was determined to resist,

The North African Theater

it had considerable resources at its disposal. In the early stage of the landing, numbers would be on its side. Though lacking in modern tanks, planes, and artillery, the French had plenty of small arms and 75's. Their coastal batteries guarding the principal ports were formidable by any standard. French naval forces were efficient and had not forgotten the bitter day in July, 1940, when the British fleet had sunk a part of their fleet at Oran. Pride demanded that resistance should be offered, and in the French navy this feeling was mixed with a natural desire for revenge. The defenders of North Africa were not caught napping; their air patrols sighted the invasion fleet and in some cases tangled viciously with the superior planes of the Allies.

As the vast armada of transports and landing craft moved toward their offshore stations, Allied diplomacy was making frenzied efforts to win over French officials in North Africa to accept the landings without resistance. In some cases the time was too short; individual French commanders operated on their own judgment. Some welcomed the Allied landings, but there was sharp if brief resistance at Casablanca, Oran, and in the harbor of Algiers. The speed and power of the landing operations, the futility of prolonged resistance, the influence of Admiral Darlan and General Giraud, however, brought resistance to an end in 48 hours.

Whatever may be said of the political embarrassments that flowed from temporary collaboration with Admiral Darlan, it was his influence that brought to an end French resistance at Casablanca where General Patton's forces were about to bombard the city. When Admiral Darlan assumed authority for the French government in North Africa on November 11, he was the only person whose orders would be honored by the forces still resisting. General Eisenhower realistically accepted this situation because military operations would not permit waiting for a solution satisfactory to all. A delay of two hours at this stage might have upset the whole subsequent timetable of events in North Africa.

Within two days after the landing, General Eisenhower could turn to the problem of Tunisia without worrying about the conquest of the vast territory of French West Africa. The military resources of that area were now placed at our disposal. Despite some initial mistakes and failures, the first phase of the campaign was a heartening success for the United Nations. It demonstrated to the Axis and the neutral world that British and American staff work was of the highest order. Many of the lessons learned in the descent upon the shores of Africa were put to good use in Sicily and Italy.

Although surprised by the events of November 8–11, the Axis reacted with vigor and speed. German and Italian troops were rushed into Bizerte and Tunis by plane and ship. With their short lines of communications, excellent wharf facilities, and airfields, the Axis forces enjoyed great advantages over the Allies in the race to secure Tunisia. General Eisenhower's forces were scattered over thousands of miles in French North Africa. Part of his armor and infantry was tied down in Morocco to guard against Axis intervention from Spanish Morocco. There was only a single-track railway leading from Casablanca to Oran. Rail facilities east of Oran were limited; motor roads were narrow; hard-surface air strips were scarce or in enemy hands.

Yet the attempt to rush Bizerte and Tunis had to be made despite German advantages. Even before French resistance had ended, Allied troops were landed at Bougie and occupied Bône on November 12. Hastily organized American and British combat teams were set in motion toward Tunis. French forces, now fighting on the Allied side, reinforced by American and British units, were sent to protect airfields in the Tebessa-Gafsa area. The whole operation had to be improvised out of the confusion following the landing.

As the Allied columns reached to within 60 miles of Tunis on November 16, they encountered German patrols for the first time. The nature of the meeting left no doubt about the character or fighting capacity of the enemy. A company of Surreys moving out from Oued Zarga into the valley of the Medjerda crossed the last crest of hills. Suddenly a German mortar battery salvo burst squarely in the center of the leading file, destroying four Bren carriers. At about the same time a group of American tanks and half tracks leading the way for a "shoestring force of British infantry" got within 12 miles of Tunis. Then a flight of Messerschmitts roared over a hill to strafe the infantry. From this time on there was no advance. We had met "the champ."

There followed a series of heartbreaking disappointments, bitter mistakes, and frustrated movements by the un-co-ordinated Allied forces. The British First Army with American reinforcements took Medjez-el-bab on November 25, and moved toward Djedeida. But on the following day a flight of American P-38's, soaring over C company of the 701st Tank Destroyers (who were rejoicing to see some Allied fighter aviation overhead), through one of those disastrous errors in recognition into which even veteran units sometimes fall, dove with blazing machine guns on the American vehicles. Five times the American planes wheeled and circled over the hapless unit, beating the life out of men and destroying machines. When the planes finally left C company had ceased to exist as a fighting unit.[2] This was a loss too sad for tears and anger, too bitter to talk about. But, as one sympathetic British observer noted, two American officers (Redding and Childs) slowly pulled the remnants of the unit together by sheer force. On the next afternoon C company, by dint of frantic cannibalization had been partially reconstituted and "spiritually reborn." Then came a confused night retreat of Combat Command B from Furna to Medjez in which most of its vehicles and heavy equipment was lost. British units like the Hampshires, the Northants, the Surreys, and the 132nd field artillery regiment fought until some of the battalions were reduced to a handful at Tebourba. Enemy air, infantry, tank, and artillery strength was increasing. Hastily organized and badly mixed units of the Allied army could no longer make headway against the tightly knit, superbly controlled enemy.

Early in December all hope of an early conquest of Tunis was abandoned. Positional warfare—with all its delays and disappointments—ensued.

IV

PART of the public disappointment over the initial failure to take Tunis and Bizerte came from a misunderstanding as to the strength of Eisenhower's forces. Early press and radio communiqués stressed the overpowering strength and modern equipment of the invading army, but these may have been issued primarily for their effect on the French and Spanish. Some correspondents were misled by the vast and elaborate headquarters establishment in Algiers, which gave rise to such expressions as "hyper-

[2] David Rame, *Road to Tunis* (New York, 1943), pp. 135–136.

thyroid Pentagon" and "never were so few commanded by so many." The troops which Eisenhower could actually put into the first battle in Tunisia were pitifully few. One might imagine from its name that the British First Army, under General Anderson, was made up of several divisions. Later a Canadian military magazine told us that until reinforced in March with two divisions, the First Army consisted of the 4th and 78th Infantry divisions and the 6th Armored Division.[3] A considerable portion of the troops employed in Tunisia were French and had not been supplied with modern equipment. The necessity to reinforce these units with American or British troops and equipment caused dispersion and the intermingling of units.

Aside from the difficulties of supply and the absence of hardsurface air strips, perhaps the greatest single source of weakness in the initial Allied thrust against Tunis was this inescapable intermingling of small units. It was the basis of Eisenhower's decision (announced to the correspondents on February 15) that henceforth American forces would not be employed in units smaller than divisions.

The decision to fight the future battles of Tunisia with integral national units was not a reflection on any of the forces engaged. True, there were numerous causes for friction between American and British troops and commanders. Nothing brings out differences in methods and temperament so sharply as the crises of battle and the boredom of inaction. American troops sometimes repeated the irritating phrase "How Green Was My Ally." British pilots scoffed at American flying techniques, the "lunatic gnattering"of American pilots over the intercom radio, their "lovely" stunting "back of the lines." But it was not all bitterness. Sometimes units of both armies would be convulsed by an American "clown" putting on a sidesplitting pantomime of a British sergeant conducting infantry drill or vice versa. It was in the comradeship of shared victories, in the fires of defeat, and in the weeks of boredom and inaction that the real basis for Anglo-American co-operation was forged.

[3] *The Tank-Canada*, July, 1943, p. 3.

From his headquarters in Algiers, Eisenhower prepared for the next phase of the Tunisian campaign. For the troops at the front it was a period of tedious fighting in the mud, of endless labor on lines of communications. Until adequate all-weather airfields could be built up, German planes seemed to have the sky to themselves. Even individual motorcyclists were strafed from the air. Ground soldiers at the front and correspondents in the rear could not understand the meaning of the period of indecisive fighting that preceded the arrival of the British Eighth Army at the Mareth line in February, but in the words of General Marshall: "The opponents [were] testing each other's strength along the partially stabilized line—matching each other's bids for air supremacy, both forces concentrating against ports and lines of communication."

These measured words do not reveal the ordeal of bitter weather, rain, sleet, mud, and cold which the troops endured. Grueling minor battles were fought in which advances and retirements were measured in yards. This was when the British Eighth Army was driving Rommel's Afrika Korps through Tripoli and measured its advances in terms of hundreds of miles. Men wondered why the American and British forces in Tunisia could not do the same. It looked so simple on the map. All we had to do was push to the sea and close the Gabes Gap behind Rommel, yet Eisenhower's army was not capable of doing it. An American and a British armored division were available, but the American division was scattered over a large area and the old cruiser tanks of the British division had to be replaced with Shermans. That took time. Allied forces were still too widely dispersed to be effective. Antitank guns and crews were not yet ready to meet the veteran enemy gunners on equal terms. Large areas had to be defended by the gallant but ill-equipped French troops. Rommel ended all hope of plugging the Gabes Gap by backing his own forces neatly into the danger spot.

Violent action soon followed. Rommel had gradually picked up strength as he retreated through Libya and Tripolitania. He took considerable material out of Tripoli before abandoning it.

By the time he reached the Mareth line he had partially reconstituted the 15th and 21st Panzer divisions and had the 90th
and 164th Light divisions ready to fight. He was still carrying
the Italian Trieste Division on his books, and had picked up the
Pistoja, Superba, Centauro, and Young Fascist divisions. There
were enough tough veterans of the desert war to give the force
confidence. These men were skilled in carrying out Rommel's
technique of swift tank strokes followed by the familiar mine
and antitank defense.

Arnim's forces in the north were also formidable. He had part
of the 10th Panzer, the Manteuffel, the Hermann Göring, the
334th and the 20th AA divisions under his command. German
troops now outnumbered the Italian forces two to one. They
had excellent training, equipment, and morale.

Leaving part of his force to hold up Montgomery on the
Mareth line, Rommel suddenly sent a strong force of tanks,
motorized infantry and antitank units, supported by dive bombers, against the American forces at Gafsa and Faïd Pass. Possibly
he wanted to test out the quality of American troops or destroy
the great Allied supply dumps at Tebessa and Thala. Perhaps
he had even larger aims. In any event his armored spearhead cut
through the American defenses like a hot knife through butter.
What happened was described by a British observer as follows:

> The American armored division was too spread out to offer concentrated
> resistance, and the strength and importance of the German drive do not
> seem to have been appreciated. The American tanks were thrown in piece-
> meal by battalions, and lost. There was no powerful screen of antitank
> guns. It must have seemed to Rommel very much like the early days in
> Libya. A retreat started which sometimes took on the proportions of a rout.[4]

Gafsa, Faïd, Kasserine, and Kasserine Pass were lost. For a
time it looked as if Rommel might capture the great Allied
supply bases built up at Thala and Tebessa. That would have
set back the campaign in Tunisia for months. Had the German
attack maintained its momentum and swept toward the sea

[4] Alexander G. Clifford, *The Conquest of North Africa, 1940–1943* (Boston,
1943), p. 399.

EISENHOWER and MARSHALL

northward behind the Allied front, it would have threatened all the Allied forces in northern Tunisia. This frightening prospect soon ended. Rommel was stopped at Thala and Sbiba on February 22. By February 24 Allied counterblows supported "by the entire Allied air force in North Africa" turned him back. Rommel recoiled swiftly, carrying a good deal of captured material with him. Arnim tried to cover Rommel's retreat by attacking the British First Army at Medjez-el-bab but made little headway.

Rommel's attack was a real body blow; two excellent American units were cut up. Eisenhower unhesitatingly shouldered the responsibility for the reverse, radioing to General Marshall on February 21:

> Our present tactical difficulties resulted from my attempt to do possibly too much, coupled with the deterioration of resistance in the central mountainous area which began about January 17th. That deterioration has absorbed the bulk of the United States 1st and 34th divisions . . . but you would have been impressed could you have seen the magnificent display everywhere by the American enlisted men. . . . The troops that come out of this campaign are going to be battle-wise and tactically efficient.

Rommel tried the same tactics that had succeeded against the Americans on the British Eighth Army at Medenine on March 6, but was stopped cold in his tracks with a loss of 52 tanks. Montgomery in turn took the offensive on March 20 in an effort to crack the Mareth line. He was assisted by American and British attacks in the north and by the concentrated force of all Allied air power in North Africa.

As the British Eighth Army approached Tunisia it became necessary to bring this splendid fighting force within the zone of the unified command. Headed by one of the most colorful soldiers in the world, the Eighth Army was a proud and highly individualistic force. Part of its esprit de corps came from Montgomery's insistence that the Eighth Army was an "independent force" taking orders fron no one but him. Sure of themselves and conscious of their skill, the men of the Eighth Army looked down tolerantly on the American troops and the British First

Army as "promising amateurs." They did not conceal their opinion that the defeat of the Axis in Tunisia would have to wait until the Eighth Army got around to it. Montgomery had worked out a technique of ground-air co-operation with Air Marshal Coningham which was the envy of all other commanders, but he gave few advance indications of being a good team-play man when it came to working with other armies. It was Eisenhower's administrative job to see that Montgomery's great talents and individualism fitted into the big pattern of the Tunisian battle.

On February 11, 1943, the command was reorganized. Eisenhower became supreme commander of the North African theater of operations with General Sir Harold Alexander as his deputy in direct command of the 18th Army Group. This army group was made up of the II American Corps under command of Major General George S. Patton and later of Major General Omar N. Bradley, the French XIX Corps under General Louis M. Koeltz, the British First Army under Anderson, and the Eighth Army under Montgomery. On February 18, 1943, a sweeping reorganization of the Allied air forces was made. Air Chief Marshal Sir Arthur Tedder was made head of the Mediterranean air command. Major General (now Lieutenant General) Carl Spaatz was placed in command of the Northwest African air force, Major General James Doolittle was placed in command of the strategic air force, and Air Marshal Coningham was given command of the tactical air force. The air coastal command was in charge of Air Vice-Marshal Lloyd. With the United Nations naval forces in the Mediterranean commanded by Admiral Cunningham under his general control, Eisenhower was now able to co-ordinate all phases of the campaign against the Axis in North Africa.

Eisenhower's ability to grasp the potentialities of air power was one of the things that marked him as a great commander. When Tedder showed him what an intelligently directed air force could do, he needed no further conversion. His method of working was simple. He used the conference method, getting ground

and air officers together in the same room. He set forth the main
objectives and let them work out the details and methods. The
only thing he demanded was results. Daily conferences permitted air and ground officers to see the whole military picture,
not just their own segment of it. Co-operation was worked out
on army and air force levels; lower echelons followed automati-
cally.

The military successes that followed were not the results of the
air reorganization alone. The whole Allied military establishment in North Africa was reaching a new peak of efficiency.
General Alexander showed great zeal and ability in unsnarling
tangled chains of local command and placing the 18th Army
Group in condition to defeat the Axis armies. American and
British military engineers doubled or tripled the capacity of
communications lines, built up advance air bases and supply
dumps, constructed 10 gasoline pipe lines, and performed many
other miracles of preparation.

On March 11 Eisenhower could radio General Marshall:
"Once we have the Eighth Army through that bottleneck [the
Mareth line], this campaign is going to assume rapidly a very
definitive form with constant pressure and drive kept up against
the enemy throughout that region." To assist Montgomery,
American forces took the offensive in the south capturing Gafsa
(March 17), El Guettar (March 18), and Maknassy (March 23).

General Montgomery attacked the Mareth position across the
almost impassable Wadi Zigzaou on March 20, but failed to hold
the bridgehead which the British 50th (Northumbrian) Division
had won. When his direct thrust failed, Montgomery sent the
1st Armored Division to support the New Zealand Division under General Freyberg which was making a flanking attack around
the enemy right wing at El Hamma, scheduled for 3:00 P.M.
March 26.

This attack was accompanied by the most concentrated and
sustained air assault delivered up to that time in North Africa.
Everything that could fly was massed to support the effort at
El Hamma: heavy bombers of the strategic air force, medium

bombers of the tactical air force, fighter planes, and new tank-busting Hurricanes armed with two 40-mm. guns. The air attack struck the enemy like a thunderbolt. The 21st Panzer, the 164th German Light, and the Italian Spezia divisions received the shock. For three hours waves of Allied planes bombed and strafed the Axis position, striking at anything that moved. German gun crews could not man their pieces; tanks were immobilized, even machine gunners took cover. The New Zealand Division opened a path for the British 1st Armored Division and the battle of El Hamma was won. The retreating Axis troops did not halt until they reached the Wadi Akarit.

On April 7 a patrol from the United States 9th Division made a juncture with the Eighth Army some 20 miles from the sea.

From this point on events developed rapidly. Sfax was captured on April 10 by the Eighth Army. Fondouk fell to the British 6th Armored Division and the Welsh Guards after severe and confused fighting. American units, which were to clear away German artillery guarding a minefield in one sector, arrived too late at the jump-off. As a result a squadron of British tanks was deliberately sacrificed to break through the minefield. One British observer later wrote: "This was the low watermark of American arms on the Tunisian front—yet these very units which failed at Fondouk were the ones that swept to a brilliant victory in the north only a few weeks later."

When enemy resistance at Fondouk collapsed the situation was so "fluid" that one officer replied to General Alexander's request for "information" by blurting out: "There's a complete madhouse in the hills over there! The American Rangers, the British Commandos and the French Goums are all stalking one another round the mountain tops. No one knows who is supposed to be fighting who. They have just ambushed the general."

After the loss of Sfax, Sousse, Pichon, Fondouk and Kirouan, the enemy retreated northward to his final position at Enfidaville. The Axis foothold in North Africa was now reduced to an area about 100 miles long and 30 miles wide, running from the coast east of Cape Serrat to Jefna, Medjez-el-bab, Pont-du-

Fahs, and Enfidaville. They had 250,000 troops to defend the last mountain ridges guarding the Tunis Plain, and the natural strength of their position gave the Germans ample reason to anticipate a prolonged defense.

Looking down on the route of the British Eighth Army from the heights of Enfidaville, the 90th and 164th Light German Infantry divisions were supported by the Italian Superba, Pistoja, Trieste, Centauro, and Young Fascist divisions. These Italian troops were making Italy's last effort to restore her military prestige, and in some instances they fought better than the German troops. Covering the approaches to the Tunis Plain through the Medjerda Valley were the 334th, the 10th and parts of the 15th and 21st Panzer divisions, plus the Hermann Göring regiments. These forces held the massive height of Long Stop Hill dominating the Medjerda Valley. In the north, the Manteuffel, 20th AA divisions, and parts of the 15th and 21st Panzer divisions held a strong position buttressed on Djebel Azag (Green Hill), Djebel Ajred (Bald Hill), and Djebel Tahent (Hill 609) which guarded the westward approach to Bizerte through the Sedjenane Valley.

The control of co-ordinate arms, the air forces and the navy, now enabled Eisenhower to cut off the flow of Axis reinforcements from Sicily. Gradually Allied air power reduced Axis airfields and destroyed its planes. Attempts to bring in supplies and evacuate German technical experts by air led to repeated massacres of Ju-52 and Me-323 transports. The waters off North Africa became the graveyard of hundreds of Axis planes and their cargoes. Heavy assaults on the Sicilian airfields in the first week in April destroyed over 150 aircraft on the ground and 50 in the air. During the next two weeks 147 large transport planes and some 30 vessels were destroyed or damaged from the air. In the opinion of General Marshall this sudden and complete "rupture of Axis communications upset their plans for delaying actions and the defense of Cape Bon Peninsula." When the time for the final attack came in the first week in May, Allied fighter planes were able to maintain patrols over enemy airfields.

Hardly a German plane made its appearance on the front.

The final plan for the destruction of the Axis armies as worked out by Generals Eisenhower and Alexander utilized the formidable reputation of the British Eighth Army to contain the Axis forces on the Southern front. They planned for a simultaneous break through the Sedjenane and Tine valleys to Bizerte and through the Medjerda Valley to Tunis. With complete control of the air, it was possible to transfer large units from one point in the Allied line to another without the enemy's knowledge. General Eisenhower was eager to have the United States II Corps, which had not yet reached its stride, distinguish itself in the final stage of the campaign. Soon after the capture of El Guettar, General Patton was relieved of command and sent to supervise preparations for the invasion of Sicily. Major General Omar N. Bradley took command of the II Corps and transferred it northward behind the First British Army to the Beja area. At about the same time General Alexander transferred the 7th British Armored Division and the Fourth Indian Division from the Eighth Army front to that of the First Army. Either the Germans were unaware of this shift or Arnim lacked Rommel's aptitude for an aggressive defense. The large Axis force opposite the now shrunken Eighth Army did not move. The stage was set for the final strokes of the campaign.

Though the break-through of British and American armored divisions on May 7 behind Tedder's "carpet of bombs" got most of the public's attention at the time, the success of these bold drives would not have been possible without the slow, slugging work of British infantrymen (the 78th Division) in capturing Long Stop Hill (April 26) and the American infantry in driving the enemy off Green and Bald hills (May 1–3). This enabled the 1st United States Armored Division to sweep into Mateur late on May 3. Eisenhower radioed General Marshall two days later that the final assault would begin on May 6.

The attack which reached its climax on May 7 achieved a high degree of strategic surprise through the unprecedented air assault that preceded and accompanied it, and by the sudden appearance of strong new British and American forces where the Germans did not expect them. The American II Corps broke into Bizerte on May 7 and the British First Army captured

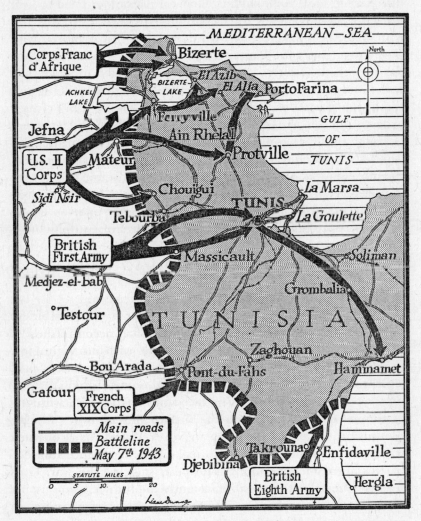

The End in North Africa

Tunis. All organization seemed to crack at once in the Axis armies. Allied armored and motorized columns streamed past large German units which were too dazed to take intelligent action. The course of the battle now depended largely on the initiative of local commanders. General Alexander tried to keep up with the advancing forces, driving his own jeep "his face whitened like a baker's boy with dust." The 7th Armored Division drove the 15th Panzer Division to the ground at Porto Farina outside Bizerte. Other German units tried to make their way to Cape Bon, but General Alexander, rightly judging that the disintegration of the enemy warranted taking a big chance, ordered the 6th Armored Division to break through the enemy position at Hammann Lif and move south to Hammamet. Except for a brief fight with a German 88 battery at Hammann Lif, the 6th Armored Division carried out this audacious move without serious opposition. That ended all hope of a German retreat and final stand on Cape Bon. By May 13, some 252,000 enemy prisoners were taken together with vast stores of equipment.

V

WHEN the North African campaign was over it was possible for the first time to survey what Eisenhower had accomplished. If American and British liberals found fault with his willingness to use Darlan and other Frenchmen of doubtful background while the campaign was being conducted, some of them came to recognize that the problems he faced in North Africa were not so simple as they seemed on the surface. Eisenhower's first responsibility was to win the battle in North Africa. His second task was to do it in such a way as to make possible France's unified participation in the coming European stage of the war. Only zealots believed it was possible instantly to produce a simon-pure democratic administration in French North Africa simply by revoking all the Vichy laws. One cannot wage war effectively at the front with the rear areas and supply routes in disorder. Patience was required to allow certain problems to settle themselves.

When the campaign was over one French liberal credited Eisenhower with having prevented a civil war in Algeria, with having forestalled a possible Moslem revolt, with nipping potential German and Italian fifth columns in the bud, and with having prevented a German invasion of Algeria by the prompt use of French forces.[5] The ultimate emergence of the French National Committee of Liberation showed the long-term wisdom of Eisenhower's early decisions.

Perhaps the greatest achievement of the North African campaign was the fusing of British, American, and French military forces into a single combat team, thus laying the basis for the invasion of Europe. In the long view of history this may well be regarded as Eisenhower's most important achievement. It was more important than the destruction of the Axis armies in North Africa, even though this was the greatest victory so far obtained by Anglo-American forces over the Axis. If British and Americans, from generals and admirals down to soldiers and seamen, went into the North African venture with expressed or unexpressed doubts about their allies, they came out of it with a mutual confidence unequaled among allies in modern war.

In an address delivered at Yale University on February 16, 1943, General Marshall stressed the importance of this achievement. Speaking of the necessity of integrating and intermingling British and American troops in North Africa and Italy, he showed that any discord in command and staff direction "would have had a fatal effect. . . . That we have been able to master these very human difficulties," he said, "that in fact we have triumphed over them to the disaster of our enemy, is in my opinion the greatest single Allied achievement of the war." Eisenhower was not solely responsible for this condition of mutual confidence and trust, but without him it would have been impossible.

[5] Gallicus, "Eisenhower Africanus," in the *New Republic*, pp. 609–612 (November 1, 1943).

The common expression in Algiers was "Eisenhower is an organizer not an improviser." After the first disappointing failure to take Tunis, he refused to launch his next effort until he was completely satisfied that it would be successful. He showed great patience under the barrage of criticism which his political decisions provoked in the early days of the campaign. Though for a time he was junior in rank to some of his subordinates, he ran the North African show with firmness, tact, and unshakable good humor. The power he exercised was never flaunted in other people's faces; he generally contrived to bring about the action desired by making it seem to come as the suggestion of the other party. Fanfare and display were not a part of his method. Subordinate American generals might roar about in flag-bedecked staff cars escorted by MP's on motorcycles but Eisenhower often made his entrance into a town so inconspicuously that it was sometime before the news of his presence got around.

Modesty was not something he used for effect; it was genuine. When he didn't understand a point he said so frankly. In a conference he might say to his deputy chief of staff (Major General J. F. M. Whitley): "Sorry, Jock, I didn't get that"—or to newsmen: "Maybe I'm dumb, repeat that please." John Gunther relates that at a press conference in connection with the Sicilian campaign Eisenhower immediately changed a snap decision which he had previously made when a mere captain on his staff pointed out its impractical nature.

Part of his success in dealing with the British came from the fact that he treated them just as he did Americans. His relations with Tedder and Cunningham were particularly friendly. Not a single dispatch was filed from his headquarters that dealt with him except in relation to other high Allied officers. Everything he did emphasized the joint nature of the enterprise.

One of Eisenhower's most valuable qualities as a theater commander is his calmness and capacity for putting aside worries about pending or current military operations. Having assured himself that the plans and preparations are as good as his staff can make them, he dismisses the matter from his mind. On the night before the Sicilian landing he was called upon to determine whether or not the operation should be postponed on account of the strong wind and heavy sea. Having decided to proceed regardless of the weather, he went to bed and slept soundly until the next morning. The only deviation from his normal routine was to give his "lucky" pocket coins an extra rub. When things go wrong—as they often do in war—he takes them philosophically, saying: "You can't draw good cards all the time!"

VI

THE decision to invade Sicily was made at the Casablanca conference and preparations were advanced even before the end of the Tunisian campaign. Shortly after the battle of El Hamma, General Patton was relieved of command of the II Corps and ordered to prepare for the invasion of Sicily. He headed a new command called the United States Seventh Army, consisting of the 1st, 3rd, 45th Infantry divisions, the 82nd Air-borne Division, and the 2nd Armored Division. General B. L. Montgomery commanded the British Eighth Army which included the 5th, 50th, and 51st Infantry divisions. Major General Guy Simons commanded a Canadian force which included the 1st Canadian Infantry Division and the 2nd armored brigade. These forces formed the 15th Army Group under the command of General Alexander.

The invasion was prepared by the Allied strategic air force which systematically destroyed Axis air bases in Sicily and southern Italy. A total of 50,000 air sorties were flown in preparation for and in direct support of the Sicilian campaign. D-day was July 10, and was to be preceded by the largest parachute troop and glider landing yet attempted by the Allies. A fleet of about 2,000 vessels was to land the Allied force on the south-central and southeastern end of the island. There was to be direct support by naval gunfire at the landing beaches.

As the immense armada left African ports on the afternoon of July 9, a heavy sea kicked up by a strong wind made the going

rough for small craft. For a time it looked as if the whole operation might have to be called off. Fortunately for the masses of
troops packed in the pitching landing craft, the weather suddenly moderated. The 'wind died down, and although many
soldiers who reached Sicily were desperately seasick, the landings
from ships took place on schedule without losses from the elements. Allied air-borne troops were not so fortunate; many were
blown off their course and landed far from their objectives.

Opposing the Allied landing was an estimated Axis force of
from 200,000 to 300,000 men under nominal command of Italian
General Alfredo Guzzoni but actually controlled by German
General Hans Hube. He commanded the Hermann Göring Division, the 15th Panzer Division, parts of the 19th Panzer Division,
the 29th Motorized Infantry Division, and the 1st Parachute
Division (now fighting as infantry).[6] There were three Italian
coast defense divisions (204th, 206th, 207th) and three Italian
infantry divisions (the 4th, the 26th, and the 54th Napoli).

The initial landings of the British and American troops took
place without serious opposition and at the end of July 10, beach-
heads were secure enough to permit the landing of artillery and
tanks. The first Axis counterattack came on July 11 when the
4th Italian Division, supported by 100 German tanks, struck
the American beachhead at Gela. The attack penetrated to
within a half a mile of the beach at one point but was finally
driven off by artillery and naval gunfire. After this attack Axis
resistance in the southern area diminished rapidly.

It soon became apparent that General Hube did not intend
to fight for southern Sicily but planned a defense of the north-
eastern tip of the island. As a result the United States Seventh
Army made rapid progress in advancing toward Agrigento,
Marsala, and Palermo. The British occupied Syracuse and

[6] The numbers or names of German divisions are switched about so radically as
to confuse the general reader. The nazis follow the practice of giving newly raised
divisions the numbers of older divisions. Thus divisions fighting in Tunisia might
have the numbers of divisions destroyed at Stalingrad and divisions in Sicily the
numbers of divisions (the 15th Panzer, the Hermann Göring) totally or partially
destroyed in North Africa.

Augusta with their port facilities almost intact. Stout resistance
was encountered only when the British Eighth Army approached
the German line near Catania. Here heavy fighting developed
and continued until August 5. Meanwhile the American Seventh
Army under General Patton was sweeping through southern
Sicily at an extremely rapid pace and capturing thousands of
war-weary Italians who acted very much as if they knew that
Italian participation in the war on the German side was about
to end.

The Axis decision to abandon Sicily was probably taken at the
Verona conference between Mussolini and Hitler on July 19.
At that time the Italians were told that it might be impossible
to defend southern Italy and that Italian troops and war industries should be moved northward beyond the Tuscan line.
This decision started a train of events that led to Mussolini's over-
throw on July 25 and Italy's withdrawal from the war on
September 8. The Allied campaign in Sicily, therefore, should
be regarded as one conducted against an opponent already committed to a general withdrawal, who was attempting to gain time
by utilizing terrain favorable for the defense.

Thus the stout resistance encountered by the British Eighth
Army at Catania and by the Americans at Troina ended as soon
as General Hube was ready to move back to a new position.
Despite the great achievements of the Seventh and Eighth armies,
the Germans carried out a masterful evacuation of the island.
They no longer seemed to care how many Italian troops went
over to the enemy, but carried out their own retreat in a rapid
and orderly manner. Few wounded Germans were abandoned;
little useful equipment was left behind. The German dead were
neatly buried. Under the protection of massed antiaircraft batteries, the crossing of the Straits to Messina went on uninter-
ruptedly for days and nights. By General Hube's orders no German soldier was permitted aboard a Seibel ferry who did not
carry a rifle, a bayonet, and ammunition. The precision, orderliness, and skill of the German units in Sicily was impressive.

If General Eisenhower could not scoop up the German defenders of Sicily, he at least had the satisfaction of conducting the best-organized campaign that the Anglo-American allies had thus far fought. The task of conquering a great island from bases across the Mediterranean in 38 days was an "organizational triumph" of the first magnitude. A total of 135,000 Axis prisoners were in Allied hands together with considerable Italian equipment. The capture of Sicily placed many air bases at Allied disposal and completed their control of the western Mediterranean. In the moral sphere it was the stroke that broke the Italian will to continue the war. Armistice negotiations followed which were concluded on September 3. On that date an armistice agreement was signed at Syracuse between Allied and Italian officers.

One of the features of the Sicilian campaign that gave Eisenhower intense satisfaction was the battle efficiency, hitting power, and mobility of the United States Seventh Army. At the end of the campaign he paid it the supreme compliment of saying that it was worthy to fight side by side with the British Eighth Army as an equal.

VII

THE Italian campaign which followed the conquest of Sicily illustrates some of the difficulties of waging modern coalition warfare. Political events now occurred at a speed that outran the military program. On September 3, 1943, Italian commissioners signed an armistice with representatives of the Allied headquarters in Sicily. This agreement provided for the surrender of the Italian navy, for placing all Italian resources and facilities at the disposal of the Allies, and anticipated Italy's ultimate participation in the war on the Allied side. Because large German forces were known to be in Italy, the announcement of the armistice was withheld until September 8.

As early as August 18, 1943, Allied leaders at the Quebec conference were said to have asked General Eisenhower to advance the date of an invasion of Italy in view of the collapse of the fascist regime and pending armistice negotiations. It may be assumed, therefore, that initial Allied steps in Italy were in the nature of improvisations.

On September 3, the same date on which the armistice was signed, the British Eighth Army under General Montgomery landed on the eastern coast of the Straits of Messina between Villa San Giovanni and Reggio Calabria. This landing was opposed only by the German 1st Parachute Division, and General Montgomery's forces made rapid progress. The important Italian naval base at Taranto was occupied by a British landing force on September 9. On the same day the units of the United States Fifth Army under command of Lieutenant General Mark Clark, together with British forces, landed on the Gulf of Salerno in a bold attempt to cut off German forces in southern Italy. General Eisenhower, realizing the hazardous nature of this attempt, used a familiar baseball expression to describe it: "It is now time to step up to the plate and try for a home run."

The Allied landing at Salerno was to provide the first example of the difficulties and disappointments that the Allies were to face in the Italian campaign. The German forces in that area were fully alert; they occupied commanding positions in the hills and subjected Allied troops on the beachhead to severe artillery fire and savage attacks. Far from being able to cut off the Germans in the south, General Clark's army was forced to fight for its life from the very outset. For seven days, from September 9 to September 16, bitter fighting raged on the Salerno beachhead. The German propaganda ministry prematurely announced the complete defeat of the Fifth Army at Salerno. Gradually Allied ground, air and naval forces turned the balance against the enemy.

After the failure of the Fifth Army to break out of the Salerno beachhead, everything depended on the rate of advance of the British Eighth Army, which now assumed the role of a relief force. On September 10, General Montgomery's army reached Pizzo, 45 miles north of Reggio Calabria. Two days later part of his army occupied the important port of Brindisi; and on September 17 advance elements of the British Eighth Army made contact with patrols of the American Fifth Army outside Salerno. The first great crisis of the Italian campaign had been successfully passed.

After the first failure to entrap German forces in the south, the immediate Allied objectives were the great Italian air base at Foggia and the port of Naples. With Naples and Foggia in Allied hands, General Eisenhower's troops would have both a first-class port of supply and a first-class air base at their disposal. Foggia was occupied by the British Eighth Army on September 28, and on October 1 advance patrols of the Fifth Army entered the outskirts of Naples. Before retreating from Naples and Foggia, the Germans had systematically destroyed these bases, and an immense amount of work was required to put them into shape for use.

Until the strength of the German defense line along the Volturno River was revealed early in October, considerable optimism existed in Allied countries over the prospect of an early capture of Rome. Contrary to expectations, the Germans did not abandon southern Italy for the strategically more advantageous Po River line in the north. Hitler's personal position required that the fiction of Italian fascism be re-created, so he rescued Mussolini by air from his place of imprisonment in Abruzzi Province and set him up as the puppet head of a new Italian "republican" fascist regime. In order to give this makeshift government some semblance of reality, Rome had to be retained as the capital of the new Italian state. Severe fighting raged along the Volturno River front throughout October. The German command in Italy brought in fresh divisions from the north and conducted a skillful and effective delaying action, first along the Volturno, then along the Garigliano, Sangro and Rapido rivers. Throughout December the United States Fifth Army was held up in the mountainous terrain in front of Cassino and the British Eighth Army had to fight desperately in order to capture Ortona.

This kind of artillery-infantry-engineer fighting was a far cry from the swift and incisive war of movement that character-

ized the last days of the Tunisian campaign. When General
Eisenhower saw the physical difficulties that faced the Eighth
and Fifth armies in Italy he made the characteristic remark:
"This is not the place for master minding!"

The ensuing period of positional warfare in Italy paralleled
that which followed the failure of the first Allied attempt to take
Tunis. Criticism of the slowness of the campaign and the political
arrangements in Italy appeared in British and American newspapers. The German propaganda ministry, quick to take advantage of these developments, rang the changes on what they
called the "slowness, lack of daring, and strategical blindness"
of Allied military leadership in Italy.

Until the full pattern of the final stage of the war is revealed,
it is impossible to speak with much definiteness about the nature
of Allied plans in Italy. It should be sufficient to point out that
in conducting the Allied campaign in Italy, General Eisenhower
was subjected to restraints that do not exist for leaders of totali-
tarian countries at war. The theater commander of democratic
allies cannot make decisions with the same disregard for risks
and losses as our enemies. His first responsibility is to carry out
the plans of Allied political leaders.

Operations in Italy, however disappointing from the territorial or political view, were not without important bearing on
the over-all picture of the war. Approximately 20 German divisions were pinned down in Italy that could not be used against
the Red army or against the main Allied invasion of Europe.
Considerable enemy resources were being expended in a non-
decisive theater. A steady attrition cut down the effectiveness of
German units, though they fought in Italy with all their veteran
skill and accustomed tenacity.

On December 24, 1943, the British and United States governments named General Eisenhower supreme commander of the
invasion forces. He turned over the Mediterranean theater to
British General Sir Henry Maitland Wilson and set up his headquarters in London. He chose Air Chief Marshal Tedder as his
deputy commander and brought along Major General Carl

Spaatz to command the United States strategical air forces. Lieutenant General Omar Bradley was appointed senior commander of United States ground forces. These choices indicated that any new invasion of Europe would be preceded and accompanied by the fullest possible use of Allied air power.

The winter and spring months of 1944 were passed in preparation for the invasion. By day and night ever growing fleets of Allied bombers struck at the centers of German aircraft production. Huge daylight raids of American bombers and fighters against Berlin and other key German cities were designed to force the Luftwaffe to fight, and so wear down its forces for the day of invasion. General Eisenhower expressed the opinion that if every soldier and civilian in Britain and America did his full duty, the power of the German army might be crushed in 1944.

As the date of invasion grew nearer, General Eisenhower could look back upon the two years that had passed since the spring of 1942 with some degree of satisfaction. He had seen the military position of the United Nations change from that of a hazardous defensive into one of general military superiority which assured final victory. Before him was the formidable task of breaking through the steel and concrete walls defending the Reich and destroying the power of the Wehrmacht. No military commander ever faced a task of greater hazard and difficulty. The German army in 1944, despite its hopeless strategical position, was still one of the most powerful forces in the world. Unless an unexpected miracle occurred, the fanatical and skillful nazi enemy could not be expected to admit defeat without a savage and bloody battle. To that end General Eisenhower was prepared to direct all the power and resources of Britain and America.

Whatever the outcome of this gigantic and hazardous venture may be, one can safely say that Eisenhower has already achieved organizational and administrative triumphs that will insure his place in military history. He has shown himself to be a military co-ordinator and administrator unequaled in modern times.

BIBLIOGRAPHY

GAMELIN

Allard, Paul, *La vérité sur l'affaire Corap* (Paris, 1941).

Bauer, Edward (Captain), "Idées de manoeuvre du haut commandement français, 1939–1940," *Revue militaire suisse* (July, 1942).

———, "Reflections sur la campagne de France," *ibid.* (August, 1943).

Belgian Ministry of Foreign Affairs, *Belgium: The Official Account of What Happened 1939–1940* (London, 1941).

Delperron, P., *Maginot of the Line* (London, 1940).

Bidou, H., *La bataille de France* (Geneva, 1941).

Chauvineau, L. (General), *Une invasion est-elle encore possible?* (Paris, 1939).

Cot, Pierre, *Triumph of Treason* (New York, 1944).

Daniker, Gustave (Colonel), "Vom Durchbruch zu Einkreisung," *Deutsche Wehr* (March 7, 1941).

Gérard, André (Pertinax), *Les Fossoyeurs*, 2 vols. (New York, 1943).

Lord Gort's Despatches (London, 1941).

Marshall, S. L. A. (Lieutenant Colonel), *Blitzkrieg: Armies on Wheels* (Washington, 1943).

Montigny, Jean, *La défaite* (Paris, 1941).

Romains, Jules, *The Seven Mysteries of Europe* (New York, 1940).

Sheppard, E. W. (Major), "The Defeat of France," the *Fighting Forces* vol. XX (December, 1943).

Soldan, George (Colonel), "Der Durchbruch uber die Maas am 13 Mai 1940," *Militärwissenschaftliche Rundschau* (November, 1940).

Thompson, Paul W. (Colonel), *Modern Battle* (New York, 1941).

Tissert, P., *The Riom Trial* (London, 1942).

Werner, Max, *The Battle for the World* (New York, 1941).

Le Procès de Riom (Lyon, 1941).

DE GAULLE

Aglion, Raoul, *The Fighting French* (New York, 1943).

Barrès, Philippe, *Charles de Gaulle* (New York, 1941).

Bénazet, E., *Défense nationale, notre sécurité* (Paris, 1938).

Bidou, H., *La bataille de France* (Geneva, 1941).

Burman, Ben Lucien, *Miracle on the Congo* (New York, 1941).

Cot, Pierre, *Triumph of Treason* (New York, 1944).

Davis, S. C., *The French War Machine* (London, 1927).

De Gaulle, Charles, *Vers l'armée de métier* (Paris, 1934), published in the United States as *The Army of the Future* (Philadelphia, 1941).

——, "Memorandum of January 26, 1940," the *National Review*, vol. CXV (October, 1940).

Gerard, Robert M. (Lieutenant), *The Tank-Fighter Team* (Washington, 1942).

Guderian, Hans (General), "Armored Forces," the *Infantry Journal*, vol. XLVIII (September–November, 1938).

Maurin, L. (General), *L'armée moderne* (Paris, 1938).

Montigny, L., "Les systèmes fortifiées dans la defense de France depuis 300 années," *Revue Militaire Française*, vols. LVII–LVIII (September–December, 1935).

Reynaud, Paul, *Le problème militaire française* (Paris, 1937).

Sheppard, E. W. (Major), "Two Generals One Doctrine," the *Army Quarterly*, vol. XLI (October, 1940).

Thouvenin, Jean, *Une anée d'histoire de France* (Paris, 1941).

WAVELL

Anon., "The Abyssinian Campaigns," the *Fighting Forces*, vol. XIX (December, 1942).

Anon., "The 4th Indian Division," the *Fighting Forces*, vol. XX (June, 1943).

Anon., "Sidi Barrani," the *Fighting Forces*, vol. XX (February, 1944).

British Information Service, *The Abyssinian Campaigns: The Official Story of the Conquest of Italian East Africa* (London, 1942).

——, *Destruction of An Army: The First Libyan Campaign, September 1940–February 1941* (London, 1941).

——, *Making an Army* (London, 1942).

Clifford, Alexander, *The Conquest of North Africa, 1940–1943* (New York, 1943).

Hill, Russell, *Desert War* (New York, 1942).

Michie, Allan A., *Retreat to Victory* (New York, 1942).

Moorehead, Alan, *Mediterranean Front* (London, 1941).

Rainier, P. W. (Major), *Pipeline to Battle: An Engineer's Adventures with the British Eighth Army* (New York, 1944).

Rowan-Robinson, H. (Major General), *With Wavell in the Middle East* (London, 1941).

Wavell, A. P. (General), *Allenby, a Study in Greatness* (New York, 1941).

—— (Field Marshal Viscount), *Allenby in Egypt* (London, 1944).

Wyndham, E. H. (Colonel), "Italy's One Victory," the *Army Quarterly*, vol. XLVI (August, 1943).

ROMMEL

Ahee, Joe (Major), "Notes on the Afrika Korps," the *Cavalry Journal,* vol. LI (November–December, 1942).

Anon., "Die Kampfe in Nordafrika," *Wissen und Wehr* (January, 1942).

Anon., "Die Schlacht in der Cyrenaika," *Deutsche Wehr* (June 26, 1942).

Anon., "Rommel's Generals," the *Fighting Forces,* vol. XIX (December, 1942).

Anon., "Von Timini nach Aegypten," *Die Wehrmacht* (September 16, 1942).

Basdorff, Herbert, "Wir werden uns durchboxen sagte Rommel," *Die Wehrmacht* (January 5, 1943).

Clifford, Alexander, *The Conquest of North Africa, 1940–1943* (New York, 1943).

Denny, Harold, *Behind Both Lines* (New York, 1942).

Diekman, Wilhelm, "Infanterie Greift An" (a review), *Wissen und Wehr* (November, 1937).

Dienstaltersliste der Generale Staboffiziere Haupleute und Rittemeister des Reichsheeres, 1922 (Berlin, 1922).

Ellington, Edward (Air Marshal Sir), "The War in the Air," the *Army Quarterly,* vol. XLVI (April, 1942).

Fredborg, Arvid, *Behind the Steel Wall* (New York, 1944).

Gordon-Finlayson, R. (General Sir), "The War on Land: The Middle East," the *Army Quarterly,* vol. XLVI (August, 1942).

Hill, Russell, *Desert Victory* (New York, 1943).

———, *Desert War* (New York, 1942).

Moorehead, Alan, *Don't Blame the Generals* (New York, 1943).

———, *The End in North Africa* (New York, 1943).

Rangliste des Deutschen Reichsheeres, 1932 (Berlin, 1932).

Rommel, Erwin (Generalmajor), *Aufgaben für Zug und Kompanie* (2nd ed., Berlin, 1940).

Rommel, Erwin (Oberst), *Infanterie Greift An* (Berlin, 1937) (American ed., Washington, 1944).

Sheppard, E. W. (Major), "The Libyan Defeat," the *Fighting Forces,* vol. XIX (August, 1942).

MONTGOMERY

Anon., "Some Experiences of an Armored Regimental Command in the Middle East," the *Tank,* vol. XXV (January, 1944).

British Information Service, *The Battle of Egypt* (London, 1943).

———, *The Eighth Army* (London, 1944).

———, *They Sought Out Rommel* (London, 1942).

Clifford, Alexander, *The Conquest of North Africa* (Boston, 1943).

Commentator, "The North African Campaign in Retrospect," *Fighting Forces*, vol. XX (August, 1943).

Crighton-Stuart, M. (Major), "The Story of a Long-Range Desert Patrol," the *Army Quarterly*, vol. XLVIII (October, 1943–January, 1944).

Freyberg, Bernard (Lieutenant General), "Dispatch on the Battle of El Hamma," *Wellington Dominion* (N.Z.) (April 14, 1943).

Gervasi, Frank, *But Soldiers Wondered Why* (New York, 1943).

Gunther, John, *D-Day: What Preceded It; What Followed* (New York, 1944).

Hill, Russell, *Desert Conquest* (New York, 1943).

———, *Desert War* (New York, 1942).

Howard-Jones, L. H. (Brigadier), "The Royal Electrical and Mechanical Engineers in the Libyan Desert," the *Army Quarterly*, vol. XLVII (January, 1944).

McMillan, Richard, *Mediterranean Assignment* (New York, 1943).

Moorehead, Alan, *Don't Blame the Generals* (New York, 1943).

———, *The End in North Africa* (New York, 1943).

Rainier, Peter W. (Major), *Pipeline to Battle: An Engineer's Adventures with the British Eighth Army* (New York, 1944).

Rame, David, *The Road to Tunis* (New York, 1943).

Ramsey, Guy, *One Continent Redeemed* (New York, 1943).

Reynolds, Quentin, *The Curtain Rises* (New York, 1944).

HITLER

Banse, Ewald, *Germany Prepares for War*, translated by Alan Harris (New York, 1941).

Barnes, N. H. (ed.), *The Speeches of Adolf Hitler*, 2 vols. (Oxford, 1942).

Beauman, A. B. (Brigadier), "France, May–June 1940," the *Army Quarterly*, vol. XLVI (April, 1943).

———, *ibid.*, vol. XLVII (October, 1943–January, 1944).

Cole, D. M., "The Politico-Military Strategy of the Nazis," the *Journal of the Royal United Service Institution*, vol. LXXXVI (August, 1941).

DeWeerd, H. A. (Captain), "Germany's Strategic Position," the *Yale Review*, vol. XXXIII (winter, 1943).

Fredborg, Arvid, *Behind the Steel Wall* (New York, 1944).

Fried, Hans E., *The Guilt of the German Army* (New York, 1941).

Harsch, Joseph C., *The Pattern of Conquest* (New York, 1941).

Heiden, Konrad, *Der Führer*, 1848–1934 (Boston, 1944).

Hitler, Adolf, *Mein Kampf* (New York, 1939).

Leudecke, Arnold, *I Knew Hitler* (New York, 1940).

Marshall, S. L. A. (Lieutenant Colonel), *Blitzkrieg: Armies on Wheels* (Washington, 1943).

Neumann, Sigmund, *Permanent Revolution: The Total States in a World at War* (New York, 1942).

Rauschning, Hermann, *The Revolution of Nihilism* (New York, 1941).

———, *The Voice of Destruction* (New York, 1940).

Reveille, Thomas (pseudonym for Rifat Tirana), *The Spoil of Europe: The Nazi Technique in Political and Economic Conquest* (New York, 1941).

Roberts, S. H. *The House that Hitler Built* (New York, 1938).

Rosinski, Herbert, *The German Army* (Washington, 1944).

Roussy de Sales, Raoul de (ed.), *My New Order* (New York, 1941).

Shirer, William L., *Berlin Diary* (New York, 1941).

Tolischus, Otto D., *They Wanted War* (New York, 1940).

Vagts, Alfred, *Hitler's Second Army* (Washington, 1943).

Wagner, Ludwig, *Hitler: Man of Strife* (New York, 1942).

Werner, Max, *Attack Can Win in 1943* (New York, 1943).

———, *Battle for the World* (New York, 1941).

———, *The Great Offensive* (New York, 1942).

———, *The Military Strength of the Powers* (New York, 1939).

CHURCHILL

Beaverbrook, W. M. I. (Lord), *Politicians and the War, 1914–1916* (New York, 1928).

Broad, C. L., *Winston Churchill* (London, 1941).

Churchill, Winston S., *The Aftermath* (New York, 1929).

———, *Life and Times of Marlborough*, 6 vols. (New York, 1934–38).

———, *Step by Step* (New York, 1939).

———, *The Unknown War*, vol. 6 of *The World Crisis* (New York, 1931).

———, *The World Crisis*, 4 vols. (New York, 1923–28).

DeWeerd, H. A. (Captain), "Churchill, Lloyd George, and Clemenceau," *Makers of Modern Strategy* (Princeton, 1943), ch. 12.

Eade, Charles (ed.), *Unrelenting Struggle,* the war speeches of Winston Churchill (London, 1942).

George, David Lloyd, *The War Memoirs of David Lloyd George,* 5 vols. (New York, 1933–37).

Guedalla, Phillip, *Mr. Churchill* (New York, 1941).

Kraus, René, *Winston Churchill* (New York, 1942).

Laski, Harold J., "Winston Churchill in War and Peace," the *Nation*, vol. CLVII (December 18, 1943).

Puleston, W. D. (Captain), *High Command in the World War* (New York, 1934).
Sydenham of Combe (Colonel Lord), Bacon, Reginald (Admiral Sir), Maurice, Frederick (General Sir), Bird, William (General Sir), and Oman, Charles (Sir), *The World Crisis by Winston Churchill: A Criticism* (London, Hutchinson, n.d.).

TIMOSHENKO

Basseches, Nikolaus, *The Unknown Army: The Nature and History of the Russian Military Forces* (New York, 1943).
Berchin, Michel, and Ben-Horin, E., *The Red Army* (New York, 1942).
Cassidy, H. C., *Moscow Dateline 1941–1943* (Boston, 1943).
Chamberlin, W. H., *The Russian Revolution, 1917–1921* (New York, 1935).
Davies, Joseph E., *Mission to Moscow* (New York, 1942).
Earle, E. M. (ed.), *Makers of Modern Strategy: Military Thought from Machiavelli to Hitler* (Princeton, 1943), ch. 14.
Engel, Leonard, "The Red Officer Corps," the *Infantry Journal*, vol. LII (June, 1943).
Kerr, Walter, *The Russian Army: Its Men, Its Leaders, and Its Battles* (New York, 1944).
Lesueur, Larry, *Twelve Months that Changed the World* (New York, 1943).
Mehring, Walter, *Timoshenko: Marshal of the Red Army* (New York, 1942).
Stowe, Leland, *They Shall Not Sleep* (New York, 1944).
Werner, Max, *The Great Offensive* (New York, 1942).
———, *The Military Strength of the Powers* (New York, 1939).
White, D. F., *The Growth of the Red Army* (Princeton, 1944).
———, "Soviet Philosophy of War," the *Political Science Quarterly*, vol. LI (September, 1936).
Wollenberg, Erich, *The Red Army: A Study in the Growth of Soviet Imperialism* (London, 1938).

MacARTHUR

Falk, Edwin A., *From Perry to Pearl Harbor: The Struggle for Supremacy in the Pacific* (New York, 1943).
Gayn, Mark J., *The Fight for the Pacific* (New York, 1941).
Hersey, John, *Men on Bataan* (New York, 1942).
Ind, Allison (Lieutenant Colonel), *Bataan, the Judgment Seat* (New York, 1944).
Irwin, C. L. (Colonel), "Corregidor in Action," the *Coast Artillery Journal*, vol. LXXXVI (January–February, 1943).

Johnston, George H., *Pacific Partners* (New York, 1944).

——, *The Toughest Fighting in the World* (New York, 1943).

Kahn, W. E. J., *G.I. Jungle: An American Soldier in Australia and New Guinea* (New York, 1943).

Lee, Clark, *They Call it Pacific* (New York, 1943).

Miller, Francis Trevelyan, *General Douglas MacArthur: Fighter for Freedom* (New York, 1942).

Report on the Army July 1, 1939 to June 30, 1943: Biennial Reports of General George C. Marshall, Chief of Staff of the United States Army to the Secretary of War (Washington, 1943).

Report of the Commanding General of the Army Air Forces to the Secretary of War (Washington, 1944), section III.

Smith, Frederic H. (Colonel), "The Papuan Campaign," the *Air Force*, vol. II (September, 1943).

Waldrop, Frank C. (ed.), *MacArthur on War* (New York, 1942).

CHIANG KAI-SHEK

Abend, Hallet, *My Life in China, 1926–1941* (New York, 1943).

Bison, T. A., *Japan in China* (New York, 1938).

Carlson, Evans Fordyce, *The Chinese Army: Its Organization and Efficiency* (New York, 1940).

——, "Strategy of the Sino-Japanese War," the *Far Eastern Survey* (May 19, 1941)

——, *Twin Stars of China* (New York, 1940).

Chiang Kai-shek (Generalissimo), *Resistance and Reconstruction: Messages during China's Six Years of War* (New York, 1943).

Chiang Kai-shek (Madame), *China Shall Rise Again* (New York, 1941).

Chinese Ministry of Information, *The China Yearbook, 1937–1943* (New York, 1944).

Fleming, Peter, "The Japanese Campaign in China," the *Journal of the Royal United Service Institution* (May, 1939).

Gasimov, N., "Japanese Landing Operations," *Krasny Flot*, English translation Army War College Library (April 14, 1939).

Gunther, John, *Inside Asia* (New York, 1942).

Hedin, Sven, *Chiang Kai-shek, Marshal of China* (New York, 1940).

Howard, Harry Paxton, *America's Role in Asia* (New York, 1943).

Infantry Journal, "How the Jap Army Fights" (Washington, 1942).

Lattimore, Owen, *The Making of Modern China* (New York, 1943).

Linebarger, Paul M. A., *The China of Chiang Kai-shek* (Boston, 1941).

Mallory, Walter H., "Strategy of Chiang Kai-shek," *Foreign Affairs*, vol. XVII (July, 1939).

Maurier, Herrymon, *The End Is Not Yet: China at War* (New York, 1941).

Ming, Chao, "Survey of China's Wartime Communications," *China Weekly Review* (April 8, 1939).

Shevielew, B., "Landing Operations on the Yangtze River," *Krasnaya Zwesda,* translation in the Army War College Library (October 24, 1938).

Smythe, Lewis S. C. (Dr.), *War Damage in the Nanking Area,* for the Nanking International Relief Committee (Nanking, 1938).

Snow, Edgar, *The Battle for Asia* (New York, 1941).

Stowe, Leland,, *They Shall Not Sleep* (New York, 1943).

Tong, Hollington, *Chiang Kai-shek, Soldier and Statesman,* 2 vols. (Shanghai, 1937).

Wu Yi-fang and Price, F. W., *China Rediscovers Her West* (New York, 1940).

EISENHOWER

Bennet, Lowell, *Assignment to Nowhere: The Battle for Tunisia* (New York, 1943).

Burba, E. H. (Lieutenant Colonel), "Sidi Bou Zid to Sbeitla, February 14–17, 1943," the *Field Artillery Journal,* vol. XXXIV (January, 1944).

Clifford, Alexander, *The Conquest of North Africa, 1940–1943* (New York, 1943).

Crawford, Kenneth, *Report on North Africa* (New York, 1943).

Gunther, John, *D-Day: What Preceded It; What Followed* (New York, 1944).

Hagood, Johnson (Major General), Bess, Demaree, et al, *These are the Generals* (New York, 1943).

Ingersoll, Ralph (Captain), *The Battle is the Pay-Off* (New York, 1943).

Lanza, Conrad (Colonel), "Finale in Tunisia," the *Field Artillery Journal,* vol. XXXIII (July, 1943).

McMillan, Richard, *Mediterranean Assignment* (New York, 1943).

Marshall, Howard, *Over to Tunis* (London, 1943).

Moorehead, Alan, *The End in North Africa* (New York, 1943).

Morris, W. H. H., Jr. (Major General), "Salerno," the *Military Review,* vol. XXIII (March, 1944).

Page, Douglas (Colonel), "Sedjenane to Bizerte," the *Field Artillery Journal,* vol. XXIII (October, 1943).

Pyle, Ernie, *Here Is Your War* (New York, 1943).

Rainier, Peter W. (Major), *Pipeline to Battle* (New York, 1944).

Rame, David, *The Road to Tunis* (New York, 1943).

Ramsey, Guy, *One Continent Redeemed* (New York, 1943).

Report on the Army, July 1, 1939 to June 30, 1943: Biennial Reports of General George C. Marshall, Chief of Staff of the United States Army to the Secretary of War (Washington, 1943).

Reynolds, Quentin, *The Curtain Rises* (New York, 1944).

Strong, E. E. (Major), "Thala Engagement, February 21–24, 1943," the *Field Artillery Journal,* vol. XXXIII (August, 1943).

INDEX

A

Abbeville, 37, 51, 85
Achtung Panzers!, 49
Adana conference, 187
Adcock, Brigadier General Clarence, 270
Afrika Korps, 53, 78, 87, 88, 89, 95, 96, 97, 99, 100, 103, 106, 109, 111, 116, 118, 123, 124, 125, 279, 280
Aldershot, 58
Alexander, General Sir Harold, 101, 104, 107, 109, 121, 123, 284, 286, 288
Alexandria, 64, 76
Allenby, Field Marshal Edmund Lord, 57, 61, 64, 80, 111
Altmark, 183
Anderson, General Sir A. K., 123
Aosta, duke of, 62, 70, 71, 73
Ardennes, 30, 32, 44, 85
Arnim, General von, 98, 99, 100, 283
Atlantic Charter, 187
Au fil de l'épée, 42
Auchinleck, General Sir Claude E., 80, 91, 95, 103
Aufgaben für Zug und Kompanie, 84

B

Bacon, Admiral Sir Reginald, 179
Bagramian, General, 211
Baker, Newton D., 215
Barrès, Philippe, 49
Bataan, 224, 225
Baudillart, Henri Cardinal, 16
Bauer, Captain E., 30
Beatty, Admiral Sir David, 177
Beaverbrook, Lord, 170, 172, 173
Beck, Colonel Joseph, 139
Beck, Colonel Ludwig, 130, 135

Belgium, 30, 31, 32, 41, 52, 143, 144, 145, 146
Below, General, 203
Bengasi, 67, 68, 69, 70, 76, 91, 118
Berthelot, General, 17
Bess, Demaree, 269
Bialystok Minsk, Battle of, 200-201
Bir Hacheim, 53, 92, 93, 103
Bird, General Sir W. S., 177
Bismarck, General, 89
Bismarck Sea, Battle of, 233, 234
Bizerte, capture of, 285-288
Blamey, General Sir Thomas, 74, 75, 229, 235, 240
Blaskowitz, General, 84
Bliss, General Tasker H., 269
Blücher, General Vassili, 245
Bock, Field Marshal Fedor von, 149, 202, 203
Boetticher, General von, 84
Boldin, General, 211
Bradley, Lieutenant General Omar N., 282, 286, 298
Brauchitsch, Field Marshal Walther von, 149, 204
Britain, Battle of, 151, 152
British army: 6th battalion Scotch Fusiliers, 74; Black Watch Regiment, 57; 7th Support Group, 89, 91, 104; 4th armored brigade, 89, 91, 93; 5th South African brigade, 91; 7th armored brigade, 89; 22nd armored brigade, 89, 93; 1st Armored Division, 123, 283, 284; 1st New Zealand Division, 109; 2nd New Zealand Division, 109; 3rd Division, 105; 4th Division, 278; 4th Indian Division, 67, 71, 88, 90, 109, 123, 286; 6th Armored Division, 278, 284; 7th Armored Division, 63, 65, 67, 68, 88, 91,

British army, *Continued*
123, 286; 9th Australian Division,
109; 44th Division, 107; 50th Division, 107, 282; 51st Division, 107;
78th Division, 278; X Armored
Corps, 109, 115; XX Corps, 57;
First Army, 120, 123, 278, 282;
Eighth Army, 53, 89, 98, 99, 103,
106, 109, 110, 117, 120, 125, 281,
282
British Expeditionary Force, 26, 56,
75
Brüning, Chancellor, 128
Budenny, Marshal, 191
Bülow, General von, 17
Bullitt, William C., 34
Butcher, Lieutenant Commander
Harry, 270

C

Cairo conference, 188
Cameroons, 53
Campbell, Brigadier Jock, 89, 104
Cape Gloucester campaign, 237, 238
Carlson, Major Evans F., 249, 250,
259
Casablanca conference, 187
Catania, 69, 124
Catroux, General, 53
Chamberlain, Neville, 142, 181, 182,
183, 184
Charleroi, Battle of, 35
Chater, Colonel Arthur, 62
Chauvineau, General L., 22
Chennault, Major General Claire,
247
Cheren, Battle of, 53, 71
Chetwode, General Sir Philip, 57
Chiang Kai-shek, 241-263
Chiang Kai-shek, Madame, 241, 245,
248
Chinese army: New Fourth Army,
257; Eighth Route Army, 257
Chu-Teh, 247
Chuikov, General, 209, 211

Churchill, Winston S., 39, 63, 65, 70,
93, 104, 106, 109, 116, 166-189
Clark, Lieutenant General Mark,
295, 296
Clausewitz, Karl von, 199
Clifford, Alexander, 68
*Command and Employment of Air
Power*, 124
Committee of National Defense,
France, 22, 23, 34, 41
Congress of the United States, 188
Coningham, Air Vice-Marshal, 101,
120, 121
Coral Sea, Battle of, 228
Corap, General André, 32, 33, 146
Corregidor, 224, 225
Crete campaign, 75, 76
Cruewell, General, 89
Cunningham, General Sir Alan, 71,
88, 90, 91, 103, 119
Cunningham, Admiral Sir James B.,
63
Cunningham, Brigadier General
Julian, 237
Curtin, Prime Minister, 239

D

Daladier, 22, 28, 34, 49
Darlan, Admiral Jean, 23, 275
De Gaulle, General Charles, 22, 28,
39-55, 145
Denikine, General, 180
Denny, Harold, 88
Dentz, General Henri, 61
Dietrich, Otto, 155
Dodd, W. E., 21
Dollmann, General, 147
Donald, W. H., 248
Doolittle, Major General James, 120
Douhet, Giulio, 199
Doumenc, General, 51
Dovator, General, 211
Dunkirk, 24, 75, 145, 146
Dyle hypothesis, 31
Dyle River line, 30, 31

E

École de Guerre, 17, 41
Edward VIII, 181
Egypt, 41, 60, 62, 70, 103
Egyptian Expeditionary Force, 57
Eisenhower, David D., 265
Eisenhower, General Dwight D., 98, 101, 120, 254-299
El Agheila, 68, 69, 86, 92, 118
El Alamein, 95, 96, 97, 104, 106, 116; see also El Alamein, Battle of
El Alamein, Battle of, 53, 98, 106-116
El Hamma, 54, 121
Ellington, Air Marshal Sir Edward, 92
Eritrea, 53, 70, 79
Ethiopia, Conquest of, 70, 79

F

Farouk, King of Egypt, 61
Faulkenhausen, General Alexander, 247
Festung Europa, 160
Field Service Regulations, 1945 (British), 57
Fighting French, 104
Finnish campaign, 195-198
Fisher, Admiral Lord John, 169, 171, 172
Foch, Marshal Ferdinand, 15, 16, 23, 56
Fort Capuzzo, 64, 65, 67
France, Battle of, 143-147
Fredborg, Arvid, 97
Frederick the Great, 161
Free French Movement, 53
French army: Trailleurs Algériens, 16; 4th Armored Division, 51; 6th Division, 16; 9th Division, 19; XIX Corps, 120, 282; First Army, 17; Fifth Army, 17; Seventh Army, 32; Ninth Army, 32, 33, 146

Freyberg, General Bernard, 54, 75, 108, 121
Friends of Europe Information Service, 25
Frunze, Michael, 192, 193
Fuller, Major General J. F. C., 47, 97, 199
Funston, Major General Frederick, 215

G

Gallieni, General Joseph Simon, 17
Gallipoli campaign, 172, 173
Gambier-Parry, General Michael, 69
Gamelin, General Maurice Gustave, 15-39, 143
Gamelin, Zephirin Auguste, 16
Gariboldi, General Italo, 69, 86
Gatehouse, General, 108
Gaza maneuver, 64, 111
Genghis Khan, 218, 230
Georges, General Alphonse, 15, 23, 28
Géraud, André (Pertinax), 34, 37
German army: 13th infantry regiment, 84; 124th infantry regiment, 81; 5th Motorized Division, 86; 7th Panzer Division, 85, 86; 10th Panzer Division, 99; 15th Panzer Division, 98, 279, 288, 292; 19th Panzer Division, 292; 20th AA Division, 280; 21st Panzer Division, 98, 99, 109, 279, 284, 292; 29th Motorized Division, 292; 90th Light Division, 109, 279; 164th Light Division, 109, 279, 284; 334th Division, 280; Hermann Göring Division, 280, 292; Manteuffel Division, 280; Sixth Army, 158
Giraud, General Henri, 28, 31, 32, 33, 54
Göring, Reichs Marshal Hermann, 137, 158
Golikov, General, 211

Gordon-Finlayson, General Sir R., 93

Gort, Field Marshal Viscount, 37, 56, 182

Gott, General W. H. E., 89, 102, 103, 104

Govorov, Marshal, 203, 211

Graziani, Marshal Rudolf, 62, 63, 66, 70, 73, 79, 81, 86, 186

Greek campaign, 74-75

Guderian, General Heinz, 49, 147

Gunther, John, 290

H

Haig, Field Marshal Lord, 177, 178, 190

Haile Selassie, 73

Haldane, George Burdon Lord, 19

Halder, General Franz, 136, 149

Halfaya Pass, Battles of, 63, 78, 87, 92, 118

Hardy, Mary, 214

Hata, General Shunroka, 253

Hentsch, Lieutenant Colonel von, 18

Hersey, John, 220, 221

Hess, Rudolf, 154

Heydrich, Reinhard, 83

Himmler, Heinrich, 165

Hindenburg, Field Marshal Paul von, 81, 128, 190

Hitler, Adolf, 25, 81, 83, 87, 96, 99, 111, 126-165, 180, 181, 183, 184, 185, 186

Hitler, Alois, 126

Hitler Youth, 137

Holland, 31, 32, 36, 143, 144, 145, 146

Horii, Lieutenant General Tomatore, 228, 229, 230

Hube, General Hans, 292

Huntziger, General Charles, 28

I

Illustrious, HMS, 69

Ind, Lieutenant Colonel Allison D., 223

Infanterie Greift An, 84

Iran, 41

Iraq, 41, 75, 76

Ironside, Sir Edmund, 56, 183

Italian army: 1st Libyan Division, 63; 2nd Libyan Division, 63; 4th Division, 292; 26th Division, 292; 54th Division, 292; Ariette Armored Division, 91, 92, 109; Bologna Division, 109; Brescia Division, 109; Catanzaro Division, 63, 67; Centauro Division, 280, 285; Cirene Division, 63; Littorio Armored Division, 109; Pavia Division, 109; Pistoja Division, 280, 285; Spezia Division, 280, 285; Superba Division, 280, 285; Trieste Motorized Division, 93, 109, 280; Young Fascist Division, 280, 285

Italian East Africa, 62, 70

Italian Somaliland, 70, 79

J

Jellicoe, Admiral Sir John, 177

Jodl, General Alfred, 153

Joffre, Marshal Jean J. C., 15, 16, 17, 18, 26, 35

K

Kasserine Pass, Battle of, 280-281

Keitel, Field Marshal Wilhelm, 149, 190

Kenney, Lieutenant General George C., 229, 232

Kesselring, Field Marshal Albert, 87, 149

Kharitonov, General, 205

King, Admiral Ernest, 213

Kitchener, Lord, 167, 169, 172

Kleist, Marshal, 147, 204, 205

Kluck, General Alexander von, 17

Kluge, Field Marshal, 84, 149

Knightsbridge, 94, 104, 108
Koeltz, General Louis M., 282
Koening, General Joseph, 53
Kolchak, Admiral, 180
Konev, General, 211
Kriebel, Colonel, 247
Krueger, Lieutenant General Walter
C., 237
Kuchler, Field Marshal, 84
Kuomintang, 240
Kuznetsov, General, 203, 211

L

Larminat, General de, 53
Laski, Harold J, 188
Lattimore, Owen, 253, 260
Lease-lend Agreements, 187
Lee, Major Ernest, 270
Lee Knowles lectures, 57
Leluishenko, General, 203, 211
Lenin, 191
Lewis, Brigadier R. R., 270
Libya, 64, 67, 68, 69, 70
Liddell Hart, Captain B. H., 25
Lindsell, General Sir Wilfred, 108,
118
Linthigow, Marquis of, 80
List, Field Marshal, 84, 149, 153
Lloyd, Air Vice-Marshal, 120
Lloyd George, David, 174, 175
Ludendorff, General Eric von, 22,
143, 156
Ludwig III, King of Bavaria, 126
Luftwaffe, 26, 32, 69, 74, 87, 136,
139, 141, 150, 151, 158, 181, 183
Lumsden, General, 108

M

MacArthur, Captain Arthur, 214
MacArthur, General Douglas, 213-
240
Maginot line, 21, 22, 27, 28, 30, 32,
44, 143, 146
Maletti, General, 63, 65

Malinowski, General, 211
Mannerheim line, 196, 197
Manoury, General, 17
Manstein, Field Marshal Fritz von,
161, 207
Mao-Tse-tung, 247
Marcks, General Erich, 154
Marcth line, 98, 119, 120, 121
Marne, Battle of, 16, 35
Marshall, General George C., 225,
265, 267, 281, 283, 286, 289
Matsui, General Iwane, 253
Maurice, Major General Sir Fred-
erick, 177
Medenine, Battle of, 99, 119
Mein Kampf, 130
Mersa Matruh, 63, 64, 65, 70, 110
Messe, General, 121
Messervy, General Frank, 89
Midway, Battle of, 228
Milch, Field Marshal Erhardt, 149
Militärwissenschaftliche Rundschau,
86
Moltke, General Helmuth Count
von, 18
Montgomery, General Sir Bernard
L., 84, 98, 100, 101, 102 125, 285,
291, 295
Morehead, Alan, 101
Moreshead, General, 108
Moscow, Battle for, 202-204
Mountbatten, Lord Louis, 80
Munich agreement, 25, 138

N

Nanking, rape of, 253
Napoleon, 16, 17
Narvik, 140, 141
Nazi party, 83, 129, 135
Neame, General Philip, 69, 87
Nehring, General Walter, 89
Newall, Air Marshal Sir Richard,
182
Nimitz, Admiral Chester W., 239
Nivelle, General Robert, 18

Norrie, General Willoughby, 89
North African landings, 272-275
Norwegian campaign, 141-143
Novikov, Marshal, 211

O

O'Connor, General Sir Richard N.,
    64, 66, 69, 87, 104
Okura, General, 195
Organization Todt, 136
Oslo, 141, 183
Osoaviakhim, 193

P

Panay incident, 254
Papen, Franz von, 128
Papuan campaign, 228-232
Patton, Lieutenant General George,
    124, 275, 282, 291, 293
Paulus, Field Marshal Friedrich,
    158, 159
Peinaar, General Daniel, 107
Pershing, General John J., 269
Pétain, Marshal Henri Philippe, 15,
    23, 36, 39, 40, 41, 48, 52, 145, 184
Philippine army, 219-220, 221
Philippines campaign, 222-225
Pilsudski, Marshal Joseph, 56
Plan XVII, 17
Platt, General, 67, 71
Polish campaign, 139-141
Puleston, Captain W. D., 180

Q

Qattara Depression, 95, 96, 97
Quebec conference, 188

R

Raeder, Admiral Erich, 141
Rangliste des Deutschen Reichs-
    heeres, 83
Ranier, Major Peter W., 91

Rauschning, Hermann, 133, 134
Red army, 155, 191-194, 195, 198,
    199, 210, 211
Reichenau, Field Marshal, 84, 149
Reichswehr, 42, 45, 130
Remisov, General, 205
Reynaud, Paul, 22, 28, 31, 34, 39, 48,
    49, 52, 142
Riom trial, 36
Ritchie, General Neil, 83, 91, 93, 103,
    107, 119
Robertson, Field Marshal Sir W.,
    177, 178
Roderick, Colonel Thomas R., 270
Rodimtzev, General, 211
Rokossovsky, Marshal, 203, 211
Romains, Jules, 20, 27, 28
Rome-Berlin Axis, 25
Rommel, Field Marshal Erwin, 68,
    69, 78, 81-101, 106, 107, 108, 109,
    110, 111, 116, 119, 120, 121, 161,
    279, 280, 281
Rooks, Brigadier General Lowell,
    270
Roosevelt, Colonel Elliott, 120
Roosevelt, President Theodore, 214
Royal Air Force, 27, 39, 70, 111, 146,
    151, 152, 181, 182, 185, 186
Royal Oak, HMS, 176, 182
Rundstedt, Field Marshal Gerd von,
    149, 161
Rupertus, Major General W. H., 237
Russian army: 4th Cavalry Division,
    191; 6th Red Cavalry Division,
    191; Ninth Army, 205; Fifty-sixth
    Army, 205
Russian campaign, 155-159
Russian-German nonaggression pact
    (August 23, 1939), 25

S

Salamaua-Lae campaign, 234-236
Salerno, Battle of, 295
Sarraut, Prime Minister, 24

Sawbridge, Brigadier General B. W., 270
Schell, General Adolph von, 84
Scherff, Colonel Walther, 157, 160
Schleicher, 128
Schlieffen, General Count von, 47
Schutzstaffel, 136, 163, 164, 165
Schwoeder, General, 205
Sedan, 24, 32, 34, 51
Seeckt, General Hans von, 42, 157, 246
Seidlitz, General, 158
Shanghai, Battle of, 252-253
Shapozhnikov, General, 192
Sheppard, Major F. W., 45
Sian affair, 248
Sicilian campaign, 291-295
Sidi Barrani, 63, 64, 65, 66, 67, 68, 70
Sidi Rezegh, Battle of, 89, 90, 91
Siegfried line, 25, 26, 27
Skagerrak, 183
Smigly-Rydz, General, 139
Smith, Major General Walter Bedell, 270
Smolensk, Battle of, 201, 202
Smuts, General Jan C., 70
Snow, Edgar, 250
Sokolovsky, General Vassili, 201, 202
Sollum, 64, 65, 70, 87, 92, 118
Soong, T. V., 248
Spaatz, Major General Carl, 282, 298
Speerle, Field Marshal, 149
Stalin, Marshal, 191, 203, 208, 211, 212
Stalingrad, Battle of, 157, 158, 208-210
Stanhope, Lord, 181
Stover, Ida, 265
Strabolgi, Lord, 82
Strong, Brigadier K. W. D., 270
Stumme, General von, 97, 111, 114
Sugden, Brigadier C. S., 270
Sun Yat-sen, 242, 245
Supreme War Council, France, 16, 17, 20, 56

Swift, Major General I. P., 239
Syria, 19, 20, 23, 53, 56, 61, 76, 78, 79

T

Taierhchwang, Battle of, 255
Taranto, 63
Tedder, Air Marshal Sir Arthur, 101, 120, 121, 290, 297
Teheran conference, 188
Terauchi, General Count, 251, 252
Thoma, General Ritter von, 97, 111, 114, 115
Timoshenko, Marshal Semion, 190-212
Tobruk, 67, 68, 70, 89, 91, 95, 118
Tolbukhim, General, 211
Transjordania, 58, 60
Tripoli, 54, 68, 69, 81, 98, 119
Tukhachevski, Marshal, 192
Tulenev, General, 211
Tunis, capture of, 285-288
Tunisian campaign, 275-288
Tweedsmuir, Lord, 37

U

United States army: 701st tank destroyers, 276; combat command B, 277; 15th infantry regiment, 266; 23rd infantry brigade, 216; 1st Armored Division, 286; 1st Cavalry Division, 239; 9th Division, 284; 32nd Division, 231; 41st Division, 231; II Corps, 120, 123, 282, 286; Fifth Army, 295, 296, 297; Seventh Army, 124, 284, 285

V

Vassilevsky, Marshal, 209, 211
Verdun, 18, 41, 52, 147
Vers l'armée de métier, 22, 42, 46, 47
Versailles treaty, 42, 130
Vichy, 36, 52, 78
Vlasov, General, 203

Voronezh, Battle for, 207
Voronov, Marshal, 209, 211
Voroshilov, Marshal K., 191
Vuillemin, General, 27

W

Wadi Akarit, Battle for, 121, 122
Wainwright, Lieutenant General
    Jonathan, 224
War Office (British), 58
Warsaw, Battle of, 56
Wavell, Field Marshal Viscount
    A. P., 56-81, 104, 186
Wehrmacht, 130, 131, 134, 136, 147,
    149, 150, 154, 181, 185, 186, 203,
    210
Werner, Max, 194
Westhoven, General, 203
Westropp, Brigadier Victor, 270
Wetzell, General, 247
Weygand line, 146, 147

Weygand, General Maxime, 15, 27,
    34, 35, 36, 37, 39, 41, 49, 56, 61, 147
Whitely, Major General J. F. M., 270
Willkie, Wendell, 105, 109
Willoughby,   Brigadier   General
    Charles A., 236
Wilson, Field Marshal Sir Henry,
    269
Wilson, General Sir Henry Mait-
    land, 63, 74, 78, 297
Wimperley, General, 108
Witzleben, General, 147, 149
World Crisis, The, 175, 176

Y

Yeremenko, General, 211

Z

Zeitzler, General Kurt, 158
Zhukov, Marshal Gregory, 209, 211

Books That Live

The Norton imprint on a
book means that in the
publisher's estimation it
is a book not for a single
season but for the years.

W · W · NORTON & CO · INC.
70 FIFTH AVENUE
NEW YORK